GMAT 词汇精选

俞敏洪　著

世界知识出版社

前　言

GMAT考试其实不考词汇，之所以要编这本词汇书，主要是为了帮助大家在学习GMAT阅读和语法时扫除词汇障碍。所有书中的词汇都来自GMAT考过的题库，是很实用的词汇。但这些词汇并不代表GMAT考试中必然要出现的词汇，也并不包括GMAT的全部词汇。我们只可以这样说：背完了这本书中的词汇，就有了学习GMAT的基础，就没有必要为学习中碰到太多的单词而苦恼了。同时大家也可以比较轻松地来对待GMAT词汇，即使不能全部背出来也不用太担心，只要留下个印象，能通过上下文猜出意思就行了。获取GMAT高分的重要途径在于反复练习阅读能力、语法能力和逻辑能力，达到熟能生巧的地步。

不过有一点大家一定要记住：词汇量是阅读的基础。从这一点讲，词汇是不能不背的。背词汇和读文章是两种完全不同的能力，又是相互依赖的两种能力。请大家记住：最愚蠢的方法就是一边查单词一边阅读。这样做的结果是单词记不住，阅读速度也上不去。我主张背单词时绝不阅读，读文章时绝不查单词。背单词在前，读文章在后。在读文章时不管有多少单词都不能去查，要尽可能地猜出它们的意思，要注重文章的整体思路，而不是中间出现的一二个单词。

背单词其实很容易。我在上大学时也怕背单词，后来为了谋生才开始专研词汇记忆；一旦入了门，才发现大量的词汇是非常容易记的。最主要的方法大概有三种，首先是词根词缀分解记忆。在本书中我对大量单词都做了词根分解，这样一来，记几个单词只需记一个单词的时间：如 commod 表示“方便”，因此 commodity（商品），commodious（宽敞的），accommodate（提供食宿）。对词根、词缀不熟悉的同学可以参考我的另一本《英语词汇速记大全——词根词缀记忆法》。其次是千方百计联想记忆法或分解记忆。如 flaunt（炫耀），可分解为 fl = fly（飞） + aunt（姑奶奶）→飞去看姑奶奶→炫耀。这样的记忆法虽然荒谬，却十分有效。最后一点一定要记住的是：凡是背过的单词一定要反复背，这是真正有效的办法。我的词汇量就是在反复教 GRE 词汇时教出来的。

中国的科学技术固然落后，但中国的管理水平和管理科学更落后。因为管理的落后才造成了让人惊心动魄的资源浪费；包括自然资源和人力资源的浪费；大批人才的聪明才智和创造能力不能市场化而造福于人民；一个科学博士后，每月只有 800 元收入；……随着改革开放的进程，我们的视野日益开阔，越来越多的人认识到生活质量的提高并不仅仅是多吃几斤猪肉，享受 VCD 和手机，而在于政府机构对公民的服务质量，商业对顾客多种需要的满足以及各种资源的合理、有效的配置。

我们的国家正在呼唤着新一代的管理人才，我们民族的伟大复兴不能缺少新一代的管理人才。令人欣喜的是，当代中国知识分子和政治家、企业家已经看到了这一点。北大、清华几乎同时成立了工商管理学院。大批的学子希望直接到国外名校去就读 MBA，把别人的管理经验学到手。新东方学校 1994 年的 GMAT 班只有几十人，现在的 GMAT 班每年几千人，这说明了中国知识分子意识的更新。有的新东方学员已经是国内知名企业家，有的学员一边苦读 GMAT，一边管理着数百万甚至是数亿元的资产。这些都表明中国人的眼光看得远了，他们已经开始注视和洞察未来了。

面对这样的一群人，我不能不心潮澎湃。我所能做的就是为他们提供哪怕一点点帮助和便利，使他们在奋斗的道路上更轻松愉快一点。这本词汇书的编辑，就是在这种心态下的结果。我个人的每一点进步，新东方学校的每一点成就和进步，都和广大学员对前途孜孜不倦的追求密不可分。

在本书编辑过程中，新东方学校写作中心的包凡一、何庆权老师提供了大量的帮助。在英文的注解和释义方面，他们做了大量的工作，使得本书日趋成熟，在此特向他们表示诚挚的谢意。

1999 年 6 月 17 日子夜

目　录

GMAT 最新词汇

A

abduct [æb΄dʌkt] v. 绑架,拐走(to take 〔a person〕 away unlawfully and by force or fraud; kidnap)
(记)ab(离开) + duct(引导)→把人带走→绑架;
n. abduction; abductor
同根词:viaduct(高架桥)
(例)The pirates abducted the princess and hid her in a castle.

abolish [ə΄bɔliʃ] v. 废除,取消(to do away with completely; to put an end to; esp., to make 〔a law, etc.〕 null and void)
(记)该词来自拉丁文 abolir,表示一点点衰退;n. abolition
(例)The committee abolished all entry requirements.

abolitionist [ˌæbə΄liʃənist] n. 废奴主义者(one who favored the abolition of slavery in the U.S.)
(记)由 abolish 而来

abrogation [æbrəu΄geiʃən] n. 废除,废止(abolition)
(记)ab(离开) + rog(问) + ate→不再问→废除
同根词:interrogation(审问)
(例)The king's abrogation of the unpopular law was welcomed by the majority of the people.

abruptly [ə΄brʌptli] ad. 突然地;无礼地(suddenly; unex-

pectedly)
(记)abrupt(突然的,生硬的)+ly→突然地
(例)He turned back abruptly when he heard noise behind him.

abstinence [ˈæbstinəns] n. 节制,禁欲(the act of voluntarily doing without some or all food, drink, or other pleasures)
(记)abs(不)+tin(拿住)→不拿住→放弃;a. abstinent(饮食有度的,有节制的,禁欲的);ad. abstinently
(例)Abstinence from fatty foods and smoking can probably lengthen your life.

absurdity [əbˈsəːditi] n. 荒谬(the quality or state of being laughable and ridiculous; nonsense)
(记)absurd(荒诞的)+ity→荒谬
(例)Dostoyevski claimed that, intellectual absurdity or not, religious belief is necessary for everyone.

accelerate [ækˈseləreit] v. 加速(to increase the speed of)
(记)ac+celer(速度)+ate→加速;n. acceleration
同根词:celerity(迅速)
(例)The car accelerated as it went downhill. / Government spending accelerates the pace of inflation.

access [ˈækses] n. 通路,途径(a way or means of approaching, getting, using, etc)
(记)ac+cess(走)→走过去→通道
同根词:procession(行列,队伍)
(例)Pickets(纠察队) blocked access to the factory.

accidental [ˌæksiˈdentl] a. 偶然的,意外的(happening by chance; fortuitous)
(记)ac+cid(落下)+ental→意外的

同根词:deciduous(落叶的)
(例)I made an accidental error on my exam.

acclimatory [ə´klæmətəri] a. 服水土的,适应的(being accustomed or becoming accustomed to a different climate, environment, or circumstances, as by physiological or psychological changes)
(记)ac(朝向)+climate→使转向气候→服水土的,适应的
(例)Plants show acclimatory signs when they adapt to new environments.

accommodation [əˌkɔmə´deiʃən] n.(常用复数)招待设备,膳宿供应(lodgings; room and board);居住舱室(traveling space, as in a railroad train or airplane; seat, berth, etc.);适应,调节(adaptation[to a purpose]; adjustment)
(记)ac(朝向)+commodate(来自 commodare,使合适,方便)→适应,调节;v. accommodate;a. accommodating
(例)The visitor was able to secure accommodations at a local hotel.

accord [ə´kɔːd] v. 同意,依允(to)(to be in agreement or harmony[with])
(记)ac+cord(心)→心心相印→一致,同意;n. accord; accordance
(例)He was accorded permission to use the library.

accordingly [ə´kɔːdiŋli] ad. 因此,因而(therefore; consequently)
(例)The snow was four feet deep. Accordingly, the boss told us to go home.

account for 指出…的用途;解释…的原因(to provide an explanation for something)
(例)The treasure could not account for the missing

money.

accrue [ə'kruː] v. 增长，增殖(to accumulate periodically as an increase)

(记)ac + crue(增加)；n. accrual(获利，利息，自然增长)；accruement

(例)The interest on my bank account accrued over the years. / My savings deposited in the bank accrue considerable interest for me every year.

acquiesce [ækwi'es] v. 勉强同意，默认(in)(to agree or consent quietly without protest, but without enthusiasm)

(记)ac + quiesce(安静)→保持安静→默认；n. acquiescence；a. acquiescent(默认的，顺从的)

同根词：quiescent(不动的，静止的)

acquired [ə'kwaiəd] a. 后天习得的(not inheritable)

(记)来自 acquire，ac + quire(得到)→得到，获得；v. acquire；n. acquirement

(例)For wolves, hunting is an acquired skill.

acquisition [ˌækwi'ziʃən] n. 获得(an acquiring or being acquired)

(记)ac + quisit(得到) + ion→得到，获得

同根词：requisite(必需品)

(例)Tom completed the acquisition of a full set of baseball cards.

acquittal [ə'kwitl] n. 宣告无罪，开释([Law] a setting free or being set free by judgement of the court)

(记)ac + quit(免除，抛弃) + tal→得到自由→开释；注意 quit 本身就是一个单词；v. acquit

(例)Max's acquittal came just when he was giving up hope.

activate ['æktiveit] v. 使活化，使激活(to put [an inactive military unit] on an active status by assigning per-

sonnel, equipment, etc. to it);【原】使产生放射性(to make radioactive)
(记)activ(积极)+ate(使成为)→使积极起来→使活化,使激活;a. active
(例)The soldier activated the bomb.

actuate [ˈæktʃueit] vt. 开动(机器)(to put into action or motion);激励,驱使(to cause to take action)
(记)由 act(行动)而来,act(行动) + u+ate(使呈…形式)→开动(机器);激励
(例)What do I press to actuate the device? / What motives actuated him?

acupuncture [ˈækjupʌŋktʃə] n. 针刺(疗法)(the ancient practice, esp. as carried on by the Chinese, of piercing parts of the body with needles in seeking to treat disease or relieve pain)
(记)acu(针)+puncture(刺,刺破)→针刺疗法,针灸
(例)Acupuncture grew out of ancient Chinese philosophy's dualistic(二元的) cosmic theory of the yin and the yang.

acute [əˈkjuːt] a. 灵敏的(sensitive to impressions);(病)急性的(severe but of short duration; not chronic; said of some diseases)
(记)acu(尖端)+te→灵敏的;急性的
同根词:acumen(敏锐)
(例)Dogs have very acute hearing. / The promiscuous(滥交的) man is suffering from an acute VD(即 venereal disease,性病).

adamant [ˈædəmənt] a. 强硬的,固执的(unyielding; inflexible)
(记)联想记忆:adam(亚当)+ant(蚂蚁)"亚当"和"蚂蚁"都是很固执的

(例)Mary was so adamant about it that she raised her voice.

addition [ə'diʃən] n. 加法(an adding of two or more numbers to get a number called the sum)
(记)由 add(加)而来

additive ['æditiv] a. 添加的,附加的(to be added);【数】加法的;n. 添加剂(a substance added to another in small quantities to produce a desired affect, as a preservative added to food, an antiknock added to gasoline, etc.)
(记)由 add(加)而来
(例)This loaf of bread contains additives.

adipose ['ædipəus] a. 脂肪质的,脂肪多的(of, like, or containing animal fat; fatty);n. 动物脂肪(fat in the connective tissue of an animal's body)
(记)adip 来自拉丁语 adeps(脂肪)
(例)Fat deposits that surround the muscles are called adipose tissue.

adjoining [ə'dʒɔiniŋ] a. 毗邻的(touching at some point or along a line; contiguous)
(记)ad(向)+join(加入)+ing→向…加入→毗邻的;同义词:adjacent
(例)We requested adjoining rooms at the hotel.

adjudication [əˌdʒu:di'keiʃən] n. 判决,裁定,宣告(a judge's decision)
(记)ad + judic(to judge 判断)+ ation →进行判断→裁决;v. adjudicate
同根词:judicious(明智的)
(例)The matter is under adjudication.(这事正在审理中。)

admonition [ˌædmə'niʃən] n. 告诫,劝告(a warning to correct some fault);温和的责备(a mild rebuke; repri-

mand)
(记)ad + mon(警告) + ish→告诫; v. admonish; n. admonitor(劝告者,训诫者)
(例) Doctors often make admonitions about the dangers of smoking. / The admonition about lying made the guilty child cry.

adopt [ə'dɔpt] v. 收养(to choose and bring into a certain relationship; specif., to take into one's own family by legal process and raise as one's own child)
(记)ad + opt(选择)→通过选择→收养; n. adoption; a. adopted(被收养的)
同根词:adoptable(可采用的,可收养的);adoptee(被收养者,被立嗣者);adopter(养父母)
(例)Because Johnsons couldn't have children, they adopted.

adulatory ['ædjulətəri] a. 谄媚的,奉承的(flattering)
(记)可以看作是成人(adult)做的坏事——谄媚; n. adulation(过分的称赞,谄媚); adulator(谄媚的人)
(例)He is being adulatory of the candidate.(他是在吹嘘候选人。)

adversarial [ˌædvə'sɛəriəl] a. 敌人的,对手的(of or characterized by opposition, disagreement, hostility, etc., as between adversaries)
(记)ad + vers(转) + arial→对着转的→对手的;n. adversary(敌手,对手);注意:adversity(灾难)
(例)The two employees became adversarial while working on the same project.

adverse ['ædvəːs] a. 逆的,不幸的,不利的(unfavorable; harmful)
(记)ad + vers(转) + e→对着转→逆的,不利的
(例)Too much stress can have an adverse effect on

one's health.

aeronautics [ˌɛərəˈnɔːtiks] n. 航空学(the science, art, or work of designing, making, and operating aircraft)
(记)aero(空气) + naut(航行) + ics→航空学; a. aeronautical(航空学的)
(例)space aeronautics(宇宙航空学)

affinity [əˈfiniti] n. 密切关系(close relationship; connection); 吸引力(the attractive force, of varying strength for various elements, that causes the atoms of certain elements to combine and stay combined)
(记)af + fin(联系) + ity→有联系→密切关系; a. affinitive(密切相关的,关系密切的)
同根词: affine(姻亲)
(例) There is a close affinity between apes and monkeys.

afflict [əˈflikt] v. 使痛苦,折磨(to cause pain or suffering to; distress very much)
(记)af + flict(打击)→一再受到打击→使痛苦,折磨; n. affliction
同根词: conflict(冲突)
(例)A disease broke out and severely afflicted the campers.

affluence [ˈæfluəns] n. 丰富,富裕(great plenty; abundance; wealth); 流入,涌入(a flowing toward; influx)
(记)af(ad 的变体)(向) + flu(flow 流)→不停地向…流→丰富,富裕
(例)The town is known for the affluence of its citizens. / an affluence of new settlers(新来定居者的涌入)

afoul [əˈfaul] ad. 纠缠着(in a collision or a tangle)(run afoul of 与…纠缠〔to get into conflict or trouble

with])
(记)a(向)+foul(缠结)→纠缠着
(例)run/ fall afoul of (与…纠缠,同…发生冲突):run afoul of the law(与法律相抵触) / run afoul of local sensibilities(触犯当地人的感情)

aftermath [ˊɑːftəmæθ] n.后果,结果(a result or consequence, esp. an unpleasant one)
(记)after(在…后)+math(=mow)(割草)→割草之后又长出来的→后果
(例)In the aftermath of the flood, people rebuilt their homes.

agenda [əˊdʒendə] n.议程(program of things to be done; specif., a list of things to be dealt with at a meeting)
(记)ag(做)+enda(表示名词多数)→做的事情→议事日程
同根词:agility(灵活,敏捷)
(例)"How many items are on the agenda?" growled the company's president.

aggravate [ˊægrəveit] v.加重,恶化(to make worse; make more burdensome, troublesome, etc.)
(记)ag(ad)(变化,添加)+grav(重)→加重; a. aggravated; n. aggravation
同根词:gravity(庄重)
(例)The lack of rain aggravated the already serious lack of food. / Don't aggravate your financial difficulties by spending more money than you make.

aggregation [ˌægriˊgeiʃən] n.集合,集中(a gathering into a whole);群体(a group or mass of distinct things or individuals)
(记)ag(ad)(变化)+greg(团体)+ation→成为团体→集合

同根词:gregarious(喜社交的)
(例)The stew was a delicious aggregation of vegetables and spices. / Forrests may become the centre of aggregation of countless animals.

agrarian [əˈgrɛəriən] a. 耕地的,土地的,土地所有的,农民的(relating to land or to the ownership or division of land; of agriculture or farmers generally);n. 主张平均地权的人(a person who advocates agrarian reform, esp. a more equitable division of land)
(记)agr(田) + arian→土地的
(例)The small town has an agrarian economy. / an agrarian movement(农民运动)

ailment [ˈeilmənt] n. (不严重的)疾病(any bodily or mental disorder; illness, esp. a mild, chronic one)
(记)ail(小病) + ment
(例)An ailment of the nervous system can be serious.

airborne [ˈɛəbɔːn] a. 空降的,空运的,空中飞行的(aloft; in the air; flying);通过电视传送的
(记)air(空中的) + borne(承受)→空中承受的→空降的,空运的,空中飞行的
(例)The airborne dust and pollen make me sneeze.

ale [eil] n. 淡色啤酒(a kind of strong beer)
(记)加上 p 就变成了 pale,可以记作"喝了淡色啤酒就脸色苍白"
(例)The Irish and English love to drink ale.

alfalfa [ælˈfælfə] n. 苜蓿,紫苜蓿(a plant that is grown to feed farm animals)
(记)不妨分开记 alf + alf + a,这种拼法跟该词的汉语写法一样独特
(例)Alfalfa is a good grazing plant for cows.

algae [ˈældʒiː] n. (alga[ˌælgə]的复数)水藻,海藻(small

plants without stems, roots, or leaves, that live in water or wet places.)
(记)alga 的复数很特殊,末尾加 e 就是了,其他不常用的复数变化特殊的词如:larva(幼虫)——larvae, fungus(菌类,蘑菇)——fungi, herring(鲱鱼)(单复数相同), quantum(量子)——quanta
(例)Bill slipped on the algae while climbing up a ladder to the dock.

alienate [ˈeiljəneit] vt. 使疏远(to make unfriendly, hostile, or indifferent while attachment formally existed); 让渡财产所有权(to convey or transfer 〔as property or a right〕 usu. by a specific act rather than the due course of law)
(记)alien(外国的,不同)+ate→使到外国→使疏远
(例)The comedian alienated his audience by making mean jokes that weren't funny.

alkaline [ˈælkəlain] a. 碱的,含碱的,碱性的
(记)由 alkali(碱)而来

allegiance [əˈliːdʒəns] n. 忠诚,拥护(loyalty, faithfulness)
(记)al+leg(法律)+iance→靠近法律→拥护;a. allegiant(忠心的,忠实的)
(例)The politician has the allegiance of the voters.

allergy [ˈælədʒi] n. 过敏症 (a physical response to a substance causing sneezing, itching, a rash, or other symptoms)
(记)all(其他)+erg(起作用,工作)+ic→起其他作用→过敏
同根词:ergophobia(厌工作症)
(例)My son recently developed allergies to dairy products.

alleviate [əˈliːvieit] v. 减轻,缓和(to make a burden lighter;

to make a problem less severe or bad)
(记)al + lev(轻) + iate→减轻
同根词:levity(轻率)
(例)Winning the lottery alleviated the couple's financial problems. / The drug alleviated the pain of my broken leg.

alligator [ˈæligeitə] n. 短吻鳄(a large reptile of the crocodile family)
(例)There are many alligators in Florida.

allow for 考虑到;估计;体谅(to take into consideration)
(例)It will take thirty minutes to get to the station, allowing for traffic delay.

allowance [əˈlauəns] n. 允许(permission);津贴,补助费(an amount of something, such as money, given to someone);折扣(a reduction from a list price or stated price)
(记)来自 allow(允许),允许拿到的或省下的钱→津贴,补助费;折扣
(例)the allowance of a claim(对要求权的允准)/ My niece's allowance is twenty dollars a week. / an allowance of 5000 yuan on an old car(一辆旧车价格中 5000 元的折扣)

almshouse [ˈɑːmzhaus] n. 贫民所,救济院(a privately financed home for the poor)
(记)alms(救济物——钱,食物,衣物等) + house→可以领到救济物的地方→救济院
同根词:alms(施舍物,救济金);almsbox(布施箱); almsman(领救济金者,受施舍者)

alternative [ɔːlˈtəːnətiv] a. 两者挑一的;选择的(offering or expressing a choice)
(记) altern (其他,改复) + ative→可以选择其他的→两者挑一的;选择的; v. alternate(交替,更

选)
(例)Her father gave her the alternative of going on to college or starting to work.

altitude [ˈæltitjuːd] n. 高度(the height above sea level)
(记)alt(来自 altus)(高)+itude→高度
(例)The pilot announced that our altitude was 30,000 feet.

alto [ˈæltəu] n. 女低音;男声最高音;中提琴
(记)alt(来自 altus)(高)+o→音质高低→男声最高音,女低音,中提琴

alumni [əˈlʌmnai] n.(alumnus 的复数)校友
(例)an alumnus of Beijing University of the class of 1986(1986 届北京大学毕业生)

amalgam [əˈmælgəm] n. 混合物(a mixture of different elements; combination)
(记)本义是"汞合金",该词来自拉丁文 amalgame(混合);联想记忆:am+alg+am,前后两者 am 结合→混合
(例)His character is an amalgam of contradictory traits. / a perfect amalgam of human and divine(人性与神性的完美结合)

amass [əˈmæs] v. 积聚(to gather people or things together; to gather or accumulate an amount of sth. else)
(记)a+mass(一团)→变成一团→积聚; n. amassment
同根词:massive(巨大的)
(例)While in college, John amassed a shelf of reference books.

amateur [ˈæmətəː] n. 业余爱好者(sb. who does an activity for fun and does not get paid for it; sb. who is not an expert)
(记)amat(=amor)(爱)+eur(人)→爱好的人→

业余爱好者；a. amateurish（业余爱好的；不熟练的）
同根词：amorous（多情的）
（例）The band was made up of amateur musicians.

ambiguity [ˌæmbiˈgjuːiti] n. 模棱两可，模糊（the quality of having more than one meaning or interpretation）
（记）来自拉丁文 ambigere，ambi（绕着，在什么周围）+ agere（做，行动）→围着什么绕来绕去→模棱两可
（例）The ambiguity of the teacher's response made us realize he did not know the answer.

ambivalence [ˈæmbiˈveiləns] n. 矛盾心理（an inability to decide; mixed feelings about something）
（记）ambi（二）+ val（强大）+ ence→两边都有力量→矛盾心理；a. ambivalent
（例）Ambivalence is natural when one makes a big decision.

ambivalent [ˌæmbiˈveilənt] a.（对人或物）有矛盾看法的（having mixed feelings about something; not being able to decide between two or more things）
（记）ambi（二）+ val（强大）+ ent→两边都有力量→矛盾看法
同根词：valiant（勇敢）
（例）They are ambivalent concerning where to go on vacation. / She has an ambivalent attitude about quitting her job.

amend [əˈmend] v. 修订（to change sth.; to modify sth.; esp. to make a change in a constitution）
（记）a + mend（补，修）→修订；另外记住：amends（赔偿，补偿）
（例）The publisher amended the contract to accommodate to the author's demands.

amiable [ˊeimjəbl] a. 和蔼的，亲切的（pleasant; kind; friendly; good-natured）

（记）其常用的同义词 amicable（友善的，温和的）和 amiable 就差一个字母

（例）I'd like to say that my niece is a very amiable girl, but her boyfriend is aloof（冷淡的）.

amnesia [æmˊniːzjə] n. 健忘症，失忆症（a condition where sb. cannot remember anything or cannot remember certain things）

（记）a + mnes（记忆）+ ia（病）→没有记忆的病

同根词：amnesty（大赦）

（例）The story is about a man trying to recapture three years of his life spent in amnesia.

ample [ˊæmpl] a. 富足的，充足的（sufficient and adequate）; n. amplitude（丰富，广阔）

（记）ampl（大，多）+ e；注意：amble（漫步）

同根词：amplify（放大）

（例）My income is small, but it is ample for my needs.

anachronism [əˊnækrənizəm] n. 年代错误（anything that is or seems to be out of its proper time in history）

（记）ana（错）+ chron（时间）+ ism→时间错误

同根词：chronicle（编年史）

（例）It is a glaring anachronism to speak of Shakespeare as riding a bicycle.

analgesic [ˌænælˊdʒesik] n. 镇痛剂（a drug that produces a fully conscious state in which a person does not feel painful stimuli）；a. 止痛的（relieving pain; making pain hurt less）

（记）an（没有）+ alg（痛）+ esic（药）→止痛药

同根词：nostalgia（怀旧，nost 家）

（例）Aspirin is an analgesic.

anatomy [ə'nætəmi] n. 解剖,分析(a detailed analysis);解剖学(the science of morphology or structure of animals or plants);人体,骨骼(the structure of an organism or body)

(记)ana(向上)+tomy(切,割)→解剖

(例)Students in medical schools must study anatomy.

ancestor ['ænsistə] n. 祖先(a person, usually no longer living, from whom one descends)

(记)an(在前面)+cest(行走)+or→在前面走的人→祖先

(例)His ancestor came to America on the Mayflower.(他的祖先是乘"五月花"号来美洲的。)

anecdotal [ˌænek'dəutl] a. 轶事的,爱谈奇闻轶事的(of or being a short, often humorous story, or a brief account of something interesting)

(记)由名词 anecdote 而来;注意不要和 antidote(解毒药)相混

(例)The speaker's anecdotal asides kept the audience awake.

anemia [ə'ni:miə] n.【医】贫血症(a lack of red blood cells, causing a lack of energy)

(记)a+nem(血)+ia→无血病→贫血; a. anemic(贫血的,患贫血症的)

(例)Bill took iron supplements to compensate for his anemia.

anesthetic [ænis'θetik] a. 麻醉的,麻醉剂的(producing the loss of the feeling of pain or any sensation)

(记)an(没有)+esthet(感觉)+ic→无感觉→麻醉

参考:aesthetic(美学)

(例)The anesthetic drug was too weak to numb the

pain I felt.

anesthetics [ˌænisˈθetiks] n. 麻醉剂(drugs, gas, etc. used to produce the loss of the feeling of pain or any sensation)

animate [ˈænimeit] vt. 使兴奋,使活跃(to make sth. come alive; to make sb. or sth. become more lively or energetic)

(记)anim(生命)+ate(动词后缀)→使有生命→使活跃

同根词:magnanimous(大度的)

(例)The wine animated the shy young man, and he sang for the guests.

annuity [əˈnjuːiti] n. 年金,年金享受权(a payment of a fixed sum of money at regular intervals of time, esp. yearly);年金保险(an investment yielding periodic payments during a person's lifetime, for a stated number of years, or in perpetuity)

(记)annu(一年)+ity→年金,年金保险

(例)Before he retired, he put his money into an annuity so that he would always have enough income to support himself.

anonymous [əˈnɔniməs] a. 匿名的(unnamed; created or done without revealing the name or identity of the creator or doer)

(记)an+onym(名称)+ous→无名称→匿名的;n. anonymity

同根词:synonym(同义词)

(例)An anonymous donor gave a million dollars to the charity.

antagonism [ænˈtægənizəm] n. 对抗,敌对(opposition; hostility)

(记) ant (反) + agon (打斗,比赛) + ism →对

着打→对抗；v. antagonize(敌对，对抗)

(例)He felt antagonism toward the winner of the contest.

antebellum [ˈæntiˈbeləm] a. 战前的；[美]南北战争以前的(relating to the period of time before a war, especially the time before the American Civil War, which began in the 1860s.)

(记)来自拉丁文 ante bellum, ante(在…之前) + bellum(战斗)→战前

(例)The antebellum period was the height of Southern culture.

antedate [ˈæntiˈdeit] v.(在信、文件上)写上较早日期(to put a date on that is earlier than the actual date)；早于，先于

(记)ante(前面) + date(日期)

(例)Some states require a person to antedate legal papers to Saturday if they are signed on Sunday. / I know you antedated the letter by a week.

anterior [ænˈtiəriə] a. 先前的，靠前的(more forward; toward the front; on the front side [of the human body])

(记)ante(前面) + rior→以前的

(例)The anterior side of the turtle's shell is lighter in color.

anthology [ænˈθɔlədʒi] n. 诗集，文选(a book that is a collection of written works on the same theme or by the same author)

(记)anth(花) + ology→像花一样的文章→文选

同根词：anthesis(开花期)

(例)This literature class uses an anthology as a text. / an anthology of 20th-century American poetry(20世纪美国诗歌选集)

anthropological [ˌænθrəpəˈlɔdʒikl] a. 人类学的(of or being the study of humans, esp. of the variety, physical and cultural characteristics, distribution, customs, social relationships, etc. of humanity)
(记)anthropo(人,人类)+logi(学科)+cal→人类学的; n. anthropology

antiaristocratic a. 反贵族统治的(opposing the rule by or the system of aristocracy)
(记)anti(反对)+aristocrat(贵族)+ic→反贵族的,反贵族统治的

antibiotic [ˌæntibaiˈɔtik] n. 抗生素(a medicine that kills inhibits the growth of disease-causing organism)
(记)anti(反)+bio(生命)+ic→反生命→抗生素
(例)The doctor gave me an antibiotic to cure my infection.

antibody [ˈæntiˌbɔdi] n. 抗体(身体中的抗病物质)(a substance made by the body in response to a foreign protein in the body)
(记)anti(反)+body(体)→抗体
(例)The vaccination caused the child's body to make its own antibodies against the disease.

anticlimactic [ˌæntiklaiˈmæktik] a. 高潮突降的;虎头蛇尾的(of or being a sudden drop from the dignified or important in thought or expression to the commonplace or trivial, sometimes for humorous effect)
(记)anti(反,抗)+climac(climax)(高潮)+tic→抗高潮的→高潮突降的,虎头蛇尾的; n. anticlimax([在重要性等方面的]突降;虎头蛇尾)
(例)After a sumptuous lunch in a restaurant the hamburger supper is anticlimactic. / The ending of this otherwise perfect play is anticlimactic.

antidote [ˈæntidəut] n. 解毒药(a substance that stops poi-

son from working)
(记)anti(抗)+dote(药剂)→抗毒的药→解毒药
注意:dote=dose(药剂),如 overdose(用药过量)
(例)The woman was given an antidote to the poison just in time. / One antidote to crime is to create jobs.

antifreeze [ˈæntiˈfriːz] n. 抗冻剂(a liquid substance that will not freeze and that is put into a car's radiator)
(记)anti(抗)+freeze(冻)→抗冻剂
(例)My dad puts this kind of antifreeze in his car's radiator each winter.

antigen [ˈæntiədʒən] n. 抗原(注射于动物体内,能使之产生抗体的物质)(a foreign substance in the body that causes the creation of antibodies)
(记)anti(抗)+gen(发生物,原)(基因)→抗原
(例)The injection contained an effective antigen.

antipode [ˈæntipəud] n. 恰恰相反的事物(of, to)(two opposite or contrary things);相对极,对极(anything diametrically opposite; exact opposite)
(记)anti(相反)+pode(做后缀用时意为 foot)→两脚相反→相对立
(例)Selfishness is the very antipode of selflessness.

antiquity [ænˈtikwiti] n. 古代,古(the early period of history, esp. before the Middle Ages);古人,古迹(the people of ancient times; 〔复〕relics, monuments, etc. of the distant past)
(记)antiqu(e)(古代的)+ity→古代;古人
(例) In antiquity, documents were written on parchment. / records left by antiquity(古人留下的文献)

antithesis [ænˈtiθisis] n. 对立,相对(the exact opposite of sth.)

(记)anti + thesis(= set)(放置)→反着放→对立
同根词:thesis(论文)
(例)My boyfriend's reaction was the antithesis of what I expected.

ape [eip] a. 无尾猿,类人猿(a large primate without a tail); 粗野的大汉,傻瓜(a person who is uncouth, gross, clumsy, etc.)
(例)The preacher refused to believe that humans are related to apes.

aperiodic [ˈeipiəriˈɔdik] a. 非周期的(not periodic; occurring irregularly)
(记)a(不,非) + period(周期) + ic→非周期的
(例)aperiodic floods(非周期性洪水)

apolitical [æpəˈlitikl] a. 不关心政治的,无政治意义的(not concerned or connected with political matters)
(记)a(不,非) + political(政治的)→非政治的→不关心政治的
(例)an apolitical attitude(不问政治的态度)

apologist [əˈpɔlədʒist] n. 辩护者(尤指卫护基督教教义的辩护者)(a person who writes or speaks in defense or justification of)
(记)来自 apology 的一个意思:正式辩解
(例)He was an apologist for slavery.(他是奴隶制的辩护者。)

apothecary [əˈpɔθikəri] n. 药剂师(a pharmacist or druggist; apothecaries formerly also prescribed drugs)
(记)拉丁语中 apotheca 是"仓库"的意思
(例) He was apprenticed by his parents to an apothecary at a very young age.

apparatus [ˌæpəˈreitəs] n. 仪器,设备(a device; equipment)
(记)ap(= ad)(向) + paratus(准备)→为…准备好→仪器,设备

(例)The science lab purchased a new piece of apparatus.

apparel [ə'pærəl] n. 衣服；服饰(clothing; garments; attire)；外观，外表(anything that clothes or adorns)
(记)appar(出现)+el→穿出来的东西→衣服；联想：apparent(明显的)
(例)Where in the store can we find women's apparel?

appliance [ə'plaiəns] n. 应用，适用(the act of applying; application)；用具，品具，装具(a device or machine for performing a specific task, esp. one that is worked mechanically or by electricity)
(记)来自 apply(运用，使用)
(例)Stoves, irons, etc. are household appliances.

applicable ['æplikəbl] a. 适用的，适宜的(that can be applied; appropriate; fitting)
(记)来自 apply 一词；n. applicability(适用性)
(例)Some questions on the questionnaire were not applicable. / a rule applicable to foreigners

apportion [ə'pɔːʃən] v. (按比例或计划)分配(to allot portions of sth.)
(记)ap(=ad)+portion(一部分，一份)→分配
(例)The church apportioned the usable clothes to needy families.

apprehend [ˌæpri'hend] v. 逮捕(to locate or arrest sb.)，恐惧，担心
(记)ap+prehend(抓住)→抓住不放→逮捕；注意：GMAT，GRE 中常考"恐惧"一义
同根词：prehensile(能抓住的)
(例)The police apprehended the criminal on the street.

apprentice [ə'prentis] n. 艺徒，初学者(someone who learns a

skill by working under an expert); v. 当学徒(be apprenticed to sb.)

(记)中世纪英语中 aprentis 意为"学习"; n. apprenticeship(学徒的身分, 学徒的年限)

(例) The plumber sent his apprentice to fix our sink.

approbation [æprə'beiʃən] n. 赞成, 同意(official approval, sanction, or commendation)

(记)ap + prob(= prove)(证实) + ation→证实是好的→称赞

参考:opprobrium(谴责, 恶名声)

(例)without the approbation of the Minister(未经部长批准) / His new play received the approbation of the masses.

appropriation [əˌprəupri'eiʃən] n. 拨款, 挪用(the process of budgeting or setting aside money for a particular purpose)

(记)ap + propr(拥有) + iation→拥有→挪用; 注意:appropriate 作形容词(恰当的)

(例)The taxpayers objected to the appropriation of more funds to fix the roads.

aquatic [ə'kwætik] a. 水的, 有水的, 与水有关的(relating to water)

(记)aqu (水) + atic→水中的

同根词:aqueous(水的;似水的)

(例)Aquatic animals can be seen at the aquarium.

arable ['ærəbl] a. 适于耕作的, 可耕的(suitable for plowing, hence for producing crops); n. 耕地(this kind of land)

(记)ar(耕种) + able→可耕的

(例)arable land(可耕地)

arbitrary ['ɑːbitrəri] a. 专横的, 不理智的(based on one's

preference, notion, whim, etc.; capricious)
(记)arbit(判断,裁决)+rary→自做判断的→专横的,不理智的
(例)If you would be less arbitrary when you deal with employees, they would be more loyal.

arbitrator [ˈɑːbitreitə] n. 公断人(someone who listens to both sides of an issue and helps resolve the issue)
(记)arbit(判断,裁决)+rator→能做判断之人→公断人;注意:arbitor(权威,泰斗)
(例)The arbitrator proposed a satisfactory compromise.

arcane [ɑːˈkein] a. 秘密的,神秘的(hidden or secret; understood only by a few; esoteric)
(记)arcan(秘密)+e→神秘的
同根词:arcanum(秘传知识)
(例)arcane rites(含义神秘的典仪) / What is arcane to them is lucid to me.(对他们来说深奥难解的东西对我却是一清二楚的。)

archaeologist [ˌɑːkiəˈlɔdʒist] n. 考古学家(someone who studies the physical remains of older human cultures)
(记)来自 archaeology,archae(古)+ology→考古学
同根词:archaic(古代的)
(例)The archaeologist speculated how ancient people prepared their food.

archenemy [ɑːtʃˈenimi] n. 天敌;主要敌人(someone or something's primary opponent)
(记)arch(主要的)+enemy(敌人)→天敌;主要敌人
(例)The candidate ran in the election against her archenemy.

archives [ˈɑːkaivz] n. 档案(a collection of documents or

records on a specific topic; a collection of important documents and historical records)

(记)联想:arch(主要的)+ives,把主要的文件放起来

(例)Please put this document in the archives with the other contracts.

ardent [ˈɑːdənt] a. 热心的,热烈的(eager; full of intense desire or passion)

(记)ard (热)+ent→热心的,热烈的; n. ardency (热心,热烈)

(例)The young lady's ardent admirer sends her flowers every day.

arid [ˈærid] a. 干旱的(very dry; without water, humidity, or rain)

(记)和 ash 一样来自拉丁语词根 arere,"使燃烧,使干燥"

(例)The desert is an arid place.

array [əˈrei] v. 使…排列成阵势;排列(to arrange things in a particular way or order);装扮,打扮(to dress sb. or sth. in fancy clothes; to adorn sb. or sth.)

(记)ar(=ad)(向)+ray(=ride)→使有顺序→使排列成阵势,排列;装扮

参考:arrange(安排)

(例)The gifts are arrayed on the table so that everyone could see them. / The king and queen were arrayed in elegant robes.

artery [ˈɑːtəri] n.【医】动脉(a vessel that carries blood from the heart to the rest of the body)

(例)If you cut an artery, you will bleed profusely.

articulate [ɑːˈtikjulit] v. 说话清晰(to speak clearly and distinctly; to describe sth., esp. an idea, logically and distinctly);以关节连接(connect by joints)

(记)articul(关节)+ate→关节之间相连→(说话)上下相连→说话清楚

(例)The six-year-old could not articulate his feelings. / bones that articulate (or are articulated) with others

artifact [ˈɑːtifækt] n. 手工艺器(any object made by human work; esp., a simple and primitive tool, weapon, vessel, etc.);文物

(记)arti(技巧)+fact→技巧做成的→手工艺器

(例)The archaeologist discovered ancient artifacts. / The museum is filled with artifacts from various cultures.

artisan [ˌɑːtiˈzæn] n. 手工业工人,手艺人(someone skilled in a craft or trade)

(记)arti(技巧)+san(人)→使用技巧的人→手艺人

(例)Blacksmiths are artisans whose craft has almost disappeared.

ascribe [əsˈkraib] v. 把…归于(to)(to identify sth. as the product of sb. or sth.; to identify sth. as the cause of sth.)

(记)a(向)+scribe(写)→写在什么上面→把…归于

(例)The monument was ascribed to an ancient civilization. / To what do you ascribe your success?

aspersion [əsˈpəːʃən] n. 诽谤,中伤(the act of defaming; a damaging or disparaging remark; slander; innuendo)

(记)a+spers(散开)+ion→散布坏东西→诽谤

同根词:intersperse (点缀)

(例)I resent your casting aspersions on my brother and his ability.

asphyxiation [æsˌfiksiˈeiʃən] n. 窒息(smothering; suffocation)
(记)来自动词 asphyxiate, a + sphyx (跳动) + iate →脉搏不再跳动→窒息
同根词: sphygmus(脉搏), sphyx = sphyg
(例)I was worried about asphyxiation from all the cigarette smoke.

aspire [əsˈpaiə] v. 渴望,热望,抱负(to have the ambition to do or be sth.)
(记)a + spir(呼吸) + e→屏住呼吸等待→渴望
同根词: respire(呼吸)
(例)I aspire to being an actress someday in the future.

assassination [əˌsæsiˈneiʃən] a. 刺杀,暗杀(the murder of sb. famous or important, esp. for political reasons)
(记)来自法语 assassin(刺杀者); v. assassinate
(例)The nation was shocked by the president's assassination.

assess [əˈses] n. 估价,评价(to estimate or determine the significance, importance, value of; evaluate)
(例) The assessor assessed the property at much less than it was worth.

asteroid [ˈæstərɔid] a. 星状的(starlike; shaped like a star or starfish); n.【天】小行星(minor planet; planetoid)
(记)aster(星星) + oid(像…的)→像星星的→星状的

asthma [ˈæsmə] v. 哮喘(an illness involving difficulty in breathing)
(记)也写作 asthema, 分割记忆: as - them - a
(例)The famous singer Deng Lijun died of asthma.

astute [əsˈtjuːt] n. 机敏的,精明的(clever; wise; intelligent; observant; insightful)

(记)来自拉丁文 astus(灵活)
(例)The astute reader noticed that the author had ignored a crucial fact. / The boss appreciated the young man's astute observations about how to improve the company's image.

asunder [ə'sʌndə] ad. 分开,化为碎片(into parts or pieces; apart or separate in direction or position)
(记)联想记忆:as + under,好像在…下面,化为碎片自然会落下去
(例)The war forced the parents and children asunder. / tear sth. asunder(把某物扯成数部分)

attorney [ə'tə:ni] n. 律师(a lawyer)
(记) at + torn (转) + er →转的人→能说会道的人→律师
同根词:tornado(龙卷风)
(例)Bob hired an attorney to get a patent for his invention.

attribute [ə'tribju:t] n. 属性,品质(a feature, a quality, or a property of sb. or sth.); v. 把…归于(to)(to ascribe as a quality or characteristic)
(记)同义词为 ascribe; a. attributable(可归于…的); n. attribution(归因)
(例)What attributes of the car enticed you to buy it? / The discovery of electricity is attributed to Benjamin Franklin.

attrition [ə'triʃən] n. 消耗,磨损(the act or process of wearing away or grinding down by friction)
(记)at(= ad)(向) + trit(磨擦) + ion→磨损
同根词:contrition(悔恨)
(例)an attrition rate(损耗率)

auction ['ɔ:kʃən] n. 拍卖(a sale where each item is sold to the person offering to pay the highest rice)

(记)auct(提高)+ion→提高价格→拍卖
同根词:augment(提高),auct=aug
(例)The charity held an auction to benefit medical research.

audit [ˈɔːdit] v.【经】审计(to go over or inspect the financial records or sb. or sth.)
(记)aud(听)+it→听…→审计; n. auditor(审计员)
同根词:auditorium(大讲堂)
(例)The company hired an accounting firm to audit the books.

aura [ˈɔːrə] n.(人或物发出的)气味,香味(atmosphere surrounding a person or object that thought to come from him or it)
(例)an aura of rosebuds(玫瑰花苞的香气)

aurora [ɔːˈrɔːrə] n.极光(南北极夜晚所放彩光)

austere [ɔsˈtiə] a. 朴素的(very simple; without luxury);(人)严厉的(stern; severe in appearance);(经济)紧缩的(financially tight)
(记)au+ster(冷)→冷面孔→一本正经的
同根词:stern(严厉的)
(例)The mountain cabin had very austere rooms and no indoor plumbing. / The austere professor never smiles. / Father was an austere man, very strict with his children.

authentic [ɔːˈθentik] a. 真的,真实的(real; genuine; known to be right or true)
(记)aut(自己)+hent(得到)+ic→自己得到的真品→真正的;n. authentication(证明,鉴定)
同根词:comprehension(理解)
(例)Is your diamond ring authentic?

automation [ɔːtəˈmeiʃən] n. 自动化

(记)auto(自己) + mat(动) + tion→自动化

autonomous [ɔː'tɔnəməs] a. 自主的,自治的(self-governing; independent)

(记)auto(自己) + nom(法则)→自己的法则的→自主的,自治的

(例)The colony wished to be an autonomous state.

auxin ['ɔːksin] n.生长素

(记)aux(aug)(提高) + in(素)→使人提高的东西→生长素

同根词:auxiliary(辅助的)

average ['ævəridʒ] n. 平均数(a sum obtained by adding several numbers together and then dividing that total by the number of figures that were added)

(记)average 作形容词用时指"通常的,平均的"

(例)The average daily rainfall for April in Beijing is quite low.

aversion [ə'vəːʃən] n. 嫌恶,憎恨(a strong dislike of sth. or doing sth.)

(记)a + vers(转) + ion→转开→厌恶的

同根词:adverse(不利的)

(例)Her aversion to buses makes it necessary for her to own a car.

B

backdrop ['bækdrɔp] n. 舞台后部的彩画,幕布(a curtain hung at the back of a stage, often painted to represent some scene);背景(background or setting, as of an event)

(记)back(后面) + drop(落下)→后面落下的→幕布

(例)Indochina is the backdrop for this story.(这个

故事的背景在印度支那。）

balk [bɔːk] vt. 阻碍，使受挫折（to stop and obstinately refuse to move or act）；vi. 畏缩不前（to hesitate or recoil）

（记）注意和 bark（犬吠）区分开来

（例）Many people do not balk at the idea of cheating on their taxes.

ballad [ˈbæləd] n. 歌谣，小曲（a poem or song that tells a story, esp. a love story）

（记）联想：ball（球）+ad→像球一样一代代滚下来→歌谣

（例）The folk singer is famous for her emotional ballads.

ballistic [bəˈlistik] a. 弹道（学）的，发射的

（记）联想：ball（球）+istic→像球一样发射出去

bankruptcy [ˈbæŋkrəptsi] n. 破产，倒闭（a state of not having enough money to pay off debts）

（记）bank（银行）+rupt（断）→破产

同根词：corruption（腐败）

（例）The failed company went into bankruptcy.

baptism [ˈbæptizəm] n.（基督教）洗礼，浸礼（a Christian rite involving immersion in or sprinkling with water, initiating a person into the church）

（记）来自动词 baptize（〔给人施行〕洗礼）

（例）The Browns presented their baby for baptism last Sunday.

bar [bɑː] v. 阻挡，拦住（get in the way, hinder）；闩上（to secure a door or window by placing across it a rigid rod of metal, wood, or some other material known as a bar）

（例）The gate was put up to bar the children from leaving. / The frightened family barred the door against the intruder.

bargain [ˈbɑːgin] n. 廉价货,好交易(sth. that was bought for less money than it would normally cost; sth. that is inexpensive)

(例)That book is a real bargain at $2.

baritone [ˈbæritəun] n. 男中音,男中音歌手(a male singer whose range is lower than that of a tenor and higher than that of bass);萨克斯号(a large brass musical instrument like a large trumpet coiled in an oval shape)

(记)bari(重,深) + tone(音质,音调)→音质重的→男中音

(例)The opera starred a magnificent baritone. / The band director recruited a little boy to play the baritone.

bark [bɑːk] n. 树皮(无复数)(the outer surface of a tree)

(记)bark 的另一个词义"犬吠"大家都很熟悉

(例)A message was etched(蚀刻) into the bark of the tree.

baroque [bəˈrəuk] a.(艺术,建筑等)高度装饰的,过分雕琢的(fantastically over decorated, gaudily ornate)

(记)通常写作 Baroque,指 17 世纪巴罗克时期的艺术,以古怪精巧为特色

barrel [ˈbærəl] n. 桶(a large, rounded wooden container with a flat top and bottom);vt. 把…装桶(put or pack in a barrel or barrels)

base [beis] n. 底,基底(lowest part or bottom)

(例)We picnicked at the base of the mountain. / the base of a machine

basketry [ˈbæskitri] n.(篮、篓、筐等的)编织术(the craft of making baskets);(总称篮子等)编织物(baskets

collectively)
(记)basket(篮子)+ry→编织术

battalion [bəˈtæljən] n.【军】营,营部(a large group of soldiers arrayed for battle);(复)部队
(记)同根词 battle

beatific [ˌbiːəˈtifik] a. 祝福的,有福的(making blissful or being blessed; showing happiness or delight; blissful)
(记)来自动词 beatify(使享福,为…祝福),beat(好)+ify(做)→做得…好→使(别人)好
(例)a period of beatific peace(太平盛世)

behest [biˈhest] n.命令,训喻(an order, command, or request)
(记)be+hest(命令,训喻)→命令,训喻
(例)carry out sb.'s behests(执行某人的命令)/at one's behest(按照某人的命令):I am ready to act at your behest.(我已准备好按照你的命令行动。)

benefactor [ˈbenifæktə] n.行善者,捐助者(sb. who gives money to an organization, institution, or person)
(记)bene(好)+fact(做)+or→做好事的人
(例)The generous benefactor remained anonymous.

beneficiary [ˌbeniˈfiʃəri] n.受益人(sb. or a group that receives money or benefits; the recipient of a gift)
(记)bene(好)+fic(做)+iary→得到好处的人→受益人
(例)The whole office was the beneficiary of the boss's good cheer.

bereft [biˈreft] a. 丧失,失去;被剥夺了的(being deprived of a person's sb. or sth. close to him)
(记)由动词 bereave 而来,be+reave(抢夺)→抢

夺掉→丧失;注意 reave 本身是一个单词,意为“剥夺”

(例)The children grieved that they were bereft of their favorite pet.

beset [bi'set] v.包围(to attack sb. or sth. on all sides; to surround sb. or sth.)

(记)be(构成动词,围绕)+set(设置)→包围

(例)The small town was beset by enemy troops.

besiege [bi'si:dʒ] n.围攻,困扰(to attack a place, as in battle; to overwhelm sb. or sth.)

(记)be(构成动词,围绕)+siege(围攻)→围攻;siege 本身是一个单词

(例)He was besieged by doubts. / The troops besieged the tiny island.

bestow [bi'stəu] vt.把…赠与(to give praise to sb.; to present an award to sb.);放置,贮藏(to put or place, as in storage)

(记)be+stow(地方)→给予地方;stow 本身是一个单词,意为“装载,收藏”

(例)The committee bestowed an engraved plaque on the winner. / Praise was bestowed on the graduate.

betray [bi'trei] v.背叛(to be disloyal or unfaithful to sb. or sth.);暴露(reveal); n. betrayal

(记)be+tray(背叛)→背叛

参考:traitor(叛徒);n. betrayal;betrayer

(例)Her red face betrayed her nervousness.(脸色通红暴露了她的不安。)/ Mary betrayed Bill by having a love affair.

better off 境况(尤指经济情况)较好(being richer or more comfortable)

(例)Since my husband was made the manager, we

are better off.

beverage [ˈbevəridʒ] n.饮料(a drink other than water)
(记)bever(喝)+age→喝的东西→饮料
(例)What sort of beverage should we serve at the party?

bicentenary [ˌbaisenˈtiːnəri] n./a.二百年(的)(happening once in a period of 200 years; bicentennial);二百多年纪念的(of a 200th anniversary)
(记)bi(二)+centenary(century)(百年)→二百年的;二百年纪念的

bid [bid] v./n.出价,喊价(to offer an amount of money for sth., esp. at an auction; an offer of an amount of money)
(记)注意:bid有两种过去时形式——bade和bid,两种过去分词形式——bidden和bid,但bid意为"出价,喊价"时过去时和过去分词都只用bid
(例)He bid $1000, but failed to buy the painting.

bilateral [baiˈlætərəl] a.双边的(involving, serving, or referring to two sides or factions)
(记)bi(二)+lateral(边的)→双边的
(例)The bilateral talks between Russia and the U.S. produced an important agreement.

bilingual [baiˈliŋgwəl] a.(能说)两种语言的([of a person] able to speak two languages)
(记)bi(二个)+lingu(语言)+al→两种语言的
(例)The bilingual child speaks both English and Chinese.

biofeedback [ˈbaiəuˈfiːdbæk] n.生物反馈(a technique of seeking to control certain emotional states, such as anxiety or depression, by training oneself, with the aid

of electronic devices, to modify automatic functions, such as blood pressure or heart beat)
(记)bio(生物的)+feedback(反馈)→生物反馈
(例)In biofeedback therapy, information is supplied instantaneously about an individual's own physiological processes.

bipartisan [baiˌpɑːti'zæn] a. 由两党成员组成的;被两党支持的(relating to two political parties; supported by both the Republican and Democratic parties)
(记)bi(二)+parti(party)(党派)+san→由两党成员组成的
(例)The bill received bipartisan support.

birch ['bəːtʃ] n. 桦,白桦;桦木(a kind of tree whose balk is often white and peels off in thin layers)
(记)注意书写时不要误写成 birth; a. birchen(桦树的;桦木制的)

bisect [bai'sekt] v. 平分(to cut sth. into two equal parts; to split sth. down the middle)
(记)bi(二)+sect(切,割)→分成两份→平分
(例)The partition bisected the room into two smaller rooms.

bizarre [bi'zɑː] a. 奇异的,古怪的(very strange; eccentric; weird)
(记)比较:bazaar(集市),集市上有各种古怪的东西
(例)A bizarre series of events preceded the murder. / He became increasingly bizarre in speech.(他言谈越来越古怪。)

blackout ['blækaut] n.(幕间或剧中)灯暗(the extinguishing of all stage lights to end a play or scene);临时眩晕(a temporary loss of consciousness or vision);新闻封锁(not allowing information about sth.,

such as an invasion or a court trial, to be covered by the press)
(记)black(黑)+out(灯灭)→灯暗
(例)I had a short blackout after I fell and broke my foot. / The judge ordered a blackout to prevent the jurors from being influenced by the media.

bland [blænd] a.(人)情绪平稳的(having no excitement; boring; dull);(食物)无味的(having no taste; not spicy)
(记)bland本身可作词根,意为"温和,奉承"
参考:blandishment(奉承,哄诱)
(例)We spent another bland evening at home last Saturday. / The cafeteria's food was really bland.

blast [blɑːst] n.一阵风(a strong, sudden gust of air; a sudden, heavy wind);爆炸(an explosion)
(记)和gust(阵风,一阵狂风)一起记
(例)The leaves were lifted into the air by a sudden blast of wind. / The building was torn apart by the blast.

bleak [bliːk] a. 苍白的,暗淡的(pale; wane);凄凉的(not cheerful; gloomy; dreary);无遮蔽的(exposed to wind and cold; unsheltered; treeless; bare)
(记)与bleach(漂白)是同根词
(例)The bleak day made us feel rather gloomy. / The bleak look on my manager's face means that he has bad news.

blemish [ˈblemiʃ] v.损害,玷污(to mark, spoil, or tarnish sth.);n. 瑕疵,缺点(a mark; a defect)
(记)blem(弄伤)+ish→把…弄伤→损害,玷污
(例)One illness will blemish your perfect attendance record. / I found a small blemish on my new

mirror, so I returned it.

blob [blɔb] n.(半流质的)粘乎乎的一团(a soft, shapeless mass of sth.);vt.用斑点弄污(to splash or mark, as with blobs)

(记)可以和下文的 blot(墨迹,污迹)一块儿记

(例)The cook kneaded a blob of dough(生面团).

blockade [blɔˈkeid] vt./n.封锁,闭塞(to start a military action that prevents people and goods from entering or leaving a place; this kind of military action, or an impediment to the movement or process of sth.)

(记)block(阻碍)+ade→阻碍物→封锁

(例)They blockaded the town to starve the people into surrendering. / The police formed a blockade on the main roads to prevent the suspect from escaping.

blot [blɔt] n.墨迹,污迹(a spot or smeared area of ink);不雅观的事物(anything that spoils, or mars, esp. by providing an unpleasant contrast)

(例)The scandalous affair was a blot on this country's president's reputation.

blurry [ˈbləːri] a.模糊的,难辨的事物(hazy; indistinct)

(记)blur(使〔视线,感觉,形状〕模糊不清)+ry→模糊的,难辨的事物

(例)The page appeared blurry to the old man, who wasn't wearing glasses.

bog [bɔg] n.泥塘,沼泽(a marsh, wet, soft, muddy ground); v.陷入泥沼,(使)停顿 (down)(to get stuck, as if sinking in mud; to come to a halt, as if mired)

(记)联想 dog 来记,狗掉进了泥塘

(例)The hikers walked around the bog. / The project bogged down because of poor management.

bolster [ˈbəulstə] n. 枕垫(a cylindrical pillow or cushion); v. 支持,鼓励(to support or uphold sb. or sth.)
(记)枕垫的功能就是支持
(例)Jane leaned her back comfortably against the bolster on the sofa. / The new comer bolstered his courage to ask for a raise.

bombardment [bɔmˈbɑːdmənt] n. 炮轰(attacking sb. or sth. constantly with sth.)
(记)来自动词 bombard, bomb(炸弹) + ard→炮轰
(例)The bombardment of the senator with letters was very effective.

bondage [ˈbɔndidʒ] n. 奴役,束缚(slavery; involuntary servitude); in bondage to(被…所奴役)
(记)bond(束缚) + age→束缚,奴役
(例)Lincoln emancipated the slaves from their bondage. / He is in hopeless bondage to his master.

bookkeeping [ˈbukkiːpiŋ] n. 簿记(the job of keeping track of the financial records and transaction of a company of an organization)
(记)book(书) + keeping(保持)→把…保持成一本书的样子→簿记
(例)Bookkeeping requires a sharp mind and a knowledge of accounting.

boom [buːm] v. 突然增加,迅速发展;兴旺,出名(to increase suddenly in size, importance, activity, etc.; undergo swift, vigorous growth; flourish)
(记)可以联想该词的读音来记,读音给人的感觉就像汤突然烧开的感觉→突然增加,兴旺
(例)The business in this area has boomed recently.

boost [buːst] vt. 提高(to make higher or greater; increase in amount, power, etc.);促进,支援(to

raise by or as by a push from behind or below; push up);(用广告)吹捧(to urge other to support; promote)
(例)boost the morale of the soldier

boreal [ˈbɔːriəl] 北的,北方的,北风的(northern; of the northwind);北半球北部山区的(of or pertaining to the northern zone of plant and animal life including the taiga and tundra)
(记)分割记忆:bo－real
(例)The North American boreal forest is one of the greatest sweeps of forest in the world.

bottleneck [ˈbɔtlnek] n.瓶颈口,[喻]交通易阻塞的狭口(the neck of a bottle; any place, as a narrow road, where traffic is slowed up or halted);妨碍生产流程的一环(any point at which movement or progress is slowed up because much must be funneled through it)
(记)bottle(瓶)＋neck(脖子)
(例)The bottleneck where two freeways merged causes large traffic jams. / Anne squeezed through the bottleneck of the doorway.

bound [baund] a. 被束缚的(confined by, as by binding; tied);密切关联的(closely connected or related);必定的(be bound to)(certain; sure; determined)
(记)bound 是由 bind(绑,捆)的过去分词演变而来的
(例)He is bound to his job.(他被工作束缚住了。) / This question is bound up with his future. / You are bound to publish a novel some day.

bountiful [ˈbauntiful] a. 慷慨的(giving freely and graciously; generous);丰裕的,充足的(provided in abundance; plentiful)

(记)bounti = bon(好) + ful→好的→慷慨的
参考:bountiful = bounteous
(例)The harvest was bountiful this year.

bounty [ˊbaunti] n. 慷慨,恩惠(generosity in giving);奖金,赏金,补助金(a reward, premium, or allowance, esp. one given by a government for killing certain harmful animals, raising certain crops, etc.)
(记)bount = bon(好) + y→好→慷慨,恩惠
(例)He had a bounty of $5000 on his head.(有人悬赏 5000 元要他的脑袋。)

bouquet [bu(:)ˊkei] n. 花束(an arrangement of cut flowers; a grouping of cut flowers that can be held in one hand)
(记)比较:bouquet(花束);banquet(宴会);另外 bouquet 为法语,要注意它的发音
(例)My boyfriend sent me a bouquet of flowers for my birthday.

bout [baut] n. 一回,一场,一阵(a period of time taken up by some activity, illness, etc.; spell);回合,较量,比赛(a specific contest or event, esp. a boxing match)
(记)原指农夫来回犁地,现在指带有反复性的活动(bouts of activity 几番活动);比较:boutique(妇女时装精品店→妇女反复走的地方)
(例)The best fighter won the bout.

bower [ˊbauə] n. 凉亭,树荫处(a place enclosed by overhanging boughs of trees or by vines on a trellis; arbor);【诗】村舍,隐居处(a rustic cottage or retreat);【古】闺房(a lady's boudoir)
(记)联想记忆:bow + er,弓:凉亭的顶部常是"弓"形的; 同义词:arbor(凉亭)

brazen [ˊbreizn] a. 无耻的，厚脸皮(shameless; impudent)
(记)braz = brass(黄铜) + en→像黄铜一样→厚颜的
同根词：brazier(炭火盆)
(例)The brazen accusation was denied.

breakthrough [ˊbreikθru:] n. 突破(a sudden discovery; a major discovery of a crucial fact)
(记)break(破) + through(通过)→穿破→突破
(例)The scientists were hoping to make a breakthrough in cancer treatments.

brevity [ˊbreviti] n. 简短，简洁(shortness; the quality of being brief)
(记)来自形容词 brief(简短的)
(例)The employees appreciated the brevity of the president's speech.

brewery [ˊbruəri] n. 啤酒厂，酿酒厂(a place where beer is made)
(记)brew(酿造) + ery→酿酒厂
(例) You can smell the neighborhood brewery a mile away.

bring about v. 产生，导致(cause to happen)
(例)bring about a war/ reforms/ sb.'s ruin

briny [ˊbraini] a. 盐水的，很咸的(very salty)；海水的(of the water of the sea)
(记)由名词 brine 而来；n. brine(盐水；海水；海)
(例)Briny pools have dissolved salts that can lower the freezing point.

brokerage [ˊbrəukəridʒ] n. 经纪业，中间人业务(a company that arranges the sale of something)；付给经纪人的经手费，佣金，回扣(a broker's fee or commission)

(记)broker(中间人,经纪人)+age→经纪业;佣金
(例)A brokerage house's job is to channel individual investors' money to the stock market.

bronze [brɔnz] n.青铜(a brownish metal made from copper and tin)
(例)The statue was cast in bronze.

browse [brauz] v./n.吃嫩叶或草(to eat by nibbling);浏览(to look through sth. casually)
(记)brow = sprout(嫩叶)+ se→吃嫩叶; n. browser(浏览器,吃嫩叶的动物,浏览书本的人)
(例)to browse in the fields/ to browse through someone's books / I browsed through the shelves at the bookstore.

brutal [ˈbruːtl] a. 残忍的,严酷的(violent and cruel; vicious)
(记)来自 brute(野兽);brutality,n. 残酷,兽行
(例)The brutal king tortured his opponents.

budget [ˈbʌdʒit] n.预算(a financial plan; an estimate of how much money will be earned and spent during a period of time)
(记)联想记忆:bud(蓓蕾,发芽)+get(得到)→得到了发芽→初步计算出来了→预算
(例)The department's budget did not include money for electricity.

buffer [ˈbʌfə] n.缓冲器(a device using padding springs, hydraulic pressure, etc. to lessen or absorb the shock of collision or impact);缓冲的人物(any person or thing that serves to lessen shock or prevent sharp impact)
(记)buff 本身是一个词,"缓冲,减震"
(例)Sue was a buffer between her boss and the angry customers.

bugbear [ˊbʌgbɛə] n. 使人恐惧的东西,妖怪(an imaginary hobgoblin or terror used to frighten children into good conduct; anything causing seemingly needless or excessive fear or anxiety)

(记)联想记忆:bug(小虫子) + bear(熊)→又是小虫子,又是熊的,自然令人恐惧→使人恐惧的东西,妖怪

(例) The general's bugbear was his soldiers' mutiny. / This frightening mask is the child's bugbear.

bulge [bʌldʒ] n. 膨胀,突出(a bump, a round swelling; a protrusion)

(记)比较:budge(让步),bilge(船底),bugle(军号)

(例)There was a bulge around my waist where I had tucked in my sweater.

bumblebee [ˊbʌmblbiː] n. 野蜂,大黄蜂(any of a number of related large, hairy, yellow-and-black social bees)

(记)联想记忆:bumble(大错误) + bee(蜂)→能犯大错误的蜂→大黄蜂

bummer [ˊbʌmə] n. 懒汉,游手好闲的人(one who lives by begging and sponging)

(记)bum 本身也是"懒汉,流浪汉,乞丐"之意

bunch [bʌntʃ] n. (一)球,束,串(a group of things that grow together or are placed together);v. 捆成一串(to gather together closely)

(记)比较记忆:bunch(束),lunch(午饭),hunch(驼背)

(例)The lady arranged a bunch of flowers in the vase.

buoyant [ˊbɔiənt] a. 易浮的(able to float);快乐的(happy, cheerful)

(记)buoy(浮标) + ant→易浮的;快乐的;n. buoy-

ancy(浮动)
(例)The plastic bathtub toys are very buoyant. / My neighbor has a buoyant personality.

bureaucrat [ˈbjuərəukræt] n. 官僚(a government worker; someone who is part of government offices and agencies and follows policies rigidly)
(记)bureau(政府的局、处等) + crat(统治参与或支持者)→官僚政治
(例)By the time John got a building permit, he was very annoyed with bureaucrats.

burgeon [ˈbəːdʒən] v. 迅速成长,发展(to grow or develop rapidly; expand; proliferate; flourish)
(记)burg = bud(花蕾) + eon→成长, burg 本身是一个单词, 意为"城、镇"→成长的地方
(例)New suburbs burgeoned all around the city. / a burgeoning industrial sector(欣欣向荣的新兴工业部门)

burglarize [ˈbəːgləraiz] v. 进行夜盗(to enter a building to steal things)
(记)burglar(夜盗) + ize(动词词缀)→进行夜盗 n. burglar(夜贼),burglary(入室行窃)
(例)The woman realized her home had been burglarized——things had been thrown everywhere.

burrow [ˈbʌrəu] n. 兔子等所掘的地洞(a hole or tunnel dug in the ground by an animal);v. 挖洞(to make a burrow or burrows in the ground; dig)
(记)和 borrow 一起记, 也可分割记忆:burro - w; burro(小毛驴)

bust [bʌst] n. 半身塑像(a sculpture of sb.'s head and shoulders);vt. 使爆裂(to burst or break);使破产,使降级(to become penniless or bankrupt)
(例)The sculptor unveiled the bust at the muse-

um.

bustle [ˈbʌsl] v. 喧闹；奔忙；活跃(to rush about busily; to hush around)

(记)记住一个与 bustle 形似意近的词 hustle; hustle and bustle(熙熙攘攘)

(例)The server bustled here and there, but she never brought us our food.

buttress [ˈbʌtris] v. 支持(to support or reinforce); n. 扶墙，拱壁(a projecting structure, generally of brisk or stone, built against a wall to support or reinforce it)

(记)分割记忆：but - tress, tress 意为"一束头发"

(例)buttress an argument(支持一个论点)

bylaw [ˈbailɔː] n. 地方法规(an official rule of an organization)

(记)by(旁边) + law→旁系法规→地方法规

(例)The city council passed a bylaw to ban smoking in all the restaurants.

C

cabin [ˈkæbin] n. (简陋的)小屋(a small house made of wood, esp. in a remote area)；船舱，机舱(a private room on a ship; or the part of airplane where passengers sit)；v. 住在小屋里(to confine in or as in a cabin; cramp)

(记)联想：cab(出租车) + in(在里面)→出租车般小的屋子→小屋，船舱

(例)It was noisy in the cabin, so no one heard the pilot's announcement.

cache [kæʃ] n. 土窖，藏物处(a hidden place)；贮藏物(a hidden supply of sth.)

(记)比较 cache 和 cash,二者读音相同,字形相像
(例)When we go on vacation, we put our jewelry in a cache under the bed. / The burglar discovered the cache of jewels.

calcium [ˈkælsiəm] n. 钙(a chemical element and essential nutrient, important for strong teeth and bones)
(记)化学元素多以 ium 或 um 结尾,如 titanium(钛),helium(氦),sodium(钠),chromium(铬)等

calamitous [kəˈlæmitəs] a. 造成灾祸的(causing or bringing a disaster)
(记)来自名词 calamity; calam(破坏 destruction) + ity→大灾祸
(例)The failure in the test could be calamitous.

caliph [ˈkælif] n. 哈里发(伊斯兰国家政教合一的领袖称号)(supreme ruler: the title taken by Mohammed's successors as secular and religious heads of Islam)

calligraphic [ˌkæliˈgræfik] a. 书法的(of handwriting or penmanship)
(记)来自 calligraphy, call = kall(美丽) + graphy(写)→写美丽的字→书法

calorie [ˈkæləri] n. 卡(热量单位)
(记)汉语中的"卡路里"是其音译

campaign [kæmˈpein] n. 战役(a series of military operations with a particular objective in a war);运动;竞选运动(a series of organized, planned actions for a particular purpose, as for electing a candidate)
(记)联想:打起战役或搞起运动来都需 camp(露营)
(例)The presidential campaign lasted for months.

campesino [ˌkæmpiˈsiːnəu] n. 农民,农业工人(a peasant or farm worker)

(记)campe(campo)(乡村)+sino→农民

(例)"Campesino" is usually refered to independent peasants who live in self-sufficient households in Latin America.

canary [kəˊnεəri] n. 金丝雀(a small, yellow bird that sings)

(记)这种鸟最初生活在大西洋的 Canary Islands

cancerous [ˊkænsərəs] a. 癌的;患癌症的(malignant; diseased with cancer)

(记)cancer(癌症)+ous→癌的

(例)The surgeon removed the cancerous tumor.

canon [ˊkænən] n. 经典,真作(the works ascribed to an author that are accepted as genuine)

(记)比较 cannon(大炮)和 canon

(例)the Shakespeare canon(莎士比亚的经典集)

canopy [ˊkænəpi] n. 蚊帐;华盖(a fabric cover that hangs over sth.)

(记)来自 canop(蚊子)+y→蚊帐

(例)There is a striped canopy over the entrance of the hotel.(旅馆入口处有一顶条纹天篷。)

canvas [ˊkænvəs] n. 粗帆布(a heavy, sturdy fabric made from cotton or hemp);帐篷(a tent or tents, esp. circus tents);一幅油画(布)(any coarse cloth of open mesh weave on which embroidery or tapestry is done)

(记)注意和 canvass(详细检查;拉选票;到处征订客户)区分开来

(例)a canvas bag

capacity [kəˊpæsiti] n. 容量(the amount of sth. that a space will hold);宽敞

(记)capac(宽大)+ity→宽敞

参考:capability(能力,才能)

(例) The maximum capacity of this room is 200 people.

capricious [kə'priʃəs] a. 反复无常的;多变的(whimsical; impulsive)

(记)由 caprice(变化,任性)而来,capriccio(随想曲)

(例)We can't go camping while the weather is so capricious. / She is a bit capricious, but she is delightful.

captious ['kæpʃəs] a. 吹毛求疵的(fond of catching others in mistakes; quick to find fault; quibbling; carping)

(记)capt(拿) + ious→拿(别人的缺点)→吹毛求疵的

同根词:caption(标题);capture(俘获)

(例)A captious debater is interested in winning the debate rather than seeking truth.

captivity [kæp'tiviti] n. 监禁,被俘,束缚(imprisonment; the condition of not being free)

(记)capt(抓住) + ivity→监禁,被俘

(例) Some animals cannot bear captivity. / the captivity of science and invention by business(企业界对科学和发明的束缚)

capture ['kæptʃə] n. / v. 捕获,占领(to catch sb. or sth.); v. 迷住 (to hold the interest of someone; captivate)

(记)capt(抓住) + ure→捕获,占领

(例)capture butterflies / His brilliant performance captured the audience's imagination. / Her beauty captured him.

carbohydrate [ˌkɑːbəu'haidreit] n. 碳水化合物;糖类

(记)carbo(碳) + hydrate(与水化合)→碳水化合

物

cardiac [ˊkɑːdiæk] a. 心脏的,心脏病的(of, near, or affecting the heart);强心剂(a medicine that stimulates cardiac action);患心病的人(a person with a heart disorder)

(记)cardi(心脏的)+ac→心脏的,心脏病的

(例)a cardiac disease(心脏病)

cargo [ˊkɑːgəu] n. 船货,货物(the load of commodities carried by a ship, airplane, truck, etc.; freight); a cargo liner 定期货轮

(记)联想记忆:装在 car 上 go 的物品→货物

(例)The ship carries cargoes of food and other goods. / The truck had no cargo, it was empty.

caricature [ˊkærikətjuə] n. 讽刺画,滑稽模仿(a picture or imitation of a person, literary style, etc. in which certain features or mannerisms are exaggerated for satirical effect)

(记)无词根,记住中间可能分解出二个单词: car－cat

(例) Caricature was a product of the Renaissance and Reformation emphasis on the importance of the individual.

carol [ˊkærəl] n. 赞美诗,赞歌(a song of joy, esp. a Christmas song)

(例)The choir sang well-known carols.

cartel [kɑːˊtel] n.【经】卡特尔(a group of businesses that conspire together to eliminate competition);为共同行动组织的政治联盟(a political bloc in certain European countries)

(记)"卡特尔"为音译

(例)The authorities are investigating the oil cartel.

cartographer [kɑːˊtɔgrəfə] n. 制图员(a person whose work is

making maps and charts)
(记)carto(图纸板)+graph(写)+er→制图员
同根词:carton(纸板箱);cartoon(漫画)

cascade [kæs'keid] n.小瀑布(a small, steep waterfall, esp. one of a series)
(记)cas(落下)+cade(落下)→一再落下→瀑布
同根词:casual(偶然的)

casualty ['kæʒjuəlti] n.严重伤亡事故(an accident, esp. a fatal one);伤亡(a member of the armed forces who is lost to active service through being killed, wounded, captured, interned, sick, or missing);受害者(anyone hurt or killed in an accident)
(记) casual (随便的) + ty →因为随随便便造成的→严重伤亡事故,伤亡
(例) Jane saw a casualty on the highway and phoned the police. / There were thousand of casualties after the powerful earthquake.

catalog ['kætəlɔg] n.(图书或商品)目录,目录册(a book or list containing descriptions of things, often of things that are for sale);vt.为…编目录(to make a catalog of)
(记)cata(下面)+log(数)→数了列在下面→按目录分类,和下面的 catalogue 是一个词

catalogue ['kætəlɔg] n.(图书或商品)目录(catalog)
(例)catalogue items for sale at auction(将拍卖的各项商品编入记录)

catalyst ['kætəlist] n.催化剂(a chemical substance that speeds up a chemical action without changing itself);促使事物发展的因素(a person or thing acting as a stimulus in bringing about or hastening a result)
(记)cata(下面)+lyst=lysis(溶解)→起溶解作

用→催化

(例) The reaction could not take place until the catalyst was added. / The new taxes imposed by the government were a catalyst for revolution.

catastrophe [kə'tæstrəfi] n. 灾难,灾祸(a very large and serious disaster)

(记)cata(下面)+strophe(使翻转)→把…翻转过来→灾难,灾祸

(例)The crash of the stock market was a financial catastrophe.

category ['kætəgəri] n. 类别,种类(a division or subdivision)

(记)cate(下面)+gory(断定)→断定怎么在下面分类→类别,种类

(例) Which literary category would this book go in?

cater ['keitə] v. 供应伙食提供娱乐节目(to provide food for an event as business);迎合,投合(to)(to be very attentive to someone)

(记)想迎合别人的人总是努力去 capture(引起注意)别人,所以是 cater

(例)An exclusive hotel catered the wedding. / I cater to my boss's every whim.

caterpillar ['kætəpilə] n. 毛虫(the creature, sth. like a worm, that is the larva of a butterfly or a moth);履带拖拉机(a tractor equipped on each side with a continuous roller belt over cogged wheels, for moving over rough or muddy ground)

(记)该词本意是 hairycat(长毛的猫),其中 pil(pile)意为 hair

(例)Susie caught a caterpillar and put it in a jar.

cathedral [kə'θi:drəl] n.(一个教区内的)总教堂,大教堂(a

large, important church, esp. a church that is the seat of a bishop); a. 大教堂的(of or like a cathedral)
(记)cathedra(主教座位)+l→有主教座位的教堂→大教堂
(例)The tourists admired the stained glass window of the cathedral.

caveat [ˈkeiviæt] n. 警告(a warning)
(记)分割记忆:cave-eat,中间少要一个 e
(例)a caveat against too much regulation(避免过多规章制度的告诫)

caviar [ˈkæviɑː] n. 鱼子酱(the salted eggs of sturgeon, salmon, etc. eaten as an appetizer)
(例)Black caviar from Russia is very expensive. / caviar to the general:曲高和寡的东西,阳春白雪(a thing appealing only a highly cultivated taste)

cedar [ˈsiːdə] n. 雪松(木材)(an evergreen tree with fragrant wood)
(记)和 cigar(雪茄)读音有些相似,汉语意思都带"雪"字

celebrity [siˈlebriti] n. 名人,知名人士(someone who is famous or well known)
(记)celebr(有名的)+ity→有名的人
(例)The unknown actress became a celebrity when her first film was released.

celestial [siˈlestjəl] a. 天体的,天空的(relating to the sky; relating to outer space, far from the earth)
(记)celest(天空)+ial→天上的
同根词:celeste(天蓝色)
(例)The picture showed the celestial bodies in position.

censure [ˈsenʃə] n./v. 责难,非难(the placing of official

blame on sb; to reprimand sb. officially)
(记)cens(评价)+ure→坏评价→指责
(例)The guard got a letter of censure for letting the prisoner escape. / The warden censured the guard for letting the prisoner escape.

census [ˈsensəs] n. 人口调查,人口普查(the process of counting the number of people who live in an area; the official number of people who live in an area)
(记)cens(评价)+us→官方评价→人口普查
(例)According to the last census, the population of this province is 220,000.

centrifugal [senˈtrifjugəl] a. 离心的(relating to a force that moves things away from the center of a rotating object)
(记)centri(中间的)+fug(逃离)+al→离心的
(例)Centrifugal force caused the child to fall off the merry-go-round.(游乐场里的转盘车)

ceramic [siˈræmik] a. 陶的,制陶的(made of hard, baked clay, able to withstand great heat)
(记)分割记忆 ce-ram-ic,ram 意为"公羊"
(例)The ceramic pot can be used in a hot oven.

cereal [ˈsiəriəl] n. 谷类,谷类食品(one of a number of plants that provides grain)
(记)分割记忆:ce-real,"真正的好东西"→食品
(例)A number of important cereals are grown in my province.

ceremonial [ˌseriˈməunjəl] a. 礼仪的,仪式的;正式的(of, for, or consisting of ceremony; ritual; formal)
(记)来自 ceremony(礼仪,仪式)
(例)ceremonial dress(礼服)/ Churches observe many ceremonial occasions.

cessation [seˈseiʃən] n. 停止(the stopping of sth.; a pause)

(记)cess(停止)+ation→不走的状态→中止
参考:cession(割让)
同根词:concession(让步)
(例)The cessation of armed conflict was a relief to the people of the nation.

chaise [ʃeiz] n. 两轮(或四轮)轻便马车(any of several kinds of lightweight carriage, some with a collapsible top, having two or four wheels and drawn by one or two horses)
(记)chase(追赶)加上 i 就成了轻便马车，我(I)坐上马车好追赶

chalice [ˈtʃælis] n.(高脚)酒杯(a cup; goblet);圣餐杯(the cup for the wine of Holy Communion)
(记)拉丁语为 calix,英语中也有 calix,和 chalice 同词根同词义

chamber [ˈtʃeimbə] n.卧室(a room, esp. a bedroom);议院(a division of a government, such as the House of Representatives or the Senate of the United States Congress, separately);chamber music: 室内音乐(music for a small number of players)
(例)The sparsely furnished chamber had only a bed and dresser. / The entire chamber voted on the proposed law. / I enjoy chamber music.

chameleon [kəˈmiːljən] n.变色龙，蜥蜴(a lizard that changes its color of its skin to match its surroundings);善变的人(someone who is very changeable)
(记)分割联想:chame 看作 shame + leon = lion,"害羞的狮子变色的龙"
(例)The chameleon turned green when it rested on the leaf. / That girl is such a chameleon. Her reactions are changeable and unpredictable.

chant [tʃɑːnt] n.歌，单调的歌(a song; melody);赞美的

诗(a simple liturgical song)
(记)enchant(使人迷)大家可能都知道,该词中的词根就是 chant(唱歌)
(例)The chant of the monks echoed through the cloister.

char [tʃɑː] n.炭,木炭(charcoal);v. 把…烧成炭(to reduce to charcoal by burning)
(记)和 charcoal(木炭)一起记

charity [ˊtʃæriti] n.上帝之爱,博爱(the love of God for humanity; or a love of one's fellow human beings);慈善事业(a welfare institution, organization, or fund)
(例)Funds were raised by the charity to help people in emergencies.

charter [ˊtʃɑːtə] n.宪章(a document setting forth the aims and principles of a united group, as of nations);特权,豁免权(a special privilege or exemption);契约,证书(an agreement);租赁(the hire or lease of a ship, bus, airplane, etc)
(记)来自 chart(航图,图表)
(例)the Charter of the United Nations(《联合国宪章》)/"The ship's no longer under charter. I've bought her,"he said.

chauvinism [ˊʃəuvinizəm] n.沙文主义,盲目爱国主义(excessive pride in one's country)
(记)来自一法国人名:Chauvin,因其过分的爱国主义和对拿破仑的忠诚而闻名;n. chauvinist(盲目的爱国者);a. chauvinistic(盲目的爱国心的,沙文主义的)
(例)The speaker's chauvinism was not welcomed by the international audience.

check [tʃek] v.阻止(to restrain or stop sb. or sth.)

(记)check"检查"一义最常用,它还可指衣服上的"方格"

(例)The policy checked politicians from abusing their power.

cheeta(h) [ˈtʃiːtə] n.(可训练来猎鹿等的)猎豹(an extremely fast, doglike cat of Africa and South Asia)

(记)和 cheese(奶酪)一起记(A cheetah doesn't eat cheese)

chicanery [ʃiˈkeinəri] n.诡计(a trick)

(记)chic(聪明)+ anery→要聪明→诡计;chic 本身是一个单词,意为"潇洒的"

chef [ʃef] n.厨师(a cook in charge of a kitchen, as of a restaurant; head cook; any cook)

(记)和 cook 的区别在于 chef 较正式,并常指地位较高的厨师

chisel [ˈtʃizl] n./v.凿子;凿(a sharp-edged tool for removing pieces from wood or stone; to shape anything with a chisel)

(记)来自古法语 cisel(割下)

(例)The artist chiseled the marble with great skill.

chord [kɔːd] n.弦(a straight line that connects two points on a curve)

(记)由 cord 变来

同根词:accord

choreography [ˌkɔriˈɔgrəfi] n.舞蹈编排(the planning of the movements of dancers)

(记)choreo(跳舞)+ graph(记录下的)→舞蹈编排

(例)The audience didn't think the choreography was good.

chromosome [ˈkrəuməsəum] n.染色体

(记)chromo(色,色素)+ some(body)(体)→染色

体

chronic [ˊkrɔnik] a. 长期的，慢性的，惯常的，经常的(persistent or ongoing, said esp. of sickness or pain)

(记)chron(时间)+ic→长期的

同根词：chronometer(计时器)；anachronism(年代错误)

(例)The employee's chronic complaint was that working conditions at the factory were unsafe.

chronicle [ˊkrɔnikl] n. 年代记，编年史(a historical record or register of facts or events arranged in the order in which they happened)；历史，记事(a narrative; history)；vt. 把…载入编年史(to tell or write the history of; put into a chronicle)

(记)chron(时间)+icle→年代史

(例)The newspaper gave a chronicle of the war.

chronology [krəˊnɔlədʒi] n. 年代学(the science of measuring time in fixed periods and of dating events and epochs and arranging them in the order of occurrence)；年表(a list or table of dates in their proper sequence)

(记)chron(时间)+ology(学科)→年代学

(例)The professor gave a chronology of the development of modern medicine.

churn [tʃəːn] n.(炼制黄油用的)搅乳器(a container or contrivance in which milk or cream is beaten, stirred, or shaken to form butter)；vt. 用搅乳器搅拌(to beat, stir, or shake [milk or cream] in a churn)

(记)不妨和 turn 一起记，正好 turn 也有"翻转"之意，churn 就指用搅乳器搅拌

cinder [ˊsində] n. 余烬；矿渣(a piece of ash from burned

coal; a small piece of mostly burned coal or wood that can cause other objects to catch fire)
(记)Cinderella(灰姑娘)的传说大家都听说过,少了后面的 ella 这样美妙的声音,就只能是灰烬了
(例)All that was left of the fire was cinders.

circulation [ˌsəːkjuˈleiʃən] n. 循环(the act of moving around in a complete circuit, specif., the movement of blood out of and back to the heart through the arteries and veins);(货币、消息等)流通,传播,发行(the passing of sth., as money or news, from person to person or place to place; dissemination)
(记)circu(圆的) + lat(构成动词) + ion(名词后缀)→使成为圆圈的过程→循环
(例) We need to increase the circulation of air through the room. / They've decided to put the new coins into circulation. / Because the magazine's low circulation, no one would advertise in it.

circumference [səˈkʌmfərəns] n. 圆周长(the distance around a circle)
(记)circum(圆的,绕,周) + fer(带有) + ence→绕着圆圈走→(量出)周长
(例)the circumference of the earth at the equator(地球沿赤道的周长)

circumscribe [ˌsəːkəmˈskraib] v. 限制;外切或外接
(记)circum(绕,周) + scribe(划线)→限制;外切或外接
(例)circumscribe a circle around a square(使圆外接于正方形)

circumspect [ˈsəːkəmspekt] a. 谨慎的(cautious; watching on all sides)
(记)circum(绕圈) + spect(spy)(仔细看)→谨慎

的

(例) The investor was circumspect when making predictions about the economy.

circumvent [ˌsəːkəm'vent] v. 用计谋战胜;规避(to find a way around sth. that one wants to avoid; to avoid sb. or sth.)

(记)circum(绕圈)+vent(来)→绕着圈儿来→用计谋战胜;规避

(例)The corrupt politician found a way to circumvent paying taxes.

civic ['sivik] a. 城市的,市民的,公民的(of or about citizenship or cities and their government)

(记)和下面的civil(公民的,市民的,国民的)为同根词

(例)It is our civic duty to vote in local elections.

civil ['sivl] a. 公民的,民用的(of or about citizens and their government, activities, rights, and responsibilities)

(例)civil rights and duties(公民的权利和义务)/a civil war(内战)

claim [kleim] n. 索赔(a document or statement requesting a payment be made)

(记)claim 另一个常用意思是"声称",声称要得到→索赔

(例) The insurance company paid the claim promptly.

clam [klæm] n. 蛤;蛤肉;寡言的人(a reticent or taciturn person)

(记)和 ham(火腿),jam(果酱),dam(水坝)一起记;clam 变化一下就成了 calm(平静的)

(例)He is a clam about his business dealing.(他对他的生意买卖守口如瓶。)

clan [klæn] n. 家族,宗派(a group of related families)
(记)和 tribe(部落,部族;[动植物的]族,类)比较记忆
(例)The two clans have been enemies for hundreds of years.

clandestine [klæn´destin] a. 秘密的,暗中从事的(secret; done in secret; concealed)
(记)分割记忆:clan(宗派)-destine(命中注定)"宗派"和"命定"都有一些"秘密"色彩
(例)The lovers had a clandestine meeting in the garden.

clarify [´klærifai] v. 澄清(to make sth. easier to understand; to explain sth. in greater detail)
(记)clar(清楚)+ify→澄清
(例)The student wanted to clarify her point for the rest of the class.

clerical [´klerikəl] a. 牧师的,教士的(of or about the clergy);办事员的(of or about the office work done by clerks: filing, typing, copying)
(记)由 clerk(教士;职员)而来
(例)The job requires excellent clerical skills. / The priest always wears his clerical collar in public.

cliche [kl:´ʃei] n. 陈词滥调(an overused expression that is trite and tiresome)
(记)法语词,e 上面一般有一点
(例)Stop speaking in tiresome cliches.

clientele [ˌklaiən´tel] n.(集合名词)律师等的委托人;商店等的顾客常客(all one's clients or customers, collectively)
(记)法语词,为集合名词,client(委托人;顾客)+ele→律师等的委托人;顾客常客
(例)The lawyer has a wealthy clientele.(这位律师

的委托人都很有钱。)/ The theatre's regular clientele.(戏院的一班常客。)

climatologist [ˌklaimə'tɔlədʒist] n. 气候学家(someone who studies the science dealing with climate and climatic phenomena)
(记)climat(气候)+olog(y)(学科)+ist→钻研气候方面的人→气候学家

clipping ['klipiŋ] n. 剪下物,剪辑,剪报(sth. cut out or trimmed off; a news story or other item clipped from a newspaper, magazine, etc.); a. 快速的(swift)
(记)clip(剪)+p+ing→剪下物,剪报
(例)a newspaper clipping / a clipping pace(快速的步子)

clockwise ['klɔkwaiz] ad. 顺时针方向(in the direction the hands of a clock rotate)
(记)clock+wise(以…方向)→以钟走的方向→顺时针方向
(例)The children walked clockwise in a circle.

clog [klɔg] n. 重物,障碍(sth. that prevents sth. else from moving through a passage; a blockage); v. 妨碍,塞满(to block the flow or passage of sth.)
(记)log(圆木)一般很重,搁在c后自然是妨碍了
(例)The sink clogged again. / Don't clog your memory with useless facts.

clone [kləun] n.【生】无性(繁殖)系,克隆;【农】无性(繁殖)系植物
(记)"克隆"是音译

clothesline ['kləuzlain] n. 晒衣绳(a rope or wire on which clothes, etc. are hung for drying or airing);[俚]私人事情,家丑
(记)clothes(衣服)+line(线,绳)→晒衣绳→晾衣

服发现的事→私人事情，家丑

clumsy [ˈklʌmzi] a. 笨拙的，拙劣的(awkward; uncoordinated; likely to trip or stumble on sth.)

(记)同义词：awkward(难使用的，笨拙的)

(例)The clumsy waiter dropped my dinner on the floor.

cluster [ˈklʌstə] n.(同类事物或人)一串，一组(a group of people or things)；v. 使成群，聚集在一起(to group people or things together somewhere)

(记)clust = clot(凝成块) + er→凝块→成群

(例)The men clustered to gather round the fire and sang songs. / A cluster of strawberries grew in the field. / I clustered the chairs near the table.

coalesce [ˌkəuəˈles] v. 合并，联合，结合(to come together; to be brought together)

(记)co + al(= ally)(联盟) + esce→一起联盟→联合；a. coalescent；n. coalescence

(例)Three old political parties coalesced to form a new one. / Eleven cities coalesced into one megalopolis.(11个城市合并为一特大的都会。)

coalition [ˌkəuəˈliʃən] n. 结合，联合(a union or alliance of things or people)

(记)co + al(= ally)(联盟) + ition→结合，联合

(例)A coalition of lawyers defended the workers in court.

cobble [ˈkɔbl] v. 补鞋(to mend or patch [shoes, etc.])；铺路(to pave with a kind of rounded stone called cobblestones)

(记)参考：cobblestone(圆石块，鹅卵石)；cobbler(鞋匠)

(例)an old cobbled street(一条古老的用大卵石铺成的街道)

cocaine [kəu'kein] n.【药】可卡因,古柯碱(a highly addictive drug made from the leaves of a South American bush)
(记)coca(古柯)+ine→古柯碱,可卡因
(例)It is easy to get addicted to cocaine.

cocoa ['kəukəu] n.可可粉(a powder made by processing cacao seeds; powdered chocolate);可可茶(a drink made by mixing powdered chocolate with sugar and milk);可可树(a tree producing this kind of cacao seeds);可可色(a reddish-yellow brown)
(记)和 coco(椰子)分开

coda ['kəudə] n.【音】结尾,符尾(a more or less independent passage added to the end of a section or composition so as to reinforce the sense of conclusion)
(记)和下面的 code(法规)一起记,并且不要和 soda(苏打)混了

code [kəud] n.法典,法规(a body of laws, as of a nation or city, organized for easy reference);规则,习俗(any set of principles or rules of conduct)
(例)the civil code of France(法国的民法)

codify ['kɔdifai] n.编辑,整理(法律)(to write out rules; to arrange rules into an organized system)
(记)cod(=code)+ify→使成为 code→编辑,整理
(例)This is the most complicated case to occur since our laws were codified.

cognitive ['kɔgnitiv] a.认识的(of or being the process of knowing in the broadest sense, including perception, memory, and judgement)
(记)cogn(认识)+itive→认识的
(例)the cognitive elements of perception(观念的认识基础)

coherent [kəu'hiərənt] a. 连贯的,一致的(clear; lucid; logical; making sense)
(记)co(一起)+her(粘上)+ent→连贯的,一致的
(例)The debater presented a coherent argument.

coinage ['kɔinidʒ] n.铸币(the act or process of coining);造币(权);货币,货币制度(metal money; coins; a system of money or metal currency)
(记)coin(币)+age(行为,结果)→铸币
(例)a decimal coinage(十进位硬币制) / The central bank recently issued a gold coinage.

collaborate [kə'læbəreit] vi.协作,合作(尤指文艺、科学等方面)(to work together, esp. in some literary, artistic, scientific undertaking);勾结(with)(to cooperate with an enemy invader)
(记)col(一起)+labor(劳动)+ate→一起劳动→协作,合作
(例)The composers collaborated on the musical. One wrote the lyrics, and the other wrote the music.

collateral [kə'lætərəl] a.并行的(side by side; parallel);附属的;旁系的;间接的(accompanying or existing in a subordinate, or indirect relationship)
(记)col(一起)+later(边缘)+al→边在一起的→并行的
同根词:bilateral(双边的)
(例)collateral mountain ranges(并行的山脉) / collateral evidence(附属证据)

combat ['kɔmbæt] n.战斗,格斗,反对(war; conflict; a battle);v.竞争(to engage in war, conflict or battle)
(记)和其同义词 war, conflict, battle, campaign

一起记

(例)The soldiers were trained for combat. / Roman Catholic churches combated the rise of socialist ideas with its own ideology of Christian corporatism (组合主义,社团主义).

combination [ˌkɔmbiˈneiʃən] n. 组合(the process of joining two or more things together)

(记)来自 combine (组合),com (一起) + bine (捆)→组合

(例)The safe combination of the two chemicals required a complicated chemical process.

combustion [kəmˈbʌstʃən] n. 燃烧(burning; catching fire)

(记)com + bust(燃烧) + ion→燃烧

参考:flammable(易燃的), inflammable (易燃的)

(例)The quick combustion of the dry forest was caused by the lack of rain.

comedian [kəˈmiːdjən] n. 喜剧演员(a performer who tells jokes or funny stories)

(记)来自 comedy(喜剧)

comet [ˈkɔmit] n. 彗星(a rapidly moving bright celestial body with a long tail)

(记)联想记忆:come + t

commercial [kəˈməːʃəl] a. 商业的(of or about commerce); n. 电视广播中的广告节目(an advertisement on television or radio)

(记)来自 commerce, com(一起) + merc(merx)(商品) + e→一起交换商品→商业的

(例)The shrewd man was very much interested in the commercial aspects of his invention. / I change the TV channel when commercials are broadcast.

commission [kəˈmiʃən] vt. 委托,委托制作(画像等)(to give the power or authority to; authorize);佣金

(记)com(一起)+mission(派…去)→派…去做什么→委托

(例)The government commissioned a group of scholars to undertake an important study.

commonplace [ˈkɔmənpleis] a. 平凡的,陈腐的(plain and ordinary);n. 平常话,平常的事物(an ordinary or plain statement)

(记)common(通常的)+place(地方)→通常去的地方→平凡的;平常的事物

(例)Access to the internet is yet to become a commonplace in China. / They are talking over the commonplaces of the day.

compact [kəmˈpækt] a. 结实的,简洁的(packed together, close together, condensed);[ˈkɔmpækt]n. 合同,协议(an agreement between two countries or parties)

(记)com+pact(打包,压紧)→一起压紧→结实的;pact 本身是一个单词,意为"契约"

(例)CD is an abbreviation for compact disks. / a compact book (writer) (文体简洁的书/作家) / The two nations made a compact to preserve the peace.(两国订立了和约。)

compactness [kəmˈpæktnis] n. 紧密,坚实,简洁(the state of being condensed, packed or small);【物】紧密度(the degree of being compact)

(记)com+pact(打包,压紧)+ness(名词后缀)→一起压紧→结实,简洁

(例)He likes his apartment for its compactness.

companionate [kəmˈpænjənit] a. 结伴,同伴的(of or like companions)

(记)com(一起)+panion(一起吃面包的人)+ate→同伴的,结伴的

(例)companionate marriage (试婚) / a companionate dog at one's heels(跟随着作伴的狗)

compatible [kəm'pætəbl] a. 相容的,和睦共处的(able to get along or function well with sb. or sth. else)

(记)com(一起)+pat(承受)+ible→一起承受→相容;n. compatibility(兼容性)

(例)This DOS-based software system is not compatible with Windows 95.

compensate ['kɔmpenseit] v. 补偿,赔偿(for)(to give sb. sth. that is equal in value to sth. else that has been taken, used or lost)

(记)com+pens(挂,花费)+ate→全部给予花费→赔偿;a. compensative(偿还的,补充的);n. compensation

同根词:expense(支出)

(例)The insurance company compensated the driver for the damage to his car.

compensation [ˌkɔmpen'seiʃən] n. 补偿,赔偿(sth. given to make up for sth. else that has been spent, taken, lost or used)

(记)来自 compensate

(例)Families of the air crash victims have received only token compensation for the loss of their loved ones.

compile [kəm'pail] v. 编辑,编撰(to assemble a collection of similar items taken from different places)

(记)com(一起)+pile(堆)→堆积→汇集

(例)We are compiling a glossary(词汇表;术语汇编)for GMAT test takers.

complacency [kəm'pleisnsi] n. 自满,自得(the state or condition of being satisfied with one's situation or achievement)

(记)com+plac(平静,满足)+ency→全部满足→

自满的；注意不要和 complaisant(随和的)相混
(例)His complacency has cost him many opportunities.

complement [ˈkɔmplimənt] n. 补足物(sth. added to complete a whole)；【数】余数；血清中的补体(any of a group of protein in the blood plasma that act with specific antibodies to destroy corresponding antigens, as bacteria or foreign protein)；vt. 补充，补足(to make complete; be a complement to)
(记)com(加强作用)+ple(装满，填满)+ment→补足物，补充；a. complementary；注意不要和 compliment(恭维)相混
(例)Wine is the perfect complement to any meal.

complementary [ˌkɔmpliˈmentəri] a. 补足的，补充的(in a way that completes or enhances sth.; making up for sth. that is lacking)
(例)complementary angle(余角) / Her first two books are complementary to her latest one.

complex [ˈkɔmpleks] n. 综合企业(a whole set of interrelated enterprises, buildings, roads or the like)；【心】情结(an integration of related impulses, ideas or emotions fixated on a particular object or activity)
(记)com+plex(重叠交叉)→综合企业；情结
(例)The once mighty Military Industrial Complex of the Soviet Union has crumbled. / Oedipus complex(恋母情结) / I had a complex about my weight.(我曾为自己的体重惴惴不安。)

compliance [kəmˈplaiəns] n. 遵守(obeying a law or command)
(记)由形容词 compliant 而来，com+pliant(柔顺的)→顺从的
(例)Compliance with the traffic laws is necessary for safe driving. / Pay your parking tickets and be

in compliance with city laws.

comply [kəm'plai] v.遵循(to obey a rule or request)
(记)a. compliant; n. compliance
(例)A good citizen complies with the laws of the country.

component [kəm'pəunənt] n.部分,零件(a part of sth.)
(记)com(一起)+pon(放置)+ent→放置在一起的东西→零件
(例)An essay question is one component of the test.

compound ['kɔmpaund, kəm'paund] n.混合物(a chemical substance made from two or more elements);a.混合的(made of two or more parts; having two or more segments)
(记)com(一起)+pound(放)→混合物
(例)Water is a chemical compound of oxygen and hydrogen. / A compound sentence has at least two clauses.

comprehend [ˌkɔmpri'hend] v.了解,领会(to understand sth.);包括(to include; take in; comprise)
(记)com(一起)+prehend(抓住)→一起抓住→领会;包括
同根词:prehensile(适于抓住的);comprehensible(容易了解的);comprehensive(全面的); n. comprehension(理解)
(例)I could not comprehend the instructions for operating the computer.

compromise ['kɔmprəmaiz] v.妥协;危害(to come to an agreement by which both sides yield a little)
(记)com+promise(保证)→相互保证→妥协;尤其要注意"危害,伤害"一意
(例)After arguing for two hours, we finally com-

promised on the issue. / The quality of our products should never be compromised.

compulsory [kəmˈpʌlsəri] a. 强制性的，命令性的(mandatory; required)

(记)com + puls(推，冲) + ory→一起推→强制性的

同根词：repulse(反击，击退)；repulsive(排斥的)；compulsive(难以抑制的)

(例)A composition class is compulsory for all college students.

conceal [kənˈsiːl] v. 隐藏，隐瞒(to hide sb. or sth.)

(记)con(一起) + ceal(隐藏)→隐瞒，隐藏

(例)conceal sth. from sb. / The criminal concealed the knife in his boot.

concentrate [ˈkɔnsəntreit] n. 浓缩，浓缩液(sth. that is not diluted)

(记)con(一起) + centr(中间) + ate→往中间收→浓缩；n. concentration

(例)The orange juice was made from a frozen concentrate.

concern [kənˈsəːn] n. 公司，企业(康采恩)(a business; a firm)

(记)"康采恩"为音译

(例)I worked for two years with an insurance concern downtown. / A business entity is usually viewed as a going concern.

concert [ˈkɔnsət] n. 一致；协作；和谐(mutual agreement; concord; harmony of action)

(记)con(一起) + cert(努力)→一起努力→协作；和谐

(例)in concert(一致，一齐) / a concert of praise (异口同声的赞颂)

concerto [kən'tʃəːtəu] n.【音】协奏曲(a piece of music written for orchestra and one or more solo instruments)

(记)concert(音乐会)+o→协奏曲

(例)The orchestra performed a violin concerto and then a piano concerto.

concession [kən'seʃən] n. 让步;特许权(an act or instance of conceding, granting, or yielding; a privilege granted by a government, company, etc.)

(记)由 concede 而来,con(一起)+cede(走,承认)→让步

参考:cede(放弃)

(例)The governor would make no concessions on the issue of crime. / the weekend concession(周末优惠价)

concrete ['kɔnkriːt] a. 具体的,有形的(actual; existing; real; definite; not abstract); n. 混凝土(a hard, compact building material formed when a mixture of cement, sand, gravel, and water dries: used in making bridges, road surface, etc.)

(记)不妨参照该词的两个意思来记:混凝土当然是具体的,有形的

(例)The scientist had no concrete data to support his theory. / concrete wall(水泥墙)

concurrent [kən'kʌrənt] a. 同时发生的(happening at the same time; simultaneous)

(记)con+current(发生的)→共同发生的

参考:occurrence(发生的事件)

(例)There were several concurrent attempts to climb the mountain. / The dates of their holidays were concurrent.(他们放假的日期是相同的。)

condense [kən'dens] vt. 使冷凝,浓缩(to make more dense or compact; reduce the volume of; compress);缩

短(to make a document or speech shorter)
(记)con(一起)+dense(稠密的)→使密到一起→使冷凝,浓缩
(例)The chemistry teacher condensed a gas into a liquid. / I condensed my speech because it was too long.

condescending [ˌkɔndiˈsendiŋ] a. 俯就的,屈尊的;有优越感的(treating other people as if they are inferior)
(记)con+de(下)+scend(爬)+ing→全部向下爬的→俯就的,贬低的
同根词:descend(下降);ascend(上升)
(例)He had a condescending attitude toward uneducated people. / I dislike his condescending manner toward his employees.

condor [ˈkɔndɔː] n.(南美产)神鹰,秃鹰(a very large vulture of the South American Andes)
(记)南美一些国家使用的金币上就是 condor 的图案,叫 condors(神鹰金币)

cone [kəun] n. 圆锥
(记)麦当劳里卖的圆锥形蛋卷冰淇淋因其形状叫 icecream cone

configuration [kənˌfigjuˈreiʃən] n. 轮廓,结构(the way that sth. is arranged)
(记)con+figur(e)(形状)+ation→全部形状→轮廓
(例)Scientists know little about the configuration of the moon's surface.

confinement [kənˈfainmənt] n. 限制,禁闭(imprisonment, putting sb. or sth. in sth. limiting)
(记)confine(限制)+ment→限制,禁闭
(例)Many wild animals cannot tolerate confinement. / She strongly resisted confinement to the

domestic sphere.

conform [kən'fɔːm] vt. 使一致,使遵照(to obey the rules); vi. 适合,适应环境(to bring into harmony or agreement; adapt: often used reflexively)

(记)con + form(形成)→一起形成→使一致,使遵照;适应环境

(例) The children conformed reluctantly to their parents' requests. / conform one's ideas to another's

confront [kən'frʌnt] vt. 使面对(stand or meet face to face);勇敢地面对危险(to face or oppose boldly, defiantly, or antagonistically)

(记)con + front(前面)→对着前面→使面对;使对质

(例) Many serious problems confronted the early pioneers. / We must confront the future with optimism. / confront the accused with the accuser(使被告与原告对质)

congenial [kən'dʒiːniəl] a. 意气相投的,宜人的(pleasant; pleasing; agreeable)

(记)con + geni = genius(才能) + al→有共同才能的→情趣相投的;注意和 congenital(天生的,先天的)区别开来,两个词就差一个字母

参考:genius (天才); n. congeniality

(例) Congenial co-workers help dispel office tedium. / The restaurant had a congenial atmosphere.

congestion [kən'dʒestʃən] n. 充血;拥挤(blockage; crowding)

(记)con + gest(管道,带来)→进入一个管道→拥挤

同根词:digestion(消化);ingest(吞咽)

(例)cerebral congestion(大脑充血) / Congestion on the highway made me late for work.

conglomerate [kən'glɔmərit] n. 集聚,企业集团(sth. that is made from a combination of things; a large corporation made up of other companies)

(记)con + glomer(球) + ate→成为一球→集聚

参考:agglomerate(凝聚)

(例)The sandwich was a conglomerate of leftovers from the refrigerator. / The conglomerate sold a few of its small companies.

congregation [ˌkɔŋgri'geiʃən] n. 集合在一起的群众(a group of people, esp. in a church service)

(记)来自 congregate,con + greg(群体) + ate→聚成群体→集合

同根词:aggregate(聚集)

(例)Half of the congregation fell asleep during the service.

congruent ['kɔŋgruənt] a. (几何)全等的(〔Geom〕 of figures, having identical shape and size)

(记)con(与) + gruent(落下)→与…一同落下→相同的→全等的;congruent 通常的意思是"一致的,适合的,和谐的",如下面的第二个例句

(例)congruent triangle(全等三角形) / Our interests are precisely congruent with yours.(我们的和你们的利益是完全一致的。)

connive [kə'naiv] v. 默许,共谋(to pretend not to see or look〔at sth. wrong or evil〕, thus giving tacit consent or cooperation; feign ignorance to sb.'s wrongdoing; conspire)

(记)con(与) + nive(眨眼睛)→互相眨眼睛→共谋,纵容

(例)The criminal spent the whole evening conniving with his wife. / The student connived with his friend to cheat on the examination.

consensus [kən'sensəs] n. 共识(the general opinion; a general agreement among people)
(记)con(共)+sensus(感觉,认识)→共识
(例)The school could not reach a consensus on the curriculum. / There can be wide differences of opinion on separate issues within a broad consensus.

consortia [kən'sɔːtjə] n.(consortium 的复数)合作,合伙,联合,会社(如国际财团等)(a partnership or association, as a temporary alliance of two or more business firms in a common venture, or an international banking agreement or association)
(记) con (合) + sort (一份) + ium →合起来管一份→合作,会社
(例)The consortium met yearly to discuss the advancement in medicine.

conspiracy [kən'spirəsi] n. 阴谋(a secret plan of two or more people to do sth. illegal or evil)
(记)con(共)+spir(e)(呼吸)+acy→共同呼吸→阴谋
(例)The police officer uncovered a conspiracy to assassinate the president. / They were arrested for conspiracy.

constellation [ˌkɔnstə'leiʃən] n. 星座,星群(a particular group of stars)
(记)con(共)+stell(星星)+ation→星星在一起→星座,星群
同根词:stellar(星的,恒星的)
(例)It was so cloudy that we couldn't see any of the constellations.

constraint [kən'streint] n. 强逼,压抑,拘束,紧张状态(restraint; limitation; holding back to one's natural behavior)

(记)con(共)+ straint(拉紧)→拉紧到一起→压抑,拘束

(例)Please exercise some constraint when you criticize your parents. / With his departure a cloud of constraint lifted from the room.

contagious [kən'teidʒəs] a. 传染的,有感染力的(easily passed from person to person)

(记)con + tag(接触)→ious→接触传染

参考:contiguous(邻近的)

(例)The flu is a highly contagious disease. / They all say that laughing is contagious.

contaminant [kən'tæminənt] n. 污染物(a substance that contaminates another substance, the air, water, etc.)

(记)con + tam(接触)+ inant→污染物;v. contaminate(污染)

contemplate ['kɔntempleit] v. 深思;(严肃)注视(to think about sth. carefully)

(记)con + templ(思考,观察)+ ate→全心思考→深思

参考:temple(太阳穴,庙宇)

(例)Philosophers contemplate the existence of humankind. / The disgruntled clerk carefully contemplated changing careers.

contemporary [kən'tempərəri] a. 当代的,同时代的,同年龄的(current; present day);n. 同时人,同龄人(someone who lived during the same time period as someone else)

(记)con(一起)+ tempor(时间)+ ary→同时代的;同代人

(例)The sociologist studied the contemporary issues of urban poverty. / My father's grandparents were contemporaries of Chairman Mao Zedong.

contemptuous [kən'temptjuəs] a. 轻蔑的,傲慢的(showing scorn or contempt; hateful)
(记)con + tempt(轻视,引诱) + uous→轻蔑的,傲慢的
参考:temptation(引诱,诱惑);contemptible(令人轻视的)
(例)She is contemptuous of people who smoke around her. / a contemptuous smile(表示轻蔑的冷笑)

contentious [kən'tenʃəs] a. 好辩的,喜争议的(eager to argue; tending to argue)
(记)con + tent(拉) + ion→你拉我夺→争论
同根词:extension(伸长,延长)
(例)The contentious students started arguments over silly matters.

context ['kɔntekst] n.(文章的)上下文(the word before and after another word that help determine its meaning);(某一事件发生的)环境,背景(the whole situation, background, environment relevant to a particular event, personality, creation, etc.)
(记)con + text(文)→接在一起的文→上下文;[转]背景
(例)Don't quote my words out of context. / It is in such a context that I got married with him.

contiguous [kən'tigjuəs] a. 接近的,接壤的(touching; adjoining)
(记)con + tig(接触) + uous→共同接触→接近的
(例)England is the only country contiguous to Wales. / The borders of the park and the school grounds are contiguous.

contingency [kən'tindʒənsi] n. 意外事件,可能性,偶发性(a

troublesome possibility)
(记)见下面的 contingent
(例)Get prepared for all contingencies. / Some unforeseen contingency must have arisen.(一定出现了某种事先没估计到的紧急情况。)

contingent [kən'tindʒənt] a. 意外的,视情况条件而定的(dependent on sth. happening)
(记)con + ting(接触 = tig) + ent→与…接触的→视…情况而定
(例)Whether or not we arrive on time is contingent on the weather. / Our offer to buy the apartment is contingent upon getting a mortgage.

contralto [kən'træltəu] n. 女低音(the range of a low female voice between mezzo-soprano and tenor; alto; a voice or singer with such a range)
(记)contra(音调低或声域窄) + alto(女低音;次高音)→女低音

control [kən'trəul] n.(实验的)对照,参照物(a standard of comparison for verifying or checking the findings of an experiment)
(记)control 作为"参照物"的意思时是专业术语
(例)a control sample(对照试样)

convalescence [ˌkɔnvə'lesns] n. 病后康复期(the period of gradual recovery after illness)
(记)con + val(强壮) + esce(开始…的)→开始强壮→康复; v. convalesce
同根词:valorous(勇猛的)
(例)a three-month convalescence in bed(3 个月的卧床疗养)

conversion [kən' vəːʃən] n. 转变,皈依(a complete change in one's beliefs; a change in religion)
(记)con + vers(= vert)(转) + ion→一起转入(新

的信仰)→皈依

(例)There were many conversions to Christianity among the ancient Romans. / The criminal underwent a conversion to Christianity in prison.

convert [kən'vəːt, 'kɔnvəːt] v. 转变,转换(to change sth. into sth. else);使皈依宗教(to have a complete change in beliefs; to change one's religion); n. 转教者(a person converted, as to another religion)

(记)con + vert(转)→一起转入(新的信仰)

(例)I used a calculator to convert miles to kilometers. / Bill, a Protestant since birth, has no desire to convert.

conviction [kən'vikʃən] n. 判罪(the act of declaring sb. guilty of crime);坚信(strong belief)

(记)来自 convict 一词,con + vict(征服)→征服罪犯→定罪;尤其注意 conviction"坚信"一义

同根词:victory(胜利);invincible(无敌的)

(例)The defendant appealed his conviction to a higher court. / The preacher spoke with great conviction.

convoluted [kənvəluːtid] a. 旋绕的,费解的(twisted and tangled; seemingly to be twisted and confused)

(记)con(一起) + volut(滚) + ed→滚在一起的→旋绕的,费解的;v. convolve(卷,缠绕);convolution(回旋,盘旋,卷绕)

(例)The rope lay on the deck of the ship, tangled and convoluted. / I had never read such an awkward and convoluted sentence.

coordinate [kəu'ɔːdinit] a. 坐标的(of or involving a kind of measurement that determines the position of a point)

(记)co(一起) + ordinate(安排)→安排在一起构

成坐标→坐标的

cornerstone [ˊkɔːnəstəun] n.【建】墙角石,奠基石(a large stone at the outside of two exterior walls);[喻]柱石,基础(a foundation; a basis; sth. that everything else is built on)
(记)corner + stone→墙角石;[转]奠基石
(例)Honesty is the cornerstone of a good relationship. / a cornerstone of foreign policy(外交政策的柱石)

cornstalk [ˊkɔːnstɔːk] n.玉米秆(a stem of corn)
(记)corn(玉米) + stalk(茎,秆)→玉米秆

corny [ˊkɔːni] a. 平淡无奇的,乡巴佬的(silly; trite; banal; unsophisticated)
(记)联想:corn(角),带角的动物随处可见,所以平淡无奇
(例)The film was just a corny comedy!

coronary [ˊkɔrənəri] a. 冠的,花冠的,冠状的(of or about the arteries of the heart)
(记)corona(冠状物) + ry→冠的,冠状的
(例)coronary arteries(心脏的冠状动脉) / a coronary heart disease(冠状动脉心脏病)

corpulence [ˊkɔːpjuləns] n.肥胖,臃肿(being fat, or obese)
(记)来自 corpulent,corp(躯体) + ulent(多…的)→肥胖的

corridor [ˊkɔridɔː] n.走廊,通道(a hallway; a passage between two rows of rooms)

corroborate [kəˊrɔbəreit] v.支持或证实,强化(to provide evidence that supports another reported fact)
(记)cor + robor(力量 strength) + ate→加强力量→支持,强化;n. corroborator(确证者)
同根词:corroborant(确证的,健身药);roborant(强壮剂)

(例)The witness corroborated the suspect's story. / These data corroborate the hypothesis of the experiment.

cortex [ˈkɔːteks] n.【解】(内部器官的)外皮(the outer layer of an internal organ; such as that of the brain or the kidneys);皮质(the outer layer of gray matter over most of the brain);【植】皮层(a layer of tissue in the roots of stems of some plants)

(记)该词也有"(植物的)皮层,树皮"之意,可以和 bark(树皮)一起记

cosmic [ˈkɔzmik] a. 宇宙的(of or about the whole universe and its enormous size)

(记)cosm(宇宙)+ic→宇宙的

同根词:cosmopolis(国际都市);cosmos(宇宙)

(例)Did the universe start with a giant comic explosion? / cosmic time and space(宇宙时空)

Cossack [ˈkɔsæk] n. 哥萨克;哥萨克人

(记)该词是音译,注意写时可记为 Cos-sack(大袋子)

cost [kɔst] n.(常用复数)成本(the sums of money needed to develop or produce sth.)

(记)注意 cost 意为"成本"时用复数

(例)We have to control costs carefully, or we will not make a profit.

counterclockwise [ˌkauntəˈklɔkwaiz] ad. 逆时针方向(in a direction that is opposite to the movement of a clock's hands)

(记)和前面列有的 clockwise 刚好相反;counter(反,抗)

counterfeit [ˈkauntəfit] v. 伪造,仿造(to make an illegal copy of sth., esp. money)

(记)counter(反)+feit(做=fact)→反着做→伪造

(例)It is against the law to counterfeit money. / The mobsters were arrested for counterfeiting bonds.

countervail [ˊkauntəveil] v. 补偿;抵销;敌过(to make up for; compensate; to counteract; avail against)

(记)counter(反) + vail(强壮)→强壮到能够敌过→敌过;补偿

(例)countervailing duty(反倾销税)

coupon [ˊku:pɔn] n.(债券等)息券(a detachable printed statement on a bond, specifying the interest due at a given time);赠券(a certificate or ticket entitling the holder to a specific right, as redemption for cash or gifts, reduced purchase price, etc.);配给券(a part of printed advertisement as for use in ordering goods, samples, or literature)

courier [ˊkuriə] n.送急件的人,信使(a messenger; someone who transports documents or other valuable items)

(记)cour(跑) + ier→跑着的人→送急件的人,信使

(例)We sent a courier to pick up the contracts.

coy [kɔi] a. 腼腆的,忸怩的(acting shy or reserved; pretending to be shy or reserved)

(记)boy 是不应该 coy 的

(例)Don't be so coy. Let me take your picture! / a coy maiden(娇羞的少女)

coyote [ˊkɔiəut] n.(美国西部的)郊狼,丛林狼

(记)美国南达科他州的别称为 Coyote State,因该州多丛林狼而得名

crack [kræk] v.爆裂(to break without separating into pieces);(健康,精神)衰退(to have a nervous breakdown)

(例)After the pitcher cracked, it would not hold water. / After the death of his wife, he cracked.

cramped [kræmpt] a. 痉挛的(tightened; contracted);狭窄的(confined; restricted; limited to space);难辨的(指字写得小而挤)(words printed too small so as to be illegible.)

(记)cramp(铁箍,夹子)+ed→箍得很紧的→狭窄的;痉挛的

(例)The physical therapist slowly rubbed the runner's cramped muscles. / No more people could fit into the cramped elevator. / Her words were cramped and her lines very close together.

crass [kræs] a. 粗糙的,粗厚的(coarse);愚钝的(grossly stupid, dull, or obtuse)

(记)可以和 grass 一起记

(例)It is crass to talk with mouth full. / crass remarks(粗话) / crass ignorance(极度无知)

crater [ˈkreitə] n. 火山口,弹坑(a large depression made by a falling bomb or meteor)

(记)去掉 r 就成了 crate(板条箱,柳条箱)

credence [ˈkriːdəns] n. 信任,相信(belief, esp. in the reports or testimony)

(记)cred(相信)+ence→相信

同根词:credibility(可信,可靠)

(例)His story lacks credence. / Such speculation gained added credence.(这种猜测被进一步证实了。)

credit [ˈkredit] vt. 相信(to believe in the truth, reliability, etc. of; trust);把…归于(to)

(例)He could not credit her explanation. / They credited him with the discovery. / The crash was credited to pilot error.

credo [ˈkriːdəu] n. 信条,信经
(记)和 creed 很像,意思也一样

crest [krest] n. 鸡冠;顶饰(any growth on the head of an animal, as a comb or feathered tuft on certain birds)
(记)分割记忆:c－rest
(例)crestfallen 冠毛垂倒→挫败的,羞愧的(with dropping crest or bowed head): He went away crestfallen.(他垂头丧气地走了。)

criminology [ˌkrimiˈnɔlədʒi] n. 犯罪学(the scientific study and investigation of crime and criminals)
(记)crimin(犯罪)+ology(学科)→犯罪学

criteria [kraiˈtiəriə] n. (criterion 的复数)标准,条件(a standard, rule, or test by which sth. can be judged; measure of value)
(记)crite(判断)+rion→判断的手段→标准,条件
(例)My primary criterion when I am buying a car is quality. / a criterion for judging intelligence(判断智力的标准)

critique [kriˈtiːk] n.(文艺等的)批评,评论(a critical analysis or evaluation of a subject, situation, literary work, etc.)
(记)为法语词;crit(判断)+ique→评论
(例)The critique praised the film's originality.

crucial [ˈkruːʃiəl] a. 决定性的,紧要关头的(of supreme importance; decisive; critical);严酷的,极困难的(extremely trying; severe; difficult)
(例)a crucial decision(关键性的决定) / a crucial experience(艰难的经历)

crumple [ˈkrʌmpl] v. 弄皱;扭弯(to make random folds in sth. while crushing it)
(记)注意不要和 crumble(弄碎)相混

(例)Take care not crumple your dress by packing it carelessly. / He crumpled the letter and threw it into the wastebasket.

crunch [krʌntʃ] v.嘎吱嘎吱地咬嚼(to bite or chew with a noisy, crackling sound);n.嘎吱嘎吱的声音(the sound of sth. snapping and breaking, esp. of sth. being chewed)

(记)crunch为拟声词,原写作 craunch

(例)The cookies made a loud crunch as the children ate them.

crusade [kruːˈseid] n.为维护理想、原则而进行的运动或斗争(a fight against sth. bad; a fight for sth. good)

(记)crus(十字)+ade→原指十字军东征

同根词:cruciform(十字形)

(例)a crusade against crime / This organization led a crusade against drunk driving.

crypt [kript] n.地窖(an underground burial room under a church);【解】腺窝,小囊(glandular cavities, or follicles in the body)

(记)crypt是秘密之意,地窖位于地下,自然是不明显的

cryptical [ˈkriptikəl] a. 秘密的,神秘的,隐义的(having a hidden or ambiguous meaning; mysterious; baffling; obscure and curt in expression)

(记)即 cryptic:crypt(秘密)+ic→秘密的

同根词:apocrypha (伪经);cryptogram(密码,暗号)

(例)I do not understand your cryptical remarks!

cube [kjuːb] n.立方体(a solid with six equal, square sides; anything having more or less this shape)

(例)a cube of sugar(一块方糖)

cue [kjuː] n.【戏】尾白,提示;暗示(sth. that is a signal for sb. to do or say sth.; a line that prompts an actor to say the next line or do the next action)
(例)The slamming of a door was the actor's cue to run on stage. / The time had come to say good night. At mother's cue, we all ascended.(到上床睡觉的时候了。在妈妈暗示之下,我们都上楼了。)

culminate [ˈkʌlmineit] vi. 达到顶点(或高潮)(to get to the highest point of sth.);告终(in)(to end with sth.);【天】到中天,到子午线
(记)culmin(顶点,高峰)+ate→达到顶点(或高潮)
(例)The evening culminated in a midnight fireworks display. / The science fair culminated in the awarding of prizes. / All his efforts culminated in failure.

culpability [ˌkʌlpəˈbiliti] n. 有罪,该受谴责(the state of deserving blame and being blameworthy)
(记)来自 culpable,culp(罪行)+able(有…的)
同根词:culprit(犯法者);exculpate(无罪释放)
(例)No culpability can be imputed to accidental homicide.

cult [kʌlt] n. 宗派;崇拜(radical system of worship or admiration)
(记)主要考第二义
(例)ancient tribal cult / the personality cult(个人崇拜) / the leadership cult

cultivation [ˌkʌltiˈveiʃən] n. 耕作(the act of preparing the using [soil or land] for growing crops);栽培(the act of growing [plants or crops] from seeds, bulbs, shoots, etc.);教养(a person's level of cultural so-

phistication)
(记)来自 cultivate, cult(培养种植) + ivate(表示动作)→种植
同根词: cultivable(可培养的); cultured(有教养的)
(例)Better cultivation of soil will result in better crops.(土地耕作得法,收成将会增加。)/ Cultivation is gained by exposure to many people, places, and things.

culture-bound a. 与文化相关的,受文化束缚的([ideas, knowledge or perspectives] conditioned by specific cultures)
(记)culture(文化) + bound(被束缚的)→受文化束缚的
(例)All our knowledge is in some sense culture-bound.

cumbersome [ˈkʌmbəsəm] a. 笨重的(big and bulky; not easily movable)
(记)来自 cumber, cumb(睡) + er→睡在(路上)的→妨碍
同根词: recumbent(斜躺的)
(例)The old, ornate furniture was cumbersome to move.

cupidity [kjuːˈpiditi] n. 贪婪,贪心,贪欲(strong desire, esp. for wealth; avarice)
(记)参考: covet(贪求); Cupid(丘比特)是罗马神话中的爱神,爱神引起人们对爱情的"贪婪";分割记忆: cupid-ity
(例)He cannot meet the cupidity that has been aroused in her. / gaze at the silverware and jewels with cupidity(贪婪地盯着银器和珠宝)

curb [kəːb] n. 马勒(a chain or strap passed around a

horse's lower jaw and attached to the bit);v.控制(to restrain; check; control)
(记)比较 curd(凝乳),curt(无礼的)
(例)to curb one's impatience(控制不耐烦) / curb inflation(控制通货膨胀)

cure-all n.万灵药(sth. supposed to cure all ailments or evils; panacea)
(记)cure(治疗)+all(所有)→万灵药
(例) Democracy is no cure-all for social and economic problems.

curriculum [kə'rikjuləm] n.学校的全部课程(all the courses offered at a school);(一门)课程(a particular course of study)
(例)They are trying to widen the college curriculum.

curtail [kəː'teil] vt.截短,缩短(to cut sth. short);削减(to reduce sth.; to lessen sth.)
(记)把 cur 看作 cut,tail 是尾巴之意,整个词可以理解为把尾巴削了,即"截短,缩短"之意
(例)The government hopes to curtail public spending in the next tax year. / The trip was curtailed because of bad weather.

customize ['kʌstəmaiz] v.定制,定做,按规格改制(to make or build according a personal or individual specifications)
(记)custom(定制的)+ize→定制,按规格改制
(例)customized hair styling(按顾客自行要求做的发式)

cylinder ['silində] n.圆柱体(a tube; a solid or hollow object with a circular top and bottom and straight sides in one dimension)

cynical ['sinikəl] a.愤世嫉俗的(believing the worst

about everything and everybody)
(记)来自古希腊哲学流派"cynicism(犬儒主义)";cyn原意为"犬"
参考:cynophobia(恐犬病)
(例)The manager's cynical attitude depresses everyone at work.

D

darn [dɑːn] v.织补(to mend [cloth] or repair [a hole or tear in cloth] by sewing a network of stitches across the gap); n.织补(处)(a darned place in fabric)
(记)darn(织补)和barn(谷仓,畜舍)、yarn(纱,纱线)一起记
(例)She darns well.(她擅长织补。)/ Can you see the darn in my stocking?

debase [di'beis] v.降低,贬低;降低(硬币)的成色,使货币贬值(to make lower in value, quality, dignity, etc.; cheapen)
(记)de + base(低)→低下去→贬低
同根词:basement(地下室);basis(基础)
(例)Such unkind action debased you. / Greed had debased his character. / debase the value of the dollar(使美元贬值)

debilitate [di'bilətet] a.使衰弱(to make weak or feeble; enervate)
(记)de + bility(= ability)→失去能力→衰弱;n. debilitation
(例)He was greatly debilitated by lack of food. / Our huge rambling country house was debilitated by its long exposure to the elements.

debenture [di´bentʃə] n. 债券(a voucher or certificate acknowledging that a debt is owned by the signer);(海关)退税凭单(a customhouse order for payment of a drawback, as to an importer)

(记)别和 debaucher(放荡,沉湎酒色)相混了

debris [də´briː] n.(破坏物的)碎片,废墟(rough, broken bits and pieces of stone, wood, glass, etc., as after destruction; rubble);【地理】岩屑,(冰川积聚的)碎石(a heap of rock fragments, as that deposited by a glacier)

(记)法语词,注意该词的发音比较特别,末尾的"s"不发音

(例)They were searching among the debris after the explosion. / There was a lot of debris in the garden.

debut [´diˇbjuː] n. [法]初进社交界(the formal introduction of a young woman into society);(演员的)首次演出(a first appearance before the public, as of an actor)

(记)法语词,末尾的"t"不发音

(例)to make one's debut(初次登台;初次参加社交活动) / The manager's youngest daughter made her debut at the dinner party.

decagon [´dekəgɔn] n. 十边形(a polygon with ten sides and ten angles)

(记)deca(十) + gon(角)→十个角的多边形→十边形

decay [di´kei] v. 腐朽,衰微(to rot; to decline in power, energy, or health)

(记)decayed(烂了的,朽了的)

(例)The empire decayed owning to a rampant corruption. / Our powers decay in old age.

decent [ˊdiːsnt] a. 正派的,可尊敬的(conforming to approved social standards; respectable);体面的(proper and fitting);公平大方的(fair and kind)

(例)When one makes a mistake, the decent thing to do is correct it. / I don't think that low-cut dress is decent. / You are decent to say so.

decimal [ˊdesiməl] n. 小数(a fraction with an unwritten denominator of 10 or some power of 10, indicated by a point〔decimal point〕before the numerator)

(记)decim(十分之一)+al→小数

(例)The number was written with a decimal rather than a fraction.

decipher [diˊsaifə] v. 破译(to translate〔a message in cipher or code〕into ordinary, understandable language; decode)

(记)de+cipher(密码)→使不再是密码→破译;a. decipherable(可破译的);n. decipherment(破译;译文)

(例)Can you decipher the cryptic message? / decipher military and diplomatic signals(破译军事和外交信号)

decrease [diˊkriːs] v. 减少(to become or cause to become less or smaller in size or strength)

(记)de+crease(增长)→使负增长→减少

(例)The pain decreased after I took an aspirin. / His influence slowly decreased.

deduce [diˊdjuːs] v. 演绎,推断(to determine sth. by looking at the facts; to come to a conclusion by studying the facts)

(记)de(往下)+duce(引导)→往下引导→推断,演绎

(例)I deduced that I would be late for the important interview when I saw how heavy the traffic was. / From her conversation, I deduced that she had a large family.

deduct [diˈdʌkt] v. 扣除,减去(to subtract sth. from a large amount)
(记)de + duct(引导)→往下引导→减去
(例)The waitress deducted the cost of the cold coffee from our bill. / They deducted the expenses from his salary.

defendant [diˈfendənt] n. 被告(与 plaintiff 相对)(someone who is the target of legal action in a court of law); a. 处于被告地位的(defending)
(记)defend(保护) + ant→保护自己→被告
参考:plaintiff(原告)
(例)The judge told the defendant to stand when the verdict was read.

deferential [ˌdefəˈrenʃəl] a. 充满敬意的(respectful; humble)
(记)defer(遵从,听从)→deference(遵从;尊敬)→deferential;注意这儿的 defer 不是"拖延"的意思
(例)A teacher should not act too deferential to the students.

deficit [ˈdefisit] n. 赤字(the amount of money by which a sum falls short of the necessary amount)
(记)de + fic(做) + it→没做好→缺陷→赤字
(例)The government tried to avoid the budget deficit.

deform [diˈfɔːm] vt. 使变形(to change the shape of sth., usually for the worse)
(记)de + form(形状)→使不再是原来的形状→使变形
(例)The intense heat from the fire deformed the metal chair.

defrost [diːˈfrɔːst] v. 除霜,解冻(to remove sth. from a freezer in order to thaw it before cooking; to thaw)
(记)de + frost(霜)→去除霜→除霜,解冻
(例)Defrost the chicken before baking it.

deft [deft] a. 灵巧的,熟练的(skillful; making quick and neat movements)
(记)由 dexter(右边)转化而来,右手较灵活,所以灵巧的
同根词:dexterous(灵巧的,惯用右手的);dexterity(技巧,灵活);ambidextrous(双手很灵巧的,熟练的)
(例)The pianist's deft fingers were delightful to watch.

degenerate [diˈdʒenəreit] v. 退步,堕落(to worsen or break down; to lose one's morals)
(记)de + gener(种类) + ate→变种→退步,degenerate 还可作形容词用,"退化的";n. degeneration(衰退,堕落,蜕化)
同根词:regenerate(使新生);generation(一代人)
(例)That fine young man has degenerated under the influence of evil company. / As the man grew older, his health degenerated. / The young man's morals degenerated due to his friends' corrupt influence.

de-ice [ˈdiːˈais] v. 除冰(to free sth., such as a car window, from ice; to scrape sth. free of ice)
(记)de(消除) + ice(冰)→除冰
(例)Now that I have a garage, I no longer have to de-ice my windshield.

deleterious [ˌdɛləˈtiriəs] a.(对身心)有害的,有毒的(harmful to health or well-being; injurious)
(例)He is wondering whether prolonged weight-

lessness has deleterious effects on human skeleton.

deliberate [di'libərit] a. 深思熟虑的(carefully thought out and formed, or done on purpose; premeditated);v. 慎重考虑(to think or consider carefully)

(记)de + liber(自由) + ate→非自由的→思考的

同根词:liberality(自由,慷慨);liberty(自由)

(例)The deliberate decision to raise taxes was welcomed by the voters. / You'd better deliberate your choice carefully.

delicate ['delikit] a. 微妙的,棘手的(needing careful handling, tact, etc.)

(例)The international situation is very delicate at present.

delineate [di'linieit] v. 描画(to mark the boundaries of sth.);描绘轮廓(to show the limits of sth. by drawing them or describing them)

(记)de + line(线条) + ate→加强线条→描绘

(例)The scientist delineated the theory's capabilities. / The scientist delineated the theory's capabilities.

delinquent [di'liŋkwənt] a. 疏忽职务的,有过失的(doing wrong, failing to perform a duty)

(记)de + linqu(= linger 闲荡) + ent→闲荡过去→疏忽职务;n. delinquency(失职罪行)

(例) The company cancelled its delinquent customers' credit. / The police often call delinquent children's parents to speak about the problem.

delta ['deltə] n.(河流的)三角洲

(记)本身是希腊语的第四个字母"Δ",也指形状像Δ的河流的三角洲

deluge ['delju:dʒ] n.大洪水,暴雨(a great flood; a heavy rainfall)

(记)de + luge(洗刷)→冲洗彻底→大洪水;the Deluge 专指基督教《圣经·创世纪》中的洪水灭世
(例)Fifty people drowned in the deluge. / The sky was blackening and making ready to release a deluge.

delusion [diˈluːʒən] n. 欺骗,谬见,妄想(a false belief)
(记)来自 delude,de + lude(玩弄)→玩弄别人→欺骗;可以和 illusion(幻觉,幻想),hallucination(幻觉,幻想)一起记
(例)Jane suffers from the delusion that she is unpopular. / He was under the delusion that he could succeed.

demise [diˈmaiz] n. 不动产的转让,遗赠(a transfer of an estate by lease, esp. for a fixed period);让位(the transfer of sovereignty by death or abdication);死亡(a ceasing to exist; death)
(记)de(往下) + mise(mit)(传送)→往下传→遗赠
(例)The country mourned the president's demise.

demobilization [ˈdiːˌməubilaiˈzeiʃən] n. 遣散(军人)(disbanding 〔troops〕);复员(discharging 〔a person〕 from the armed forces)
(记)来自 demobilize,de + mobilize(动员)→反动员→遣散,mob(动)
同根词:mobility(能动性);mob(暴民)

demographic [ˌdiːməgræfik] a. 人口统计的,人口学的(of the study of statistics of births, deaths, diseases, etc)
(记)来自 demography,demo(人) + graphy(写)→写出人口有多少→人口统计
参考:census(人口普查)
(例)Our country has very serious demographic problems. / Measures were decided to change the

demographic composition.

demolition [ˌdeməˈliʃən] n. 破坏,拆除(a pulling or tearing down, eg. old buildings; destruction)

(记)来自 demolish,demol(破坏) + ish→摧毁

参考:demon(魔鬼)

(例)the demolition of the buildings / Demolition work has begun on the old building.

demonstrable [ˈdemənstrəbl] a. 可论证的,可表明的(able to be proved)

(记)来自 demonstrate(论证,证明),de(向外) + monstrate(展示)→向外展示→论证,证明

(例)Though intriguing, the theory's conclusions were not demonstrable.

demur [diˈməː] v. 表示异议,反对(to raise an objection to sth.)

(记)de + mur(墙)→竖起墙→反对

同根词:mural(壁画);demure(严肃的)

(例)The teacher demurred at the suggestion that she assigned too much homework. / The majority were in favor of the plan, but a few demurred.

denationalization [ˌdiːˌnæʃənəlaiˈzeiʃən] n. 非国有化(placing [an industry owned or controlled by the government] under private ownership)

(记)来自 denationalize,de(解除) + nation(国家) + lize→解除国有化→非国有化

denigrate [ˈdenigreit] vt. 使黑(to blacken);抹黑,贬低(to disparage the character or reputation of; defame)

(记)de + nigr(黑) + ate→弄黑→贬低

同根词:negrophile(同黑人友好者);nigrify(使变黑)

(例)She was dismayed by the denigrating remarks that her friend made about her behind her backs.

denote [di'nəut] v. 指示,表示,意味着(to be a sign of; indicate; to signify or refer to explicitly)
(记)de(下面)+note(做记号)→在下面做记号→指示表示
(例)A frown often denotes displeasure. / The sign X denotes an unknown number.

denouement [dei'nuːmɔːŋ] n. (小说的)结尾,结局(the outcome, solution, unraveling, or clarification of a plot in a drama, story, etc.; any final revelation or outcome)
(记)法语词:de+noue(=knot 结),解开结→结尾;注意不要和 denouncement(谴责)相混

dentition [den'tiʃən] n. 出牙,长牙(the teething process); 【动】牙系,牙列,齿式(the number and kind of teeth and their arrangement in the mouth)
(记)dentist(牙医);denture(假牙);indented(锯齿状的);dent(缺口,凹痕)
(例)Dogs and wolves have the same dentition.(狗和狼有相同的牙列。)

denunciatory [di'nʌnsiətəri] a. 指责的,谴责的,恐吓的(reproaching; accusing; threatening)
(记)de(强调性的)+nunci(宣告)+atory→指责的,谴责的,恐吓的;v. denunciate(=denounce)(谴责);n. denunciation(谴责)

depart [di'pɑːt] v. 离开(to leave; to start a journey by leaving a place)
(记)de(离开)+part(分开)→离开;n. departure
(例)The President is scheduled to arrive at 4:00 p.m. and depart after dinner. / The train departs the station at 6:00 p.m. sharp.

depict [di'pikt] v. 刻画,描述(to show sb. or sth., esp. by using a picture; to portray sb. or sth.)

(记)de(起强调作用)+pict(画)→刻画,描述
(例)Mary depicted a beautiful sunset in her painting. / depict a government as inept(把一个政府描绘成无能而不称职)

deplete [diˈpliːt] v. 倒空,耗尽(to use up all or most of a supply of sth.)
(记)de+plete(满)→不满→倒空
同根词:replete(饱满的);plentiful(大量的)
(例)The cost of this journey has depleted our small store of money. / The drought depleted the village's water supply.

depletion [diˈpliːʃən] n. 耗尽,弄空(a depleting or being depleted; drain, exhaust)
(例)a depletion of coal deposits(耗尽煤藏)

deploy [diˈplɔi] v.【军】展开,调度,部署(to position soldiers and their equipment [somewhere] before an attack)
(例)After the general deployed the soldiers and tanks, they attacked the village.

depreciation [diˌpriːʃiˈeiʃən] n. 贬低(a decrease in the value of the currency of a country; disparagement)
(记)来自 depreciate,de+preci(价值)+ate→贬低
同根词:appreciate(赞成)
(例)The gradual depreciation of the dollar was fueled by rising imports. / The depreciation of a car is greatest during its first year.

depress [diˈpres] v. 降低(to weaken the force or effect of sth.);使抑郁(to make sb. sad; to send sb. into despair)
(记)de(往下)+press(压)→往下压→降低,使抑郁
(例)Some drugs depress the functions of the hu-

man body. / The cold, grey weather depressed the students on campus.

deride [di'raid] v. 讽刺,讥讽(to insult or mock sb. or sth.; to ridicule sb. or sth.)

(记)de + ride(笑)→嘲笑, ris = rid; n. derision

同根词:ridicule(奚落,嘲笑);risible(爱笑的)

(例)He was derided for his horrid taste in furniture. / The politician derided his opponents at every opportunity.

derision [di'riʒən] n. 嘲笑,嘲笑的目标,笑柄(mockery; ridicule)

(例)This guy is famous for his clever derision of government officials.

derivative [di'rivətiv] a. 派生的,无创意的(using or taken from sources; not original)

(记)来自下面的 derive(派生,推知)

derive [di'raiv] v. 派生(to get or receive from a source);推知,推论出(to get by reasoning; deduce or infer)

(记)de + rive(= river 河流)→支流→派生

(例)What language does the word "pathos" derive from?

derogatory [di'rɔgətəri] a. 不敬的,诽谤的(belittling; disparaging; showing contempt)

(记)de(坏) + rog(问,说) + ate→说坏话→贬低

同根词:arrogate(声称);rogation(祈祷)

(例)I can't bear his derogatory remarks about my character. / Mike's derogatory statement to the police officer almost got him arrested.

descend [di'send] v. 传下,遗传(to come from an earlier time)

(记)de + scend(爬)→爬下→下降→传下,遗传

参考:ascend(上升)

(例)This practice descends to us from the sixteenth century.

descendant [di'sendənt] n. 子孙,后裔(someone's child, grandchild, great-grandchild and so on)
(记)descend(传下)+ant→子孙
(例)This gentleman is the descendant of the last emperor in China.

desegregation [di:segri'geiʃən] n. 取消种族隔离(the ending of the separation of the races)
(记)来自 desegregate, de(解除)+segregate(隔离)→解除隔离→取消种族隔离
(例)After desegregation, children of all races attended the same schools.

desktop n.(计算机)桌面系统
(记)desk(桌子)+top(上面)→桌面系统

despise [dis'paiz] v. 轻视,轻蔑(to have a strong dislike for sb. or sth.)
(记)de+spis(看)+e→不值得看→轻视
参考:despicable(可鄙的);conspicuous(显著的)
(例)Many people despise greasy food. / He despises flattery.

detached [di'tætʃt] a. 分开的(separate; not attached);超然公平的(impartial; indifferent; unbiased)
(记)来自 detach(分离、拆开),de(不)+tach(接触)→不接触→分开
同根词:attachment(附件;依恋)
(例)The detached nozzle of the hose lay in the grass. / Bob's detached attitude about school often gets him in trouble.

detection [di'tekʃən] n. 察觉,发现(noticing or discovering sb. or sth.)
(记)来自 detect(察觉,发现),de(去除)+tect(遮

盖)→去掉遮盖→发现
同根词:protection(保护)
(例)The FBI agent took credit for the detection of the crime. / the techniques of crime detection(犯罪侦察技术)

detergent [di'tə:dʒənt] a. 净化的(cleansing);n. 清洁剂(a product used for cleaning clothes and dishes)
(记)de+terg(擦)+ent→擦掉→清洁剂
(例)put the detergent in the dishwasher before starting it

deterioration [diˌtiəriə'reiʃən] n. 变化;恶化;退化(falling apart; becoming worn or damaged; declining in strength, quality or condition)
(记)来自 deteriorate, deterior(糟糕的)+ate→变糟,恶化
参考:superior(高级的);inferior(低级的)
(例)After your caustic remarks, the deterioration of our friendship is inevitable. / He had trouble with bone deterioration and walked with a cane.

deterrent [di'terənt] n. 制止(因素);威慑物(sth. that keeps sb. or sth. from doing sth.; sth. that encourages sb. or sth. not to do sth.);a. 制止的;威慑的(deterring or tending to deter)
(记)来自 deter, de+ter(使害怕)→使吓得离开→威慑
(例)Thoughts of his parents' anger served as a strong deterrent when the naughty boy considered misbehaving. / I do not think that prison is much deterrent to those people.(我认为监狱对那些人没有多大的威慑作用。)

detractor [di'træktə] n. 贬低者(sb. who criticizes, ridicules or heckles)

(记)de + tract (拉) + or→向下拉的人→贬低者, detract 就是"诽谤,贬低"之意

(例)The popular writer answered both to her detractors and her admirers.

detrimental [ˌdetriˈmentl] a. 有害的,不利的(to)(damaging; harmful); n. 有害的人或物(an undesirable or harmful person or thing)

(记)来自 detriment,分割记忆:de - trim(修剪) - ent→剪坏了→伤害

(例) Smoking cigarettes is detrimental to your health. / belligerent actions detrimental to the cause of peace(不利于和平事业的好战行动)

devastate [ˈdevəsteit] vt. 使荒芜,破坏(to ruin sth.);压倒(to cause emotional distress to sb.)

(记)de + vast(大量) + ate→大量弄坏→破坏;vast 本身是一个单词,意为"广阔的、大量的";a. devastating(破坏性极大的,毁灭性的);n. devastator(破坏者,蹂躏者)

(例)The loss of his wife devastated him.

diabetes [ˌdaiəˈbiːtiːz] n.【医】糖尿病(a disease where there is too much sugar in the blood and urine)

(记)dia(通过) + betes→老是有尿通过→老是需要排尿→糖尿病

diagonal [daiˈægənl] n. 对角线(a line that goes from one corner of a four-sided figure to the opposite corner)

(记)dia(通过) + gon(角) + al→通过两个角的线→对角线

(例)A diagonal splits the square into two triangles.

dialect [ˈdaiəlekt] n. 方言(a regional variety of a language distinguished by features of vocabulary, grammar, and pronunciation)

(记)dia(在…之间) + lect(谈话)→在有的人之间说的话→方言
(例)His Southern dialect is hard for me to understand.

diameter [daiˈæmitə] n. 直径(the length of a straight line going through the center of a circle)
(记)dia(通过) + meter(量)→穿过…量的→直径
(例)How wide is the tyre in diameter? (这轮胎直径有多少?)

diaper [ˈdaiəpə] n. 婴儿尿布(a piece of cloth or other fiber that a baby wears between its legs before the baby has learned to use a toilet)
(例)Many people now use disposable diapers instead of cloth ones.

dichotomy [diˈkɔtəmi] n. 两分;本质对立(a division of sth. into two parts, groups or classes, esp. when these are sharply distinguished or opposed)
(记)dicho(二份) + tom(切、割) + y→切成二份→二分;a. dichotomous(分成两个的,叉状分枝的)
(例)The two characters in the play formed an interesting dichotomy.

didactic [diˈdæktik] a. 教诲的,说教的(used or intended for teaching or instruction; morally instructive or intended to be so)
(记)注意:didact (好说教的人)来自 didactic
(例)The pupils are tired of their teacher's didactic lectures. / didactic manner(好说教的态度)

die out 灭绝,绝种(become extinct; come to a complete end)
(例)Many old customs are gradually dying out.

diesel [ˈdiːzəl] n. 内燃机,柴油机(a type of internal-combustion engine that burns fuel oil)

(记)由德国的发明家 Diesel 而来
(例)diesel engine/ motor

difference [ˈdifrəns] n. 差(the amount by which one quantity differs from another; remainder left after subtraction)
(记)比较记忆:subtraction(减法),minuend(被减数),subtrahend(减数),difference(差)
(例)The difference between 90 and 60 is 30.

dilution [daiˈljuːʃən] n. 稀释,渗水(thinning down or weakening as by mixing with water or other liquid)
(记)来自 dilute,di + lute(冲洗)→冲洗掉→稀释

diminish [diˈminiʃ] v. 减少,减弱;削弱(to become or cause sth. to become smaller or less important; reduce)
(记)dimin(小) + ish→减小;削弱
(例)Unexpected expenses diminished the size of my bank account. / Her illness diminished her strength.

dine [dain] v. 吃饭(to eat a meal, esp. to eat dinner);招待…吃饭(to provide a dinner for);(房子,桌子)可容…吃饭([a room, or table] to be enough for a certain number of people to eat dinner)
(例)We dined our friends at home. / This table dines ten comfortably.

dinosaur [ˈdainəsɔː] n. 恐龙(a large, prehistoric reptile that is now extinct)
(例)A dinosaur's skeleton is displayed in the museum's main hall.

dioxide [daiˈɔksaid] n.【化】二氧化物(an oxide containing two atoms of oxygen per molecule)
(记)di(二) + oxide(氧化物)→二氧化物
(例)carbon dioxide 二氧化碳

dip [dip] n. 倾斜;下降,下沉(an abrupt downward slope);浸渍(a quick plunge into water or other liquid);溶液(a liquid in which sth. is soaked shortly, as for dyeing)

(例)hear the dip of the oars(听见桨入水的声音) / the dip of the sun(日落) / cattle dip(牲畜药浴用的药液)

diphtheria [dif´θiəriə] n.【医】白喉(症)(a type of severe, contagious throat infection)

(例)Outbreaks of diphtheria used to kill many people.

diploma [di´pləumə] n.毕业文凭;学位证书(a certificate of graduation from a school or college)

(记)diplo(双)+ma→原指双折的信件→文凭

(例)award/ grant a diploma(授毕业文凭/学位证书)

directive [di´rektiv] n.命令,指令(an official order or instruction);a.指示的,管理的(directing; tending or intended to direct)

(记)来自 direct(指导,命令)

(例)The manager sent a directive stating that all employees had to work overtime. / a directive to the armed forces(给武装部队的命令)

disarm [dis´ɑːm] vt.使人消除敌意(或怀疑,怒气等),使友好(to make sb. feel more at ease or less suspicious)

(记)dis(消除)+arm(武器)→消除武器→使人消除敌意,使友好

(例)The thief uses charm to disarm people before swindling them. / She disarmed him by saying that her behavior had been unforgivable.(她说自己过去的行为是不可饶恕的,这就消释了他的怒

气。)

disavow [ˌdisəˈvau] vt. 不承认,抵赖,拒绝对…承担责任(to deny any knowledge or approval of, or responsibility for; disclaim; disown)

(记)dis(不) + avow(承认)→不承认

(例)The boy disavowed his promise to marry his innocent fiancee.

discern [diˈsəːn] v. (费劲)识别,看出(to be able to perceive or distinguish sth. clearly)

(记)dis(分离) + cern(=sift 筛)→筛出来→识别; a. discernible(可辨别的)

同根词:concern(关注)

(例)He was just able to discern the road in the dark. / I can't discern the difference between ice cream and frozen yogurt.

discharge [disˈtʃɑːdʒ] v. 流出(to let sth. out; to pour sth. out);释放(to release sb. or sth.);解雇(to dismiss sb. from employment)

(记)dis(离开) + charge(古语指车)→从车里出来→流出,释放,解雇

(例)The engine discharged a stream of oil onto the floor. / The judge found him not guilty and discharged him. / The company discharged 200 employees to cut costs.

discount [ˈdiskaunt] vt. 不全信,对…持怀疑态度(to disregard sb. or sth.; to disregard what sb. says or does; to not believe sth.)

(记)dis(不) + count(计算)→不计算在内→不全信,持怀疑态度

(例)The jury was told to discount the false testimony. / Much of what he says must be discounted.

discourse [dis'kɔːs] n. 演讲；论述(a formal speech; a lecture; the process of discussing sth.)
(记)dis(离开)+course(跑)→跑开→论述，演讲
同根词：concourse(汇合，合流)
(例)The priest delivered a long discourse on the evils of untruthfulness. / The doctor presented a discourse on patient management.

discrete [dis'kriːt] a. 个别的；不连续的；不相关联的(separate; not connected; distinct)
(记)注意不要和 discreet(小心的，谨慎的)混了
(例)A computer can perform millions of discrete functions per second. / The word "heart" has several discrete meanings.(这个词有好些不相关联的词义。)

discretionary [di'skreʃənəri] a. 随机行事的，处理自由的(left to one's own choice or decision)
(记)由 discretion 而来，discretion(谨慎；斟酌决定的自由)
(例)an ambassador with discretionary powers(有随机行事权的大使)

discrimination [disˌkrimi'neiʃən] n. 歧视，偏见(treating people differently because of prejudice)
(记)来自 discriminate(辨别)，dis(分开)+crimin(罪行)+ate→分开对待有罪的人→辨别，歧视
同根词：incriminate(连累)
(例)Different groups of people in many countries of the world face discrimination. / The applicants were judged without discrimination as to race, color or creed.(评审申请者时不因种族、肤色或信仰而加以歧视。)

disenfranchise ['disin'fræntʃaiz] vt. 剥夺…的公民权(to deprive sb. of the right to vote in a political election; disfranchise)

(记) disenfranchise = disfranchise, dis (剥夺) + franchise(选举权)→剥夺权力

(例)a law to disenfranchise the illiterate(剥夺文盲公民权的法律) / These people are culturally disfranchised.(这些人在文化上被剥夺了权利。)

disguise [dis'gaiz] vt. 把…假扮起来(to change the appearance of a thing or a person to make identification difficult);隐瞒(to conceal sb. or sth.)

(记) dis (不同) + guise (姿态,伪装) → 掩饰"guise",本身是一个单词

(例)The woman disguised the gift so that her son could not guess what it was. / Bill disguised himself as a soldier for Halloween. / She disguised her sadness with a happy smile.

disinclination [ˌdisinkli'neiʃən] n. 不愿意;厌恶(a dislike or lack of desire; aversion; reluctance)

(记)dis(不) + inclination(愿意,偏好)→不愿意

(例)have a disinclination for hard work / Disappointment gave him a disinclination to the fair sex.(失恋使他厌恶女性。)

dislodge [dis'lɔdʒ] v. 取出(to remove sth. that is stuck or jammed);逐出(to drive from a position)

(记)dis + lodge(小屋)→逐出(小屋等)

(例)dislodge a fishbone from a cat's throat / The city workers dislodged the tree trunk that was damming the river. / The enemy troops were finally dislodged from the fort.(敌军终于被逐出要塞。)

dismal ['dizməl] a. 忧郁的;凄凉的;阴沉的(dreary; bleak; depressing)

(记)dis + mal(高兴)→不高兴

(例) I cried during the dismal movie. / dismal weather(阴沉的天)

dismantle [disˊmæntl] vt. 拆除…的设备(或装备、防御工事等)(to strip〔a house, ship, etc.〕of furniture, equipment, means of defense, etc.);拆开,拆散(to take apart; disassemble)

(记)dis(去掉) + mantle(覆盖)→去掉覆盖→拆除…的设备等

(例)The child dismantled the toy and then could not reassemble it.

dismember [disˊmembə] vt. 割下(动物)的肢体(to move the limbs of by cutting or tearing),肢解(to pull or cut to pieces; separate into parts);割裂(to mutilate);

(记)dis(去掉) + member(人或动植物的一部分)→割下(动物)的肢体,肢解

(例)The murderer dismembered his victim in order to hide his hideous crime. / dismember a country (瓜分某国)

disorder [disˊɔːdə] n. 杂乱;异常(lack of order; irregularity);不舒服(an upset of normal function; ailment)

(记)dis(不) + order(正常状态)→不是正常状态→不适;异常

(例)The disorder caused by the hecklers disrupted the political debate. / a mild stomach disorder(轻度胃病)

disorient [disˊɔːriənt] vt. 使迷失方位(to confuse, esp. about directions);使迷惑(to perplex or mystify with respect to time, place or the identity of people)

(记)dis(使…不) + orient(定向)→使不能定向

(例)The strange streets disoriented him.(陌生的街道使他迷失方向。) / After several bottles of beer, he looked disoriented.

disparaging [dis′pæridʒiŋ] a. 贬低的,轻蔑的(belittling, unkind, contemptuous)

(记)来自 disparage, dis(不) + par(平等) + age→不平等→贬低

同根词:parity(平等)

(例)The teacher gave her noisy pupils a disparaging look.

disparate [′dispərit] a. 迥然不同的,不可并论的(varied or distinct; unequal)

(记)dis(不) + par(平等) + ate→不等的→不同的

(例)The witnesses gave disparate accounts of the incident.

disparity [dis′pæriti] n. 不同,差异(difference; incongruity)

(记)参考 disparate

(例)The two scientists could not reconcile the disparity between their respective findings. / Income disparities have narrowed sharply.

dispassionate [dis′pæʃənit] a. 平心静气的(calm, free of emotions or attachment; impartial)

(记)dis(不) + passionate(激情的)→不表现激情→心平气和的; n. dispassion(冷静, 公平); 注意千万别把 dispassionate 看成"冷漠的"意思

(例)The politician's dispassionate speech failed to generate any tangible support for his party.

displace [dis′pleis] vt. 迫使离家(或祖国)(to force people to move, esp. during the war)

(记)dis(离开) + place(地方)→使离开自己的地方→迫使离家(或祖国)

(例)displaced person(被迫离家的人) / Many of the inhabitants were displaced by the rising floodwaters. (许多居民由于越涨越高的洪水而离开了

家园。）

dispose [dis'pəuz] vt. 配置，安排（to place in a certain order or arrangement）；使倾向于，有意于（to make willing; incline）；dispose of 处理（deal with conclusively, settle）

（记）dis（分开）+ pose（布置）→安排

（例）His interest in nature disposes him to go hiking regularly. / Your words of cheer disposed me for the task.（你说的一番鼓励话使我愿意接受这一任务。）/ The ruthless leader disposed of the prisoners arbitrarily.

dissemination [diˌsemi'neiʃən] n. 散布，传播（the spreading of information）

（记）来自 disseminate，dis（分离）+ semin（种子）+ ate→散布（种子）

同根词：seminal（种子的；生殖的）

（例）The Internet is speeding up the dissemination of news across international borders.

dissenter [di'sentə] n. 持异议者（someone who disagrees with the authority or the majority）

（记）dis（相反）+ sent（感觉）→反感觉→不同意

同根词：assent（同意）；sentiment（情感）

（例）Dissenters were severely punished under the emperor's harsh rule.

dissipate ['disipeit] v.（使）驱散（to disperse or dilute）；浪费（to spend money foolishly; to squander money）

（记）分割记忆：dis（分离）- sipate（扔）→扔开→（使）驱散；浪费；n. dissipator（放荡者，浪子）；a. dissipative（消耗的；浪费的；放荡的）

（例）The rising sun dissipated the heavy fog. / The company dissipated its funds buying unnecessary equipment.

distill [dis'til] v. 蒸馏(to vaporize liquid by heating it and the vapor)
(记)di(分离)+still(点滴落)→分离出来的水滴→蒸馏;注意:n. distillate(馏出液,精华)
(例)It is debatable whether distilled water is good for our health.

distinct [dis'tiŋkt] a. 不同的,有差别的(different; separate; able to be distinguished)
(记)di+stinct(促使=sting)→促使分开的→有差别的
(例)The twins may look alike, but they have very distinct personalities.

distort [dis'tɔːt] vt. 弄歪(脸、嘴)(to twist sth. out of shape);歪曲(to misrepresent the facts of a matter);把…弄得不正常
(记)dis(起强调作用)+tort(扭曲)→弄歪,歪曲
(例)a face distorted by pain / This mirror is not good, it distorts our reflections. / Don't distort the fact. Just tell the truth.

distraction [dis'trækʃən] n. 精神涣散;发狂(a mental intrusion or cause of confusion);消遣,娱乐(anything that gives mental relaxation; amusement; diversion)
(记)dis+tract(拉)+ion→(精神)被拉开→精神涣散,发狂
同根词:tractable(温顺的,随和的)
(例)After several days of toiling and moiling, his girlfriend's visit was a welcome distraction.

distribution [ˌdistri'bjuːʃən] n. 分配;销售;分布(the giving out of sth.; dispersing sth.)
(记)来自 distribute,dis(分开)+tribute(给)→分配;销售

(例)an equal distribution(平均分配) / Our distribution is bad.(我们的销售情况不佳。)

diva [ˈdiːvə] n.[意]歌剧女主角;主要女歌手(a leading woman singer, esp. in grand opera)

divergence [daiˈvəːdʒəns] n.分歧;岔开(a diverging, separating, or branching off; departure from a particular viewpoint, practice, etc)
(记)来自 diverge, di + verg(转向)→分开转→分歧
同根词:converge(聚集,集中)
(例)The divergence of their opinions has made it difficult for them to work together.

divergent [daiˈvəːdʒənt] a. 有分歧的;岔开的(breaking off into two or more different paths)
(例)A series of divergent paths wound through the woods.

diverse [daiˈvəːs] a. 不同的,多种多样的(varied; different)
(记)di + vers(转) + e→不同的
(例)China's top leadership is made of people of diverse background.

diversify [daiˈvəːsifai] v.使多样;使不同(to give variety to; vary)
(记)di + vers(转) + ify→使转开→使多样,使不同
同根词:adversity(苦难); versatile(多才多艺的)
(例)The company is diversifying its products to meet the demands of the consumers.

divest [daiˈvest] v.使卸下,使脱去(to strip[of clothing, equipment, etc.]);剥夺(to deprive or dispossess [of rank, rights, etc.])
(记)di(去掉) + vest(穿衣)→脱衣→剥夺; n. divestment

同根词:vested(穿着衣服的);vestment(外衣,法衣)

(例)The servants helped to divest the king of his royal garments. / They divested the king of all his power. / The congress divested the dishonest president of all his authority.

divestment [daiˈvestmənt] n. 卸下盛装(the stripping of sth.);剥夺(dispossession or deprivation)

dividend [ˈdividend] n.(股份的)红利(a part of the profit of a company given to the shareholders of the company)

(记)divid(分开)+end→分享的利润→红利

(例)When its profits increased, the company raised its dividend.

dividend [ˈdividend] n. 被除数(a number that is divided by another number)

(记)是数学术语,和下文的 division(除法)、divisible(可整除的)、divisor(除数)一起记

divine [diˈvain] a. 神的,神性的(of or about God; holy; sacred);天赐的(given by God);非凡的(fabulous; excellent; wonderful)

(记)div(神)+ine

(例)Every Sunday the minister preached about the divine world. / A divine dress is hanging on the mannequin in the store window.

divisible [diˈvizəbl] a. 可整除的(able to be divided by another number with no remainder)

division [diˈviʒən] n. 除法

division [diˈviʒən] n. 部门;科(a particular department of a government, business, school, or other organization);区域(a particular section of a country, state, etc. divided off as for administration);【军】师(an

army unit larger than a regiment and smaller than a corps)
(记)分出来的→部门,区域,师
(例)the sales division of a company(公司的销售科)/ a court in the seventh division(第七区的一个法院)

divisor [diˊvaizə] n. 除数

divulge [daiˊvʌldʒ] vt. 泄漏(秘密等)(to tell a secret; to reveal sth.; disclose)
(记)di + vulge(普通)→使…普通→透露
同根词:vulgar(粗俗的, 普通的)
(例)The traitor divulged the secret plans to the enemy. / The secret has been divulged to no one.

docile [ˊdəusail] a. 驯服的;温顺的(tame; submissive; obedient)
(记)doc(教) + ile→可教的
(例)It is often said that men like docile women best.

doctrine [ˊdɔktrin] n. 教条,教义(a statement of policy; a set of beliefs)
(记)来自 doctor(博士)
(例)The manager promoted her doctrine of management.

dogma [ˊdɔgmə] n. 教条(the beliefs taught by a particular religion)
(记)分割记忆:dog(狗) - ma→像狗一样顽固的教条
(例)The religion that I am a member of has no dogma at all.

dogwood [ˊdɔgwud] n. 荚,木属植物,山茱萸(designating a family of small trees and shrubs)
(记)分割记忆:dog(狗) - wood(木)→山茱萸

donor [ˊdəunə] n. 捐献者(someone who gives sth.)
(记)v. donate(捐献),don(给予)+ate
(例)The hospital asked for blood donors.

doom [duːm] n. 厄运;死亡(a horrible fate; a death that cannot be avoided);法令(a judgment, esp. a sentence of condemnation);(上帝)最后审判日(Judgment Day)
(例)The little boy felt that doom and disaster were in his future.

dope [dəup] n. 粘稠物,胶状物(any thick liquid or pastry substance);添加剂(any additive, as a food preservative)
(记)和 rope,hope,lope(大步慢跑)一起记

dose [dəus] n.(药的)剂量;一服(the amount of medicine that is to be taken at one time)
(例)The sick woman forgot to take her second dose of medication, and started to feel worse.

doubtless [ˊdautlis] ad. 无疑地(without doubt; certainly; surely);很可能地(probably)
(记)doubt(疑问)+less(无)→无疑地
(例)The lost cat will doubtless find its way home again.

drab [dræb] a. 枯燥的,无味的,单调的(dull; gray; boring; not exciting)
(记)和 grab(夺取)一起记; n. drabness(枯燥)
(例)The prison cells were painted a drab color.

drain [drein] vt. 排水(to draw water or any liquid gradually from so as to dry or empty);喝干(to drink all the liquid from [a cup, glass, etc.]);消耗(to remove sb.'s energy, endurance, or other quality); vi.(水)流掉(to become dry by the drawing or flowing off of liquid)

(记)d + rain→把雨水排掉→排水,消耗
(例)To drain the bathtub, just pull the plug out. / Watching the sentimental movie drained me emotionally.

drastic [ˊdræstik] a. 激烈的(acting with force; having a strong or violent effect);(法律)极端的,严厉的(severe; harsh; extreme)
(记)dra(做) + stic→做得激烈→激烈的,严厉的
(例)The principal felt that the cheater's punishment should be drastic.

drizzle [ˊdrizl] n. 毛毛雨(misty rain; rain that falls in tiny drops)
(例)The children continued to play, even in the drizzle.

dropout [ˊdrɔpaut] n.[美]中途退学;中途退出的人(one who drops out, specif. a person who withdraws from school, esp. high school, before graduating);退出社会的人(one who withdraws from the mundane world)
(记)drop(掉) + out(出来,出去)→掉出来→中途退出的人;中途退学
(例)It is very difficult for a dropout to find a good job in a big city like Beijing. / a political dropout (退出政界者)

dubious [ˊdju:bjəs] a.(对事物)半信半疑的,怀疑的,犹豫不决的(feeling doubt; hesitating; skeptical);未定的(with the outcome undecided or hanging in the balance)
(记)du(二) + bious→有两种想法→半信半疑的,怀疑的
(例)I am dubious that a new stove will improve my cooking. / He felt dubious as to what to do next.

ductile [ˊdʌktail] a. 易拉长的;易变形的,可塑的(that can be stretched, drawn, or hammered without breaking; easily molded; pliant; tractable)
(记)duct(引导)+ile→可引导的→可塑的
参考:induction(就职,入伍)
(例)Silver is a ductile metal.(银是韧性金属。)/the ductile minds of youth(青年人的思想可塑性大)

dummy [ˊdʌmi] n. 哑巴;笨蛋(a person unable to talk; mute;〔Slang〕a stupid person);(服装店里的)人体模型;(足球训练、劈刺用的)人形靶(a figure made in human form, as for displaying clothes, practicing tackling in football, etc.)
(记)dum(dumb)(哑的)+my→哑巴;笨蛋
(例)The kids made fun of the boy who they thought was a dummy./The designer dressed the department store dummy in the window.

dump [dʌmp] n. 垃圾堆(a junkyard; a landfill; a place where trash is thrown away);堆存处(〔Mil.〕a temporary storage center in the field, as for ammunition, food, clothing)
(记)dump 还经常作动词用,意为"倾倒",如:dump the garbage(倒垃圾)
(例)We went to dump to look for the diamond ring my mother lost yesterday.

dump [dʌmp] vt. 倾销(to sell〔a commodity〕in large quantity at a low price, esp. in a foreign market at a price below that of the domestic market)
(例)dump surplus goods abroad(向国外倾销过剩货物)

duplicate [ˊdju:plikit] a. 复制的(an additional copy of sth.);n. 副本,抄件;复制品(a copy; a replica;

sth. that looks and works exactly like sth. else); vt.复写;复制(to make an exact copy of sth.)
(记)du + plic(重叠) + ate→使重叠→复制
(例)The duplicate is hard to read. Would you please give me its original? / I need to duplicate the key.

durability [ˌdjuərəˈbiliti] n. 耐久性(the quality of being strong, hard, able to withstand rough use)
(记)dur(持续) + ability(能力)→持续的能力→耐久性
(例)The watch has doubtless durability, since it is both waterproof and shatterproof.

dwelling [ˈdweliŋ] n.住处,寓所(a residence; a place where someone lives)
(记)dwell(居住) + ing→住处,寓所
(例)A dormitory is the typical dwelling of a college student.

dwindle [ˈdwindl] v.日渐减少;变小(to decrease piece by piece)
(记)注意不要和 swindle(欺骗,诈骗)相混

dynamics [daiˈnæmiks] n.力学;动力学;动态(the branch of mechanics dealing with the motion of material bodies under the action of given forces; kinetics; the various forces, physical, moral, economic, etc., operating in any field)
(记)dynam(力量) + ics→有活力的→力学;动力学;动态
同根词:dynamo(发电机);dynamite(炸药)
(例)The dynamics of the business cycle were evident in the economic reports from the past decade.

dysfunction [disˈfʌŋkʃən] n.【医】机能障碍(abnormal, impaired or incomplete functioning, as of a body or-

gan or part)
(记)dys(不良)+function(功能)→功能不全→机能障碍，也可以写成：disfunction
(例)brain dysfunction / sexual dysfunction

dyskinesia [ˌdiskiˈniːʒiə] n.【医】运动障碍(impairment of body movement)
(记)dys(不良)+kinesia(运动)→运动不良→运动障碍
参考：kinetics(运动学)

E

echelon [ˈeʃələn] n.【军】梯队(a steplike formation of ships or troops, in which each unit is slightly to the left or right of the one preceding it);组织系统中的等级(any of the levels of responsibility or importance in an organization)
(记)来自古法语：eschile (梯子)
(例)The government's lower echelon consists of career bureaucrats.

ecology [i(ː)ˈkɔlədʒi] n.生态学(the study and science of living things and the way they interact with their environment)
(记)eco(环境)+logy(学科)→生态学
(例)The sixth graders discussed ecology in their science class.

economical [ˌiːkəˈnɔmikəl] a. 勤俭的，节省的，节约的(money-saving; thrifty)
(例)Comparing prices is an economical way to shop for groceries.

economy [i(ː)ˈkɔnəmi] n.经济(the system and management of industry and trade within a country);节省

(thriftiness; spending time, energy or money wisely);a. 经济实惠的(costing less than the standard or traditional kind)
(例)Not known for her economy, the housewife often spends money on things she doesn't need.

ecosystem [ˌi:kəˈsistəm] n. 生态系统(a specific environment in which certain plants and animals interact)
(记)eco(ecology)(生态学)+system(体系)→生态系统
(例)Logging (伐木) has destroyed the ecosystem of the forest.

edge [edʒ] n. 优势;优越条件(an advantage)
(记)跟别人比多一个边→多一个优势→优势;优势条件
(例)A good education will give you an edge in the job market. / competitive edge(竞争优势)

effigy [ˈefidʒi] n. 假人,模拟像(a crude representation of a disliked person, usually made for ridicule or mocking)
(记)ef(=ex)(出)+figy(=figure)(外形)→做出外形→假人,模拟像
(例)The angry mob burned an effigy of their ruler. / burn(hang) sb. in effigy(烧掉〔绞死〕某人的模拟像)

effluent [ˈefluənt] a. 发出的,流出的(flowing out or forth);n.(从河、湖、阴沟等)流出的水流;流出物(a thing that flows out and forth)
(记)ef(=ex)(出)+flu(流)+ent→往外流的→流出的;流出物
(例)Industrial effluents have gravely contaminated the scenic river.

egalitarianism [ˌi:gæliˈtɛəriənizəm] n. 平均主义(advocating, or

believing that all people should have equal political, social, and economic rights)
(记)来自 egalitarian, egalit(平等) + arian→平均主义的，等于 equalitarian

eggnog [ˈegˌnɔg] n. 蛋奶酒(a thick drink made of beaten eggs, milk, sugar, and nutmeg, often containing whiskey, rum, wine, etc.)
(记)egg(蛋) + nog(浓啤酒)→蛋奶酒

egregious [iˈgriːdʒəs] a. (缺点等)过分的；惊人的(remarkably bad; flagrant)
(记)e(出) + greg(团体)→ious→超出一般人→过分的
同根词：gregarious(喜社交的)；aggregate(集合)
(例)He said he was an egregious fool to have bothered about me. / The story seemed too egregious to be believed.(这故事似乎离奇得令人难以置信。)

elaborate [iˈlæbərit] v. 详尽说明，阐明(to explain〔sth.〕using many details)；a. 精致的(highly wrought or ornamented; complicated)
(记)e + labor(劳动) + ate→(努力)劳动出来的→精致的
(例)Don't elaborate! I don't want to hear every little detail. / She wore an elaborate costume to the party.

elective [iˈlektiv] n. 选修课(an optional course in one's schooling; a course that can be taken but is not required)
(记)e(出) + lect(选择) + ive→选择出的→选修课
(例)This university offers a lot of interesting electives.

electorate [iˈlektərit] n. 全体选民(all those qualified to vote in an election)

(记)elector(选举人)+ate→全体选民
(例)The electorate voted the corrupted politician out of office. / The president appealed directly to the electorate.

electron [i'lektrɔn] n.【物】电子(a negatively charged atomic particle)
(记)electr(电)+on→电子
(例)Atoms are made up of electrons, neutrons, and protons.

elevate ['eliveit] vt. 抬起;使升高(to raise or lift sb. or sth. from a lower level to a higher level);提高;振奋(to raise sth., such as sb.'s spirits or hope)
(记)e(出)+levate(抬起,举起)→抬起;使升高
(例)I elevated my arm over my head. / Materials are elevated to the top floor by a hoist.(材料由起重机吊到顶楼。) / I elevated my aunt's spirits by visiting her in the hospital.

elicit [i'lisit] v. 引出;探出(to draw out information from sb.; to bring out a response from sb.)
(记)e(出来)+licit(诱导)→引出
(例)At last I elicited an explanation of what was bothering my fiance.

eligible ['elidʒəbl] a. 合格的;适宜的(having met the proper requirements)
(记)e+lig(=lict 选择)+ible→能够选出来的→合格的
(例)Because of my nephew's medical problem, he was not eligible to join the army. / Only native-born citizens are eligible to the office of president.(只有本国出生的公民才有资格当选总统。)

eliminate [i'limineit] v. 淘汰;消除(to get rid of sb. or sth. completely)

(记)e + limin(门槛) + ate→扔出门槛→除去
(例)The new mayor tries to eliminate the gang activity in the city. / eliminate poverty(消除贫困)

elite [eiˈliːt] n. 精华;中坚(the group or part of a group selected or regarded as the finest, best, most distinguished, most powerful, etc.)
(记)e(出) + lite(挑选)→挑选出的→精华;中坚
(例)These intellectuals are the elite of our country.

elliptical [iˈliptikəl] a. 椭圆形的(oval; shaped like an ellipse)
(记)来自 ellipse,el + lipse(离开)→离开中心→不圆→椭圆
(例)Goose's eggs are usually elliptical.

elongate [ˈiːlɔŋgeit] v. 延长,伸长(to become or make sth. longer; to lengthen; to extend)
(记)e(出去) + long(长) + ate→长出去→伸长
同根词:longevity(长寿);longitude(经度)
(例)The fire engine's ladder elongated, reaching to the top of the building. / elongate a rubber band (拉长橡皮筋)

elongation [ˌiːlɔŋˈgeiʃən] n. 延伸(being extended or lengthened)
(例)The elongation of the garden made it possible for me to plant more trees in it.

eloquent [ˈeləkwənt] a. 雄辩的;演说动人的(capable of beautiful expressive public speaking; beautiful and expressive)
(记)e + loqu(说) + ent→说出的→雄辩的
参考:elocution(演讲术,演讲技巧)
(例)The eloquent lecturer was interesting to listen to. / The president is famous for his eloquent

speeches.

elude [iˈljuːd] vt.(巧妙地)逃避(to evade or avoid capture, often by cunning);使难倒,困惑(to escape detection, notice,or understanding by)

(记)e+lude(玩弄)→捉弄人→使困惑

(例)The robber's immediate goal was to elude capture. / Do you know who that man is? His name eludes me right now. / The cause of that disease has yet eluded all research.

elusive [iˈljuːsiv] a. 逃避的;难懂的([of sb. or sth. that is] hard to find or catch)

(记)来自 elude

(例)The elusive butterfly escaped the scientist's net. / an idea too elusive to be put into words(很难用语言表达的思想)

emanate [ˈeməneit] vi.(气体等)发出,发散(to send forth; emit);发源(from)(to come forth; issue, as from a source)

(记)e(出来)+man(流)+ate→流出来→发出;发源

(例)Dense fumes emanated from the exhaust pipe. / Much of the criticism against him emanated from his political opponents.

emancipation [iˌmænsiˈpeiʃən] n. 释放;解脱;解放(setting sb. free from authority or control; gaining one's freedom)

(记)来自 emancipate,e(出来)+man(手)+cip(落下)+ate→把手(从锁链中)放下→解放

参考:manuscript(手稿);manumission(释放)

(例)The young movie star took parents to court to obtain legal emancipation at age 16. / the struggle for the emancipation of women(争取妇女解放的

斗争）

embalm [im'bɑːm] vt. 以香油（或药料）涂尸防腐（to apply chemicals to a corpse to preserve it）；使不朽；使铭记（to preserve in memory）；使充满香气（to make fragrant; perfume）

（记）em + balm（香油，香膏）→把香油涂在…上→以香油涂尸防腐；[转]使不朽

（例）Ancient Egyptians used oils and natural substances to embalm their dead. / His memory is embalmed in the hearts of his people.（他永远被铭记在人民心中。）

embargo [em'bɑːgəu] n. 禁运令；封港令（a restriction on trade with a particular country）

（记）em + bar（阻挡）+ go→阻拦（船等）进入→禁运令

（例）The trade minister placed an embargo on goods from the hostile country. / lift (raise/ remove) an embargo（解禁／重新开放贸易）

embark [im'bɑːk] v. 从事，开始搞（on）（to engage 〔a person〕or invest 〔money, etc.〕 in an enterprise; to engage in an enterprise）

（记）em（= in）+ bark（三桅船，四桅船）→进到船里→开始做，从事

（例）He has embarked on an adventure no one else has dared.

embellish [im'beliʃ] v. 装饰（to decorate sth. with some extra ornamentation）；润色（to make a story more exciting by adding small details that are not true）

（记）em + bell（美）+ ish→使…美→装饰

同根词：belle（美女）

（例）The jeweler embellished the ring with a few extra stones on each side of the diamond. / I'm not embellishing the story. I'm describing how things happened exactly.

embody [im'bɔdi] v. 使具体化;体现(to give bodily form to; make corporeal; to make concrete);使集成一体,编入,包含(to bring together into an organized whole; incorporate)

(记)em + body(身体)→(思想)变成身体→体现

(例)a speech embodying democratic ideals/ The latest findings have been embodied in the new book.

embrace [im'breis] v. 拥抱(to hug sb. closely);接受(to accept sth., such as a belief, tenet, or policy);包括(to include, contain)

(记)em(= in) + brace(胳膊)→搂进胳膊里→拥抱

(例)She embraced her son tenderly. / She embraces vegetarianism because it is healthy. / Biology embraces botany and zoology.

embroider [im'brɔidə] v. 刺绣(to make a design on a piece of fabric by stitching colored thread onto it in a specific pattern);修饰(to add details to sth., to make a story sound better)

(记)em + broider(刺绣)

(例)embroider stars on the dress / He has a tendency to embroider a story to make it more interesting.

embryo ['embriəu] n. 胚胎(the earliest stage of an unborn creature's development);事物的萌芽期(the beginning, first stage, or first step of sth.)

(记)em(= in) + bryo(胀满)→逐渐长大胀满的东西→胚胎

(例)The embryo is attached to the uterine wall(子

宫壁). / The idea for my new book is just an embryo.

emerald [ˈeməræld] n.【矿】祖母绿(a bright green gem stone)

(例)The sparkling stone in this ring is an emerald.

emission [iˈmiʃən] n. 发出;发光(the sending out of sth., such as a gas or fluid);发射物(sth. that is discharged)

(记)来自 emit(发出,发光),e(出来)+mit(送)→送出→放出(味道等)

(例)An emission of smoke showed that there was a fire in the house. / The emissions from the power plant were dangerous.

empirical [emˈpirikəl] a. 经验的,经验主义的(based on observation instead of theory; based on experience in the real world)

(记)来自 empiric,原指单凭经验而行医的医生;分割记忆:empire(帝国)-ical

(例)The scientist considered the empirical evidence before writing a report.

emulate [ˈemjuleit] v. 努力赶上或超越(to try to be like sb. or sth. else; to try to do sth. as well as sb. or sth. else)

(记)emul(竞争)+ate→努力赶上或超越;a. emulous(好胜的)

(例)The proverb tells us to emulate the industry of the ant. / set a standard for sb. to emulate(为某人树立一个赶超的标准)

encapsulate [inˈkæpsjuleit] v. 装入胶囊(to enclose in or as in a capsule);压缩(to put in concise form; condense)

(记)en+capsul(胶囊)+ate→装入胶囊

(例) The machine encapsulated the medication,

making thousands of bright yellow pills. / encapsulate a period of history(概括一个时期的历史)

encode [inˊkəud] vt. 把(电文等)译成电码(或密码)(to convert 〔a message, information, etc.〕 into code)

(记)en + code(电码,密码)→把…译成电码

encompass [inˊkʌmpəs] v. 包围,围绕(to shut in around; surround; encircle)

(记)en + compass(罗盘;范围)→进入范围→包围

(例)He is encompassed with doubts. / The fugitives were encompassed by the police.

encounter [inˊkauntə] v. / n. 遭到;意外地遇见(朋友等)(to meet sb. or sth. by chance)

(记)en(= in) + counter(对着)→对着撞进→遇到

(例)While skipping school, the naughty boy encountered his principal at the mall. / The two high-school friends had an unexpected encounter.

encroach [inˊkrəutʃ] v. 侵犯,侵占;蚕食(on)(to trespass or intrude 〔on or upon the rights, property, etc. of another〕, esp. in a gradual or sneaking way)

(记)en + croach(钩)→钩进去→侵占

同根词:crochet(用钩针编织),croch = croach

(例)The sea is encroaching upon the land all along the coast. / The reporter encroached on my privacy.

endeavor [inˊdevə] n. 尽力,努力(an attempt or a struggle to do sth.); v. 努力,力图(to try very hard to do sth.)

(记)en(放进) + deavor(责任)→放进责任→尽力,努力

(例)Would you please make an endeavor to stay out of trouble? / I endeavored to be the best student in my class while I was at this school.

endemic [en'demik] a. 地方性的(native to a particular country, nation, or region: said of plants, animals, and, sometimes, customs, etc.)
(记)en + dem(人民) + ic→在人民之内→地方性的
同根词:epidemic(流行性的);pandemic(广泛的)
(例) Cotton is endemic to the southern United States. / This is a problem endemic to the Western world.(这是西方世界普遍存在的问题。)

endorse [in'dɔːs] v. 同意,赞同(to support sb., to approve sb. for sth.);背书(to write one's name on the back of a check when cashing it)
(记)en + dorse(背)→在背后签名→赞同
(例)I do not endorse your choice of friends. / The bank teller reminded me to endorse the check I was cashing.

endorsement [in'dɔːsmənt] n. 同意;保证(approval; a statement of approval);背书(a name written on the back of a check, indicating who guarantees payment of the check)
(例) Without your endorsement, I would never have gotten the permission to carry out the plan. / The bank teller verified the endorsement before cashing the check.

endothermic [ˌendəu'θəːmik] a.【化】吸热的(designating, of, or produced by a chemical change in which there is an absorption of heat)
(记)endo(到…里面) + therm(热) + ic→把热吸到…里面→吸热的

endowment [in'daumənt] n. 捐赠;捐款(基金)(a large sum of money given to a school, charity, hospital, church, or fund to support the institution for a pe-

riod of time);才能,天资(a good quality or talent that is present at one's birth)
(记)en(=in)+dow+ment(给)→捐赠
(例)The endowment helped the hospital buy new equipment. / His quick mind was an endowment that served him well in college. / men of great endowments (才能出众之辈)

enervation [ˌenəːˈveiʃən] n.虚弱,无力(the condition with reduced vigor)
(记)e+nerv(神经)+ation→使神经软弱了→虚弱,无力
(例) His enervation is due to long illness.

engender [inˈdʒendə] v.产生;造成;引起(to produce sth.; to bring about the existence of sth.)
(记)en+gender(产生)→使产生
(例)dirt engenders disease / I hope my actions will engender your trust. / Angry words engender strife.(恶言怒语引起争吵。)

engrave [inˈgreiv] vt.雕上,刻上(to cut or incise letters, designs, etc. in or on 〔a surface〕);铭记(to impress deeply or permanently on the mind or memory, as though by engraving)
(记)en+grave(雕刻,铭记)→雕上,刻上
(例)My boyfriend engraved a heart on the tree. / My grandmother's words were engraved in my memory.

engulf [inˈgʌlf] v.吞噬(to swallow up or overwhelm sb. or sth.)
(记)en+gulf(深渊,吞没)→吞噬
(例)The flames engulfed the building. / An almost unbearable loneliness engulfed her.(她陷入了一种几乎难以忍受的寂寞。)

enhance [inˈhɑːns] v. 提高，增加(to add to the quality of sth.; to cause sth. to appear more important, valuable, functional, or beautiful)

(记)en + hance(高)→提高

(例)Small improvements enhanced the value of the house. / The book is enhanced with illustrative photographs.(这本书因有了插图而更加精彩。)

enlist [inˈlist] v. 使服兵役，征募(to sign up for military duty; to enroll for service in the military)

(记)en + list(名单)→进入(战士的)名单→入伍

参考:induction(入伍)

(例)He enlisted when he was 18. / Determined that the boy needed discipline, his father enlisted him in the army.

enormous [iˈnɔːməs] a. 极大的，巨大的(huge; large; very big)

(记)e(出) + norm(正常) + ous→出了正常状态的→极大的，巨大的；注意:n. enormity(巨大，穷凶极恶)

(例)We ate an enormous dinner because we were very hungry. / The rent and cost of maintenance of such a building are enormous.

enrich [inˈritʃ] v. 使富裕；使丰富；装饰，增美；浓缩(to make rich or richer)

(记)en + rich(富足)→使富裕；增美

(例)I enriched my coffee by cream and sugar. / The taxes you pay will enrich the treasury. / Many foreign words and phrases have enriched the English language.

enslave [inˈsleiv] vt. 使…成为奴隶(to make sb. a slave; to take sb.'s freedom away)

(记)en + slave(奴隶)→使成为奴隶

(例)The addict was enslaved by drugs. / be enslaved by poverty(受贫困奴役)

ensue [in'sjuː] vi. 接着发生(to come afterwards; following immediately);结果是(to happen as a consequence; result)

(记)en + sue(向…请求)→(基督教《圣经》用语)追求→[转](请求的结果)接着发生;结果是

(例)A serious traffic jam ensued after the accident / He spent his allowance the first week and a lean month ensued.(他第一周就把津贴用完,接着过了一个月拮据的日子。)

entail [in'teil] v. 必需;使承担(to cause or require as a necessary consequence; involve; necessitate)

(记)en + tail(尾巴)→给加上尾巴→必需;使承担

(例)The project will entail many hours of overtime at the office.

enterprise ['entəpraiz] n. 事业;计划(a business or company; a plan or a project)

(例)The new enterprise will require additional staff and equipment. / Our department's new enterprise is fraught with(充满) problems.

entice [in'tais] v. 引诱(to lure, attract, tempt, or lead sb. or some creature into doing what one wishes)

(记)en(= in) + tice(烙铁)→使烧热,烧烫→引诱

(例)The fisherman enticed the fish with a big, fat worm.

entity ['entiti] n. 实体;统一体(a being, sth. like an organization or a business, that has its own rights and responsibilities)

(例)My brother works for a large banking entity.

entrant ['entrənt] n. 进入者;新成员;参加竞赛者(sb. who takes part in a contest or competition)

(记)entr(=enter)+ant→进入者
(例)Five entrants were disqualified because they were professionals. / Entrants include leading athletes from many countries.

entree [ˊɔntrei] n. 进入;入场权(the act of entering; right, permission, or freedom to enter, use or take part in; access);[美]主菜(the main course of a meal);
(记)entr(=enter)+ee→进入;入场权
(例)His wealth gave him the entree into upper-class society. / The entree consisted of shrimp and lobster.

entrepreneur [ˌɔntrəprəˊnəː] n. 创业者;企业家(someone who develops a business)
(记)来自法语,等于 enterpriser
参考:enterprise(事业)
(例)The entrepreneur in the international export business made a lot of money.

enumeration [ˌinjuː məˊreiʃən] n. 列举,枚举(naming one by one)
(记)来自 enumerate,e+numer(数字)+ate→数字出来→列举
(例)A census is essentially an enumeration of people, houses, firms, or other important items in a country or region at a particular time.

envelope [ˊenviləup] n.【天】包层(a cloudy mass surrounding the nucleus of a comet; coma);信封
(记)en(放进)+velope(包)→包层

envious [ˊenviəs] a. 妒忌的(feeling envy; wanting sth. that someone else has)
(记)由 envy 一词而来
(例)I don't like to have envious feelings about

others.

envision [en'viʒən] v. 想象；展望(to imagine [sth. not yet in existence]; picture in the mind)

(记)en(放进) + vision(景象)→把景象放进去→想象

(例)The company envisioned opening the sides of two mountains to extract coal. / envision a bright future(展望光明前途)

enzyme ['enzaim] n.【生化】酵素，酶(any of proteins, formed in plant and animal cells or made synthetically, that act as organic catalysts in initiating or speeding up specific chemical reactions)

(记)en + zyme(酶)→酵素，酶

同根词：zymic(酶的，酵母的)

epic ['epik] n. 史诗，叙事诗(a long narrative poem in a dignified style about the deeds of a traditional or historical hero or heroes)；a. 史诗的；英雄的(of a long narrative poem; heroic)

(例)Homer's Iliad and Milton's Paradise Lost are epics.(荷马的《伊利亚特》和弥尔顿的《失乐园》是史诗。)

epicenter ['episentə] n.【地】震中(the area of the earth's surface directly above the place of origin, or focus, of an earthquake)；中心，集中点(a focal or central point)

(记)epi(向) + center(中心)→中心→震中

epidemic [ˌepi'demik] a. 传染的，流行性的(prevalent and spreading rapidly among many individuals in a community at the same time: said esp. of a serious human contagious disease)

(记)epi(向) + dem(人) + ic→在人之间传染的→传染的，流行性的

(例) The disease quickly reached epidemic proportions.

episode [ˈepisəud] n. (文艺作品中的)一段情节;插曲,(one thing that is part of a series; one incident; a separate event)

(例) The long lecture I got from my boss was an episode I did not want to undergo a second time.

epochal [ˈepɔkəl] a. (新)时代的;划时代的,开新纪元的(of a period of time considered in terms of noteworthy and characteristic events, developments, persons, etc.)

(记) epoch(时代) + al→划时代的,开新纪元的

(例) the epochal voyages of Zheng He(郑和划时代的几次航海)

era [ˈiərə] n. 时代;年代(a period of time characterized in a particular way);纪元(a system of reckoning time by numbering the years from some important occurrence or given point of time);【地】代(any of the five main divisions of geologic time)

(例) In United States, the last years of the 1960s were an era of unrest and turmoil.

eradicate [iˈrædikeit] v. 根除,杜绝(to completely get rid of; destroy sb. or sth.)

(记) e + radic(根) + ate→把根挖出来→根除

同根词:radical(基本的);radix(根本)

(例) The mayor wanted to eradicate crime within five years. / Cholera(霍乱) has been eradicated in China.

erratic [iˈrætik] a. 反复无常的;古怪的(not regular; irregular; uneven)

(记) err(跑) + atic→跑出去→反复无常的

(例) Mary's behavior becomes erratic when she

drinks alcohol. / His erratic moods upset everyone in our office.

ersatz [ˈɛəzæts] a. 代用的;假的(substitute or synthetic)
(记)德语词,原词为 ersetzen,er(=re)+satz(setzen)(放)→代替放→代用的;假的
(例)ersatz coffee(代用咖啡) / ersatz materials(代用材料) / All guests, real and ersatz, were put up at the inn.

erudition [ˌeru:ˈdiʃən] n. 博学(learning acquired by reading and study; scholarship)
(记)来自 erudite,e(出)+rud(原始,无知)+ite→走出无知→博学的
同根词:rudiments(基础知识)
(例)Erudition is a fine quality in a professor. / He possessed a considerable legal erudition.(他法律知识相当渊博。)

eschew [isˈtʃu:] v. 避开;戒绝(to shun sb. or sth.; to avoid associating with sb. or sth.)
(记)分割记忆:es(出)-chew(咀嚼)→通过深思而去掉→戒绝
(例)She eschews both alcohol and tobacco.

espionage [ˌespiəˈnɑ:ʒ] v. 间谍活动(the use of spies to get useful information; the work of spies)
(记)e+spion(=spy 看)+age→出去看→间谍活动
(例)He committed industrial espionage for his corporation. / Three persons have been arrested on espionage charges.

espouse [isˈpauz] vt. 支持,拥护(to undertake to support a belief or a cause)
(记)e+spous(配偶)+e→出来做配偶→支持,拥护

(例) I do not espouse your beliefs on the death penalty. / His party espouses radical reform.

estrange [is'treindʒ] vt. 使疏远(to remove, as from usual surroundings or associates; keep apart or away)

(记)e + strange(陌生)→使…陌生→使疏远

(例) His foolish behavior estranged all of his friends.

et al 拉丁文 et alibi 的缩写:以及其他地方(and elsewhere)

eternal [i'təːnl] a. 永久的,永恒的(without ending; existing forever)

(例)The bride and groom pledged their eternal love to each other.

ethnicity [eθ'nisiti] n. 少数民族(ethnic classification or affiliation)

(记)ethn(种族) + icity→少数民族

ethnocentric [ˌeθnəu'sentrik] a. 种族(或民族)中心主义的(of an excessive or inappropriate concern for racial matters);种族(或民族)优越感的(about the emotional attitude that one's own ethnic group, nation, or culture is superior)

(记)ethn(种族) + o + centr(中心) + ic→种族中心主义的

(例) Myths of origin are always ethnocentric; they explain the creation, by supernatural powers, of the people possessing the myth.

ethnographic [ˌeθnə'græfik] a. 人种学的,人种论的(of the branch of anthropology that deals descriptively with specific cultures, esp. those of non-literate peoples or groups)

(记)ethn(种族) + graphy(学科)→人种学

同根词:ethnical(种族的)

ethnologist [eθ′nɔlədʒist] n. 人种学者,民族学者;人类文化学者(one who study the branch of anthropology that studies comparatively the cultures of contemporary, or recent, societies or language groups)

(记)ethn(种族)+olog(学科)+ist(做…的人)→人种学者,民族学者

ethnomusicology [ˌeθnəuˌmju:zi′kɔlədʒi] n. 民族音乐(学)(the study of the music of a particular region and its sociocultural implications, esp. of music outside the European art tradition)

(记)ethno(民族)+music(音乐)+ology(学科)→民族音乐学

etymology [ˌeti′mɔlədʒi] n. 语源学(the branch of linguistics dealing with word origin and development)

(记)来自 etymon(词源,词根)

(例)While studying etymology, I saw how many English words are related to German.

euphoria [ju:′fɔ:riə] n.【心】欣快症;幸福愉快感(a feeling of vigor, well-being or high spirits)

(记)eu(好)+phor(带来)+ia(病)→带来好处的病→欣快症;a. euphoric(心情愉快的;心满意足的)

同根词:semaphore(信号灯)

(例)I cannot describe the euphoria I felt when my daughter was born. / After he won, he lived through a day or two of euphoria.(取胜后,他过了一两天兴高采烈的日子。)

evacuation [iˌvækju′eiʃən] n. 撤退,撤离(removing all people from an area that is danger)

(记)来自 evacuate, e+vacu(空)+ate→空出去→撤离

同根词:vacant(空的);vacuum(真空)

(例)The police evacuated the citizens before the hurricane came. / The evacuation was done in a calm and orderly manner before the village was flooded.

evaporate [i'væpəreit] v. 蒸发(to turn into a gas or vapor)

(记)e + vapor(蒸发) + ate→蒸发

(例)The steaming water evaporated quickly. / The sun evaporated the dew.(阳光使露水蒸发掉了。)

evict [i'vikt] v.(依法从租地或租屋中)逐出(to force a tenant to vacate a rented or leased space)

(记)e + vict(征服)→把…征服出去→驱逐

同根词:victor(胜利者);victory(胜利)

(例)The landlord tries to evict the tenant for failing to pay the rent. / We evicted the enemy from the town.

exacerbate [eks'æsəbeit] v. 加重,恶化(to make sth., as a problem, worse)

(记)ex + acerb(苦涩) + ate→出现了苦涩→恶化

同根词:acerbic(酸苦的);acerbate(激怒)

(例)The accident exacerbated the slow flow of traffic. / The three-day's strike exacerbated the relationship between the employer and the workers.

exaggerate [ig'zædʒəreit] v. 夸张,夸大(to make sth. seem larger or more severe than it really is)

(记)ex(出) + ag(一再) + ger(带) + ate→一再带出去→夸张

(例)No exaggerating, please. We've known every detail. / Keep to the facts and don't exaggerate.

excavate ['ekskəveit] v. 挖掘;挖出(to uncover sth. buried in the ground by digging)

(记)ex + cav(洞) + ate→挖出洞→挖掘
同根词:cavity(洞,腔)
(例)The archaeologist and his team excavated the ruins. / Over a million tons of rich ore were excavated from that one pocket.(从这一处矿穴中挖出了百万吨以上的富矿石。)

excerpt [ˈeksəːpt] v./n. 摘录,节录;引用(from)(to extract or quote a passage from a text)
(记)ex(出) + cerpt(选择)→选择出的→摘录
(例)The musician excerpted a short section of the concerto for performance. / read several excerpts from the President's speech.

excise [ekˈsaiz] v. 切除(to cut sth. out surgically);删去(to cut out parts of a text)
(记)ex(出) + cise(切)→切出去→切除;n. excision
同根词:concision(简洁);incisive(一针见血的)
(例)The surgeon excised the cancerous tumor. / The editor excised the unconfirmed statements from the reporter's article.

exclusionary [iksˈkluːʒənəri] a. 排斥的(that tend to exclude)
(记)exclude→exclusion→exclusionary; ex + clude(关闭)→关出去→排斥的
同根词:occlude(堵塞); preclude(预防,排除)
(例)exclusionary rule(【律】排斥规则)

excrete [eksˈkriːt] vt. 排泄;分泌(to release solid waste from the body; to defecate)
(记)ex(出) + crete(滤出)→滤出→分泌;排泄
(例)The baby excreted waste into a diaper.

excruciate [iksˈkruːʃieit] vt. 使受酷刑;折磨(to cause intense bodily pain to; torture);使苦恼(to subject to mental anguish; torment)

(记)ex(起强调作用) + cruci(+ 字) + ate→放在十字架上折磨→使受酷刑;使苦恼

(例)The very sound of his voice excruciates me.(一听到他的声音就教我苦恼。)

excursion [iks'kəː ʃən] n.远足(a trip, a journey)

(记)ex(出) + curs(跑) + ion→跑出去→旅行

同根词:incursion(闯入); cursive(草书的)

(例)Our family took a two-week excursion to the South.

executioner [ˌeksi'kjuː ʃənə] n.刽子手(someone who carries out the sentence of death on sb.)

(记)来自 execute(执行,实施),execute 来自拉丁文 exsecutus, secu(跟随),ex(出来)→跟着出来→实施,执行

(例)In earlier times, the executioner wore a black mask.

exempt [ig'zempt] vt.免除,豁免(from)(to free sb. from a rule, duty, or obligation which applies to others; excuse; release)

(记)ex + empt(拿,买)→拿出去→免除

同根词:exemplar(榜样,empl = empt);preempt(以先买权取得,占先)

(例)The teacher exempted the smartest students from taking a quiz.

exhaustive [ig'zɔːstiv] a.彻底的,无遗漏的(complete; comprehensive; thorough)

(记)ex + haust(拉) + ive→(用力)拉出→彻底的,无遗漏的

同根词:exhaustion(彻底,耗尽)

(例)The real-estate agent gave the prospective buyers an exhaustive tour of the new house.

exhort [ig'zɔːt] v.力劝,激励(to urge sb. to do sth.; to

advice sb. strongly to do sth.)
(记)ex + hort(=incite 激励)→激励出来→力劝
同根词:hortative(劝告的,忠告的)
(例)The teacher exhorted the students to study for the final exams.

exigency [ˈeksidʒənsi] n. 紧急(状态),危急(关头)(the condition or quality of being urgent or critical)
(记)来自 exigent(紧急的,迫切的)
(例)After the earthquake, the government sent food to the people in this exigency.

exile [ˈeksail] v./n. 放逐(to banish sb.; to force one from one's homeland; someone who has been banished)
(记)ex(出)+il(无目的地游荡)+e→使…出去无目的地游荡→放逐
(例)They exiled Napoleon to the island of St. Helena. / The political exile went into hiding.

exodus [ˈeksədəs] n. 大批离去,成群外出(a departure of many people; a mass emigration)
(记)ex(出去)+(h)odus(路)→都到路上去→大批离去,成群外出
(例)The refugees made an exodus to a safe place.

exoneration [igˌzɔnəˈreiʃən] n. 免除责任;确定无罪(freeing sb. from a charge or a blame)
(记)来自 exonerate,ex + oner(负担)+ate→走出负担→无罪
同根词:onerous(费力的,繁重的)
(例) The disgraced official now seeks exoneration.

exotic [egˈzɔtik] a. 珍奇的;来自异国的(not native to a country; foreign)
(记)exo(外面)+tic→外面来的
(例)I enjoy eating spicy and exotic food dishes.

expatriate [eks′pætrieit] v. 驱逐出国;脱离国籍(to drive [a person] from his or her native land; exile)
(记)ex + patri(父亲,国家) + ate→驱逐出国
同根词:patriotism(爱国主义);patricide(杀父)
(例)The government expatriated the political dissidents.

expedient [iks′pi:djənt] a. 方便的,快速的;权宜之计的(profitable; efficient; or advantageous, rather than right)
(记)ex + ped(脚) + ient→把脚拔出去→权宜之计的
同根词:centipede(蜈蚣);podiatrist(足病医生,ped = pod)
(例)Hiring temporary workers provided an expedient answer to my company's labor shortage.

expedite [′ekspidait] v. 加速;促进(to make sth. happen faster or more efficiently)
(记)ex + ped(脚) + ite→把脚跨出去→加速
(例)He used my credit card to expedite the ticket purchase. / The person I talked to on the phone promised to expedite the shipment of the book I ordered.

expedition [ˌekspi′diʃən] n. 远征;探险(a trip; a journey; a specific course of travel to a place)
(例)The explorers started a half-a-year-long expedition in the largest val|ey of the world.

expertise [ˌekspə′ti:z] n. 专门知识,专长;专家鉴定(the skill, knowledge, judgement, etc. of an expert)
(记)expert(专家) + ise→专家的知识→专门知识
(例)Do you have the expertise required to tune the piano?

explicate [′eksplikeit] v. 清楚,明确地说明(to make clear or

explicit [something obscure or implied]; explain fully; explain)

(记)参考:explicit

(例)He wrote a book to explicate and help interpret the constitution.

explicit [iks´plisit] a. 清楚的;明确的(specific; clearly stated)

(记)ex(出)+plic(重叠)+it→重叠在一起的意义出来了→清楚的

(例)The directions I gave her to get here were very explicit.

expound [iks´paund] v. 解释;阐述(to explain or interpret; clarify; to make a statement)

(记)ex+pound(=pon 放)→把(道理)放出来→解释

(例)I expounded on the budget proposal for half an hour.

expressly [iks´presli] ad. 清楚地;特意地(clearly; distinctly; definitely)

(记)来自 express(表达,明白的,特殊的)

(例)This book was written expressly for the GMAT test. / The children are expressly forbidden to go out at night by themselves.

expulsion [iks´pʌlʃən] n. 驱逐(removal of sb. from an office, status, or location);开除(removal of sb. from school or membership in an organization)

(记)ex(出)+puls(推)+ion→推出去→驱逐

(例)The expulsion of the dictator was accomplished by the army. / the expulsion of sb. from school

exquisite [´ekskwizit] a. 精致的(of an excellent beauty; very fine)

(记)ex + quisit(要求,寻求)→按要求做出→精致的
同根词:requisite(必要的);inquisitive(好问的)
(例)The exquisite lace dress was very expensive.

exterior [eks'tiəriə] a. 外部的,外面的;exterior angle:外角(an angle formed by any side of a polygon and the extension of the adjacent side)

exterminate [eks'tə:mineit] v. 根除,灭绝;消灭,扑灭(to kill all of a group of living creatures; to kill insects, rats, and other pests in an area)
(记)ex + termin(范围,结束) + ate→从范围中出去→消灭
同根词:terminate(结束,中止);terminus(终点站)
(例)The soldiers exterminated the enemy troops. / I exterminated the ants with pesticide.

external [eks'tə:nl] a. 外部的(outside; outer)
(记)exter(在外边) + nal→外部的
(例)The crab's external shell must be removed before you eat the meat inside.

extinguish [iks'tiŋgwiʃ] v. 灭绝,消灭(to put out a fire or a flame; to put an end to sth.)
(记)ex(出去) + (s)tingu(压制,破坏) + ish→灭绝,消灭
(例)The fire fighters extinguished the fire in the building. / The married woman extinguished the young man's hopes of going out on a date.

extradite ['ekstrədait] v. 引渡回国,拿获归案(to order an accused criminal moved from one jurisdiction to another for trial)
(记)ex + tradit(传递)→传递出去→引渡
同根词:tradition(传统)
(例) The English murderer was caught by the

French police and extradited to Britain.

extraneous [eks'treinjəs] a. 外来的;无关的(not belonging or related to sth.; foreign or alien to sth.)

(记)extran(外面)+eous→外来的

(例)The editor cut the extraneous material from the first chapter.

extrapolation [eksˌtræpə'leiʃən] n. 预测,推测(making a guess about sth., based on what is really known)

(记)extra(外面)+pol(放)+ate→放出想法→推测

同根词:interpolate(插入,窜改)

(例)The stock broker made an extrapolation of the future price of the stock based on its historical growth patterns.

extraterrestrial [ˌekstrəti'restriəl] a. 地球外的,地球大气圈外的(from outer space; existing on another celestial body; alien)

(记)extra(在…外边)+terrestrial(地球上的)→地球外的,地球大气圈外的

(例)Do you think that extraterrestrial life exists?

extricate ['ekstrikeit] v. 拯救,救出(to remove sb. or sth. from a delicate situation; to remove sth. that is stuck; to untangle sb. or sth.)

(记)ex+tric(复杂,迷惑)+ate→从复杂中出来→救出

同根词:intricate(复杂的,难懂的);trick(诡计)

(例)The wrecked car had to be lifted before the driver could be extricated. / The emergency rescue crew extricated the injured people from the wrecked vehicle.

extrinsic [eks'trinsik] a. 外在的;外部的(additional; not inherent; coming from the outside of sth.)

(记)参考:intrinsic(内部的)

(例)the extrinsic difficulties caused by unknown outside forces / We discussed the extrinsic difficulties associated with the project.

F

fabrication [ˌfæbriˈkeiʃən] n. 制作,装备(construction; manufacture);捏造,伪造(a lie; an excuse; a story that is made up or invented)

(记)fabric(构造)+ate→构造出来→捏造

参考:prefabricate(预制)

(例)Fabrication of the huge machine took three months. / Your story of being caught in traffic is a fabrication, isn't it?

facade [fəˈsɑːd] n. 建筑的正面;外表(The front of a building; the part of the building that faces the street)

(记)fac(=face 正面)+ade→正面

(例)a facade of honesty (装诚实的虚伪外表)/ During the earthquake, the facade of the small shop collapsed.

faction [ˈfækʃən] n. 派系(a small section of a larger group of people);派系斗争(partisan conflict within an organization or a country; dissension)

(例)The president negotiated a cease—fire among the opposing factions.

factor [ˈfæktə] n.【数】因数(a whole number multiplied by another whole number to make a specific number)

(记)factor 还有"因素"之意

fad [fæd] n.(流行一时的)狂热,时尚(a short-lived

fashion; a very popular thing that everyone does or has for a short period of time)
(记)可以和 fan(狂热爱好者)一起记
(例) Popular celebrities often start fads unintentionally.

fade [feid] v. 褪色;消退(to lose color, to become less bright; to wither; to become weak)
(例)An old soldier never dies. He just fades away. / Over the years, the bright red carpet faded.

fake [feik] a. 假的(false; not genuine; artificial; made in order to deceive);n. 赝品(sth. made to take the place of an original in order to deceive; a fraud)
(记)fake 还可用作动词,"伪造,佯装"之意,如:She faked illness so that she did not have to go to school.
(例)He tried to buy things with fake bills and got caught. / The new painting in the art museum was found to be a fake.

fallacy [ˈfæləsi] n. 谬误(an error in one's thinking);谬见(a false belief)
(记)fall(错误)+acy→谬误
同根词:fallible(易犯错误的)
(例)The badly written article about taxes contains numerous fallacies. / The fallacy of your thinking is based on ignorance.

fallow [ˈfæləu] a. 休耕的;休闲的([of land] not farmed for a period of time, usually in order to help to replenish the soil with nutrients)
(记)和 fellow(伙伴,同伙)一起记
(例)Don't let your talent fallow! / Much of the land in the country was fallow during the war.

falter [ˈfɔːltə] vi. 蹒跚,摇摆(to move or talk unsteadily;

stumble);踌躇,畏缩(to act hesitantly; show uncertainty; waver; flinch)

(记)fal(l)(摔倒)+ter(使害怕)→欲摔倒的样子让人害怕→蹒跚,摇摆

(例)The untrained soldiers faltered as they neared the battlefield.

famine [ˈfæmin] n. 饥荒;饥饿(a period of time when there is little food or no food available);严重缺乏(any acute shortage)

(记)famin(=famina)(饥饿)+e→饥荒

(例)A severe famine was caused by a terrible drought.

fanatic [fəˈnætik] a. 狂热的,盲信的(unreasonably enthusiastic; overly zealous);n. 狂热者(someone who is too enthusiastic about sb. or sth.; zealot)

(记)fan(迷,狂)+atic→入迷的→狂热的

(例)Several doctors who perform abortion have been killed by religious fanatics.

fanfare [ˈfænfɛə] n. 虚张声势,大吹大擂(noisy or showy display);嘹亮的喇叭声(a loud flourish of trumpets)

(记)无词源,分割记忆:fan(迷)-fare(车船费)

(例)A military band played a lengthy fanfare before the president's speech.

farce [fɑːs] n. 闹剧,胡闹(an absurd play or movie written to make people laugh; sth. absurd or ridiculous, as an obvious pretense)

(记)分割记忆:far(远), ce 看作 voice(声音),声音传远→闹剧

(例)The talks were a farce since the minister had already made the decision. / After writing light romantic comedies, he decided to write a farce.

fare [fɛə] v. 过活；进展(get on; go through an experience)；进食(to eat or be given food)

(例)I could offer the unexpected guests only modest fare.

far-reaching [fɑːˊriːtʃiŋ] a. 影响深远的(influencing many things or people; having an effect over a large area)

(例)The nuclear bomb explosion had serious, far-reaching effects.

fatal [ˊfeitl] a. 致命的(causing death; resulting in death)

(记)fat=(fate 命运)+al→致命的

(例)A fatal accident blocked traffic on the freeway for hours.

fatality [fəˊtæliti] n. 命运决定的事物(fate or necessity; subjection to fate)；死亡事故(a death caused by a disaster, as in an accident, war, etc.)；致命性(a deadly quality or effect)

(记)fat=(fate 命运)+ality→宿命

参考:fatal(致命的)

(例)The traffic accident resulted in six fatalities.

fault [fɔːlt] n.【地】断层(a fracture or zone of fractures in rock strata together with movement that displaces the sides relative to one another)

(记)fault 一般指"错误,缺点",有错→断层

fauna [ˊfɔːnə] n. 动物区系(某一地区或时期的动物群)(the animals of specified region or time)

(记)来自 Fannus(潘纳斯),罗马神话中动物之神,Fauna 是 Faunus 的妹妹

参考:flora(植物区系)

feat [fiːt] n. 功绩,壮举(a remarkable accomplishment; an act or deed that shows skill or talent)

（记）和 feet 读音相同
（例）It was quite a feat to move that piano by yourself. / brilliant feats of engineering（工程上的伟绩）

fecundity [fiˊkʌnditi] n. 肥沃；多产（the state of being fruitful or fertile）
（记）由 fecund 而来；fecund（肥沃的）
（例）In the minds of primitive peoples, numerous earth goddesses were associated with the fertility of the soil and with the fecundity of women.

feeble [ˊfi:bl] a. 虚弱的，无力的；微弱的（weak; frail; lacking force）
（记）记住和 weak, frail 为同义词
（例）My teacher ignored my feeble excuse for being late.

feline [ˊfi:lain] a. 猫科的（of or about cats or members of the cat family）
（记）来自 felid（猫科动物）
（例）In biology class today, we studied feline body structure.

feminist [ˊfeminist] n. 女权主义者（someone, typically a woman, who advocates the principle that women should have economical, political, and social rights equal to those of men）
（记）femin（女人）+ ist→女权运动者
同根词：feminine（女性的）
（例）Feminists believe in equal work for equal pay, regardless of the worker's sex.

ferret [ˊferit] n. 雪貂（a small furry animal similar to the weasel, sometimes kept as a pet）；v. 搜寻（out）（to search for persistently and discover〔facts, the truth, etc.〕; search）

(例)The detective ferreted the information out by reading through the papers.

fervent [ˊfəːvənt] a. 炽热的,热烈的(passionate; showing a warmth of spirit or sincerity)
(记)ferv(热)+ent→热的
参考:fervid(热情的)
(例)a fervent desire to win / I used to be a fervent admirer of that famous writer.

fetal [ˊfiːtl] a. 胎儿的(of, pertaining to, or like the unborn young of an animal while still in the uterus or egg, esp. in its later stages)
(记)fet(胎儿)+al→胎儿的
同根词:fetology (胎儿学);feticide(堕胎)
(例)Fetal surgery corrected the child's deformity before it was born.

feudal [ˊfjuːdl] a. 封建的(of or about the system used in western Europe during the Middle Ages where people who farmed land, served, and protected by the owners of the land)
(记)来自 feud(封地)
(例)The feudal system flourished in Europe a thousand years ago.

fickle [ˊfikl] a.(爱情或友谊上)易变的,不坚定的(changing often for no reason; liking sb. or sth. one moment and not the next)
(记)和 tickle(呵痒)一起记
(例)Bill is a fickle man. Every time I see him, he's with a new girlfriend.

fiction [ˊfikʃən] n. 小说(literature that is written about imagined events, as opposed to real events; a story that is made up)
(记)fict(做)+ion→做出来的→小说

(例)The school library keeps fiction on the second floor.

fictitious [fik'tiʃəs] a. 假的,虚构的(imaginary; invented)

(记)fict(做)+itious→做出来的→假的

同根词:fiction(小说);figment(虚构)

(例)Although loosely based on fact, the TV program about the hostages was mostly fictitious.

field studies 实地考察

fierce [fiəs] a. 残酷的;凶猛的(violent; cruel; untamed; wild)

(记)和 coerce(强制、强迫)一起记

(例)fierce animals(猛兽)

filibuster ['filibʌstə] v./n. 妨碍议事,阻挠(to speak endlessly to prevent or delay the passage of a bill in Congress by making a very long speech; this kind of act)

(记)分割记忆:fili-buster(破坏者),破坏者阻挠别人发展

(例)If you want to delay the bill, I suggest you filibuster. /The senator filibustered for three days to prevent the bill from passing.

finale [fi'nɑːli] n.【音】终曲,乐曲的最后部分(the ending of a piece of music or a musical production)

(记)来自 final(最后的)+e(表示名词)→终曲

(例)For the grand finale, the singer was surrounded by sixteen tap dancers.

financial crash 金融危机

fiscal ['fiskəl] a. 财政的;国库的(financial; of or about money or taxes)

(记)fisc(国库)+al→财政的

同根词:confiscate(充公,没收)

(例)We have a treasurer who keeps track of our

fiscal responsibilities.

fjord [fjɔːd] n. 峡湾(尤指挪威海岸边的)(fiord: a narrow inlet or arm of the sea bordered by steep cliffs)
(记)和其同义词 fiord 就差一个字母

flawed [flɔːd] a. 有缺陷的(damaged; not perfect; in error)
(记)组合词:flaw(缺陷)+less→有缺陷的
(例)The jeweler sold the flawed diamond at a very good price.

fleck [flek] n. 斑点;微粒(a small particle of sth.)
(记)和 freckle(雀斑,小斑点)一起记
(例) There are flecks of chalk on the teacher's pants.

fledgling [ˈfledʒliŋ] a. 乳臭未干的(inexperienced; beginning; new)
(记)和动词 fledge(长羽毛)、fledged(羽毛长成的,成熟的)一起记
(例)The fledgling author did not like the editor's comments.

flippant [ˈflipənt] a. 无礼的;轻率的(rude; casually disrespectful)
(记)flip 本身就是一个词,意为"无礼的;冒失的"
(例) If your flippant attitude doesn't improve, you're going to be fired.

flora [ˈflɔːrə] n.(某地区或时代的)植物群(the plants of specified region or time)
(记)flor(花草)+a→植物群
参考:fauna(动物群)

florid [ˈflɔrid] a. 华丽的(highly decorated; gaudy; showy; ornate);(脸)红润的(flushed with red or pink; rosy; ruddy: said of the complexion)
(记)flor(花)+id→像花一样的→华丽的

(例) That music is too florid for my taste. / After a cup of wine, her face turned florid.

fluctuation [ˌflʌktjuˈeiʃən] n. 波动(going up and down uncertainly)

(记)由 fluctuate 而来,fluct(= flu 流动) + uate→波动,变化

(例)Many theories have been established to explain the economic fluctuations.

fluorescent [fluəˈresnt] a. 萤光的;发光的(producing light when acted upon by radiant energy)

(记)fluor(荧光) + escent(发生…的)→发萤光的

同根词:fluorometry(荧光计)

(例)fluorescent light(荧光灯,日光灯)

foe [fəu] n. 敌人,敌军(the enemy in general; individual enemies)

(记)和 hoe(锄头),toe(脚趾)一起记

(例)The soldiers fought with the foe on the battlefield. / a foe to health

folly [ˈfɔli] n. 愚笨,愚蠢(stupid behavior; foolishness)

(记)fol(fool)(蠢) + ly→愚蠢,傻念头

(例)Why are we standing in line in the cold? This is folly!

forage [ˈfɔridʒ] n. 饲料,粮草(animal food; fodder);v. 搜寻,翻寻(to search for sth.)

(记)分割记忆:for(为了),age (年龄),为了年龄(成长)需要的粮草

(例)The farmer poured the forage into the trough (饲料槽). / I foraged through the refrigerator for sth. to eat.

forebear [ˈfɔːbɛə] n. 祖先,祖宗(an ancestor)

(记)fore(前面) + bear(生〔孩子〕)→前面出生的→祖先,祖宗

(例)All of my forebears were farmers.

forecast [ˈfɔːkɑːst] v. 预测,预报(to say what sth. is going to be like)

(记)fore(前面) + cast(计算)→提前计算出→预测,预报

(例)The economic forecast a sharp drop in unemployment for the next year.

foreclose [fɔːˈkləuz] v. 排除;取消抵押品赎回权(take away the right of a borrower to repay a loan and to take possession of the property that secured the loan)

(记)fore(出去) + close(关闭)→关闭在外面→排除

(例)The bank foreclosed on our house because we couldn't make the payments.

foreign [ˈfɔrin] a.【医】外来的;异质的(alien)

(记)此处 foreign 作为专业术语的意思

foresee [fɔːˈsiː] v. 预见(to be aware of sth. before it happens; to envision that sth. will happen)

(记)fore(前面) + see(看见)→预见

(例)I foresaw that there would be trouble with my neighbors shortly after they moved in.

foreshorten [fɔːˈʃɔːtn] vt. (绘画中)按照透视法缩短(〔Drawing, Painting, etc.〕to represent some lines of〔an object〕as shorter than they actually are in order to give the illusion of proper relative size, in accordance with the principles of perspective)

(记)fore(前面) + shorten(缩短)→往前画就需缩短→按照透视法缩短

forestall [fɔːˈstɔːl] v. 预先阻止(to prevent sth. from happening; to delay or postpone sth.)

(记)fore + stall(停止)→使提前停止→预先阻止

(例) Financial problems were forestalled because

the manager was alert.

forge [fɔːdʒ] vt. 锻造(to make sth. out of heated, softened metal);伪造(to counterfeit 〔a check, signature, etc.〕);n. 铁匠铺;锻炉(a place where metal is heated and hammered or wrought into shape; a furnace for heating metal to be wrought)

(记)forge 和 forget 就差一个字母,忘了"t"就开始伪造

(例)The blacksmith forged horseshoes from iron. / He forged his father's name on a check.

formidable [ˈfɔːmidəbl] a. 可怕的;困难的(causing fear or dread; hard to defeat)

(记)formid(可能来自 formic"蚂蚁的")→蚂蚁成群骚扰→可怕的

(例)Cancer is a formidable disease, killing thousands each year. / The army surrendered to its formidable enemy.

forthcoming [fɔːθˈkʌmiŋ] a. 将来的(appearing soon; approaching);愿意帮忙的(helpful; ready to help; accommodating)

(记)forth(前面) + coming(即将到来)→将来的;愿意帮忙的

(例)The couple eagerly awaited their forthcoming wedding. / The pleasant and forthcoming police officer gave me excellent directions to the train station.

forthwith [ˈfɔːθˈwið] ad. 即刻(immediately; at once)

(记)forth(前面) + with(带上)→带上…就往前冲→即刻

(例)Any member guilty of such conduct will be suspended forthwith.

fortitude [ˈfɔːtitjuːd] n. 刚毅(courage or bravery, esp. when

one is suffering)
(记)fort(刚强)+itude
(例)I admired the fortitude of the citizens who were trapped in the war zone.

fortress [ˈfɔːtris] n.堡垒,要塞(a fortified building)
(记)fort(坚固)+ress→坚固的地方→堡垒,要塞
(例)Soldiers attacked the enemy fortress.

foster [ˈfɔstə] v.养育,抚养,培养;促进(to encourage the growth and development of sb. or sth.; to help sb. or sth. grow and develop)
(记)foster 还可作形容词用,专指为某人的养父母,养子女,如:foster brother,foster parent
(例)My interest in science was fostered by my parents.

foul [faul] a. 恶臭的(so offensive to the senses as to cause disgust; stinking; loathsome);邪恶的(very wicked; abominable); v. 弄脏(to make sth. dirty);n.【体育】犯规(an infraction of the rules, as of a game or sport)
(例)The sewers have a foul smell. / Everyone hated the foul ruler. / The baby fouled its diapers. / The umpire determines whether a ball that is hit is a foul.

fraction [ˈfrækʃən] n.分数(a part of a whole number)
(记)fract(破开)+ion→破开的数→分数

fracture [ˈfræktʃə] n.骨折;裂口;折断(a break or crack, esp. a break in a bone)
(记)fract(破开)+ure→裂开,破开→骨折;折断
(例)The doctor told me that my fracture would heel in 8 weeks. / I turned the vase around so that its fracture faced the wall.

fragile [ˈfrædʒail] a. 脆的;易碎的(easily broken; deli-

cate)
(记)frag(=fract 断裂)+ile(易…的)→易碎的
同根词:fragment(碎片)
(例)Don't drop those glasses! They are fragile.

fragment [ˈfreigmənt] n. 碎片(a part broken away from a whole; broken piece);部分(a small piece of sth.)
(记)见上面的 fragile
(例)I cleaned up fragments of glass from the carpet.

fragrance [ˈfreigrəns] n. 芳香(a smell or scent that is pleasant)
(记)fra+grance; a. fragrant
(例)The fragrancu of chocolate lured me into the kitchen.

frame [freim] v. 构筑(to put together the parts of; construct)
(例) She is a woman of slim frame.(她身材弱小。)/The new windows have metal frames.

framework [ˈfreimwəːk] n. 框架(a structure that serves as a frame or skeleton)
(记)frame(结构)+work(工作)→框架
(例)The decorations were mounted on a wooden framework.

fraternal [frəˈtəːnl] a. 兄弟的;友善的(of or about brothers or brotherhood)
(记)fratern(兄弟)+al→兄弟的
参考:fratricide(杀兄弟,自相残杀)
(例)My brother gave me some fraternal advice.

fraudulent [ˈfrɔdjulənt] a. 欺骗的,不诚实的(deceiving; false; dishonest)
(记)来自 fraud(欺骗,不诚实),分割记忆:frau 是德语"妻子,太太"之意,如果妻子欺骗丈夫,那就

是 fraud
(例)The fraudulent doctor was taken to court.

fresco [ˊfreskəu] n.壁画(the art or technique of painting with watercolors on wet plaster)
(记)来自 fresh(新鲜的)+cool(凉爽的),原指"凉爽的新鲜空气"→湿壁画
(例)This artist's specialty is fresco.

fretful [ˊfretful] a. 烦躁的(worried; upset; anxious)
(记)来自 fret(v./n.〔使〕烦躁,焦虑)
(例)The fretful stayed awake until their children were safely home.

Freudian [ˊfrɔːidjən] a. 弗洛伊德学说的,精神分析学的(of or according to Freud or his theories and practice)
(记)来自德国著名的精神分析专家 Freud

frivolous [ˊfrivələs] a. 轻浮的,轻佻的(silly; not serious)
(记)friv(愚蠢)+olous→愚蠢的→轻佻的
(例)The teacher was annoyed by frivolous questions.

front [frʌnt] n.(企业集团等)挂名负责人(a person who serves as a public representative of a business, group, etc., usually because of his or her prestige)
(记)front 最常用的意思是"…的前面",在前面的经常起掩护或装饰作用,所以该词还指"(企业集团等)挂名负责人"和"掩护物"

frugal [ˊfruːgəl] a. 节约的,节俭的(saving money carefully; not spending much money)
(记)和其同义词 thrifty(节约的),economical(节约的,经济的),abstemious(有节制的,节约的)一起记
(例)The frugal bought only the most inexpensive food.

frustrate [frʌsˊtreit] v. 挫败;使沮丧(to cause sb. to feel

disappointed; to discourage sb.)
(例)The difficult exam frustrated the whole class.

fume [fjuːm] v./n. 愤怒(to be upset; to be angry);冒烟(to emit fumes; to give off smoke or gas); fumes(强烈而刺激的气味,气体)
(记)fume经常指冒出的浓烟,也指特别生气,汉语里开玩笑也说"气得冒烟"
(例) He fumed at the delay of his order. / Fumes in the factory posed a health hazard to workers.

fungi [ˊfʌŋgai] n. (fungus的复数)真菌(a plant that does not have leaves and is not green, such as the mushroom or toadstool);突然发生并迅速发展的东西(sth. that grows suddenly and rapidly like a fungus)
(例)Don't eat that fungus. It might be poisonous.

funnel [ˊfʌnl] n. 漏斗(an instrument consisting of an inverted cone with a hole at the small end);漏斗形物(a thing shaped like a funnel);烟囱(a cylindrical smokestack, as of a steamship; a chimney)
(记)参考tunnel(隧道)记,二者在形状上有相似之处,都是为通过什么而造
(例)a funnel of smoke(漏斗状的烟雾)

furnace [ˊfəːnis] n. 熔炉(an oven that can be heated at very high temperatures to melt metal, heat a building, etc.);严峻的考验(a grueling test or trial)
(例)We have our furnace inspected each year for carbon monoxide leaks.

fusion [ˊfjuːʒən] n. 熔化(a melting together);【原】核聚变(nuclear fusion: energy created by combining the centers of two atoms);联合(the union of different things by or as if by melting; blending; coalition)

(记)与 fuse (v. 熔化)形状接近，虽然 fusion 不是 fuse 的派生词

(例) The scientist worked to develop a reliable source of energy from nuclear fusion.

futile [ˊfjuːtail] a. 无益的，无用的(useless; worthless); (人)没出息的(hopeless)

(记)fut(流出，倒出) + ile(能…的)→能倒出去的→无用的

同根词：refute(反驳，驳倒)

(例)It would be futile for you to explain it to me again. I just don't understand algebra.

G

galaxy [ˊgæləksi] n. 银河星群(any of the large-scale clusters of stars in outer space); 显赫的人群(brilliant company of persons)

(记)gala(乳) + xy，银河像乳汁

同根词：galactic(银河的；乳汁的)；galactogogue (催乳剂)

(例)the Galaxy(银河系；天河)/ a galaxy of talent/ beautiful women(一群才子/ 美女)

gauge [geidʒ] n. 标准尺寸，标准规格(a standard measure or scale of measurement); 容量，范围(dimensions, capacity, thickness, etc.)

(记)不要和 gouge(半圆凿，v. 敲竹杠)相混

(例)agricultural production as a gauge of the economy's effectiveness/ The IMF failed to gauge the severity of the Asian financial crisis.

gear [giə] v. (使)适合(to be adjusted to the working of another; be made dependent on)

(记)ear 在词尾读音相同的有 gear, fear, dear,

near, year 和 hear,其他词都很简单常用,不妨再记住 gear

(例)The country's economics must be geared to wartime requirements.

gender [ˊdʒendə] n. 性别(sex)

(记)和 sex 不同,gender 没有性爱的意思

(例)I wrote my name, address, age, and gender on the application form.

genetic [dʒiˊnetik] a.【生】基因的,遗传的(of or about genes; of or about the cell that determines traits)

(记)注意不要和 generic(种类的、类属的)相混

(例)Bill doesn't want to have children because he has an genetic disorder.

genetical [dʒiˊnetikl] a. 基因的(genetic)

(记)即 genetic

genuine [ˊdʒenjuin] a. 真正的(real; actual; not fake; not artificial);真诚坦率的(sincere; not pretending to act a certain way);纯血统的(purebred)

(例)My necklace is made with genuine pearls. / I was touched by his genuine display of sympathy.

geometrid [dʒiˊɔmitrid] n. / a.【动】尺蠖(的)(any of a family [Geometridae] of moths whose larvae are called measuring worms)

(记)geo(土地)+metrid(测量)→能测量的虫→尺蠖(的)

geometry [dʒiˊɔmitri] n. 几何学(the part of mathematics that deals with the relationships and properties of points, lines, curves, angles, surfaces, and solids)

girdle [ˊgəːdl] n. 腰带,环形物(a belt or sash for the waist);vt. 束,围绕(to surround or bind)

(记)来自 gird(束腰)+le→束腰物→腰带

(例)He girdled the world twice.(他两次周游全

球。)

glacier [´glæsiə] n. 冰河,冰川(a vast body of ice that moves very slowly)

(记)glac(冰)+ier→冰河,冰川

(例)This huge lake was carved out by glaciers during the last Ice Age.

gland [glænd] n.【解】腺(a group of cells or an organ of the body that produces fluids [or secretions] of various types)

(例)My throat glands were sore and tender, so I went to bed early.

glean [gli:n] v. 收集,采集(to collect bit by bit)

(记)和 clean 差一个字母

(例)The detective gleaned some important details from nosy(爱打听的) neighbors.

glut [glʌt] v./n. 供过于求(to supply too much to);过多(an overabundance of sth.; too much of sth.)

(记)参考:glutton(贪吃的人)

(例)Our office is glutted with paper supplies. / I dislike the glut of violence in this movie.

GNP (Gross National Product) 国民生产总值

(记)注意:GDP (Gross Domestic Product), 国内生产总值,包括外国投资创造的财富

gorilla [gə´rilə] n. 大猩猩(the largest kind of ape);[美俚]打手,暴徒(a gangster, thug)

gourmet [´guəmei] n. 美食家(a person who likes and is an excellent judge of fine foods and drinks; epicure)

(例)The waiter asked the gourmet if the wine was suitable.

grade-school n. [美]小学(a school for young children)

(例)Usually grade schools have kindergartens and first through fifth grades, first through sixth grades, or first through eighth grades.

gradient [ˈgreidjənt] n. (道路等的)斜坡,坡道(a slope, as of a road or railroad);
(记)gradi(迈步) + ent→往下迈→斜坡,梯度

grandiloquent [grænˈdiləkwənt] a. 夸张的,夸大的(using high-flown, pompous, bombastic words and expressions)
(记)grand(盛大的) + loquent(讲话)→夸张的,夸大的
(例) The administration bequeathed upon him a stream of grandiloquent titles without granting any real power.

grandiosity [ˌgrændiˈɔsiti] n. 宏伟壮观(having grandeur or magnificence; being imposing and impressive);铺张;浮夸;沾沾自喜(seeming or trying to seem very important; being pompous and showy)
(记)grand(盛大的,豪华的) + iosity→宏伟壮观
(例) Herb's penchant for flamboyance in writing propelled him to pursue extremes of grandiosity and hyperbole.

granular [ˈgrænjulə] a. 粒状的;含颗粒的(containing or consisting of grains and small grains called granules; like grains or granules)
(记)gran(= grain 颗粒) + ular→粒状的;含颗粒的

graveside [ˈgreivsaid] n. 坟墓边(the area alongside a grave)
(记)grave(坟墓) + side(边)→坟墓边

gravitate [ˈgræviteit] v. 受重力作用(to move lower owing to the pull of gravity);受吸引(to / toward)(to move toward sb. or sth. because of an attraction)
(记)grav(重) + itate→受重力作用
(例)The kite gravitated toward the ground. / The

screaming fans gravitated toward the rock star. / Why is it that people who come to my parties always gravitate to the kitchen?

graze [greiz] vt. 喂草;放牧(to feed on 〔growing grass, herbage, etc.〕; to allow or to cause animals to search for and eat grass, as in a pasture)

(记)来自 grass(草),和 glaze(装玻璃,上釉彩)一起记

(例)The shepherd grazed the herd of sheep in the meadow.

gregarious [greˊgɛəriəs] n. 群居的(living in herds or flocks); 喜社交的(fond of the company of others; sociable)

(记)greg(群体)+arious→群体的→群居的

同根词:egregious(异乎寻常的,极坏的)

(例)Sheep and cattle are gregarious. / She is very gregarious and loves parties.

grievance [ˊgriːvəns] n. 委屈;抱怨(a complaint; the problem that cause a complaint)

(记)griev(悲痛)+ance→委屈

(例)I think you have several saved-up grievances. (我看你心里积了不少牢骚。) / Overwork is the employee's main grievance.

grim [grim] a. 冷酷的;可怕的(〔looking〕 stern and harsh)

(例)The students disliked their teacher's grim attitude.

ground [graund] n. 原因(the logical basis of a conclusion, action, etc; valid reason, motive, or cause)

(例) His application for a visa was refused on the ground that he did not have enough money to pursue the proposed studies.

gruesome [ˊgruːsəm] n. 令人毛骨悚然的;恶心的(causing

horror and disgust; sickening; revolting)
(记)来自 grue(可怕)+some(…的)→可怕的
(例)I left the gruesome movie before it ended.

gullible [ˈgʌləbl] a. 易受骗的(likely to believe anything; easy to be tricked; naive)
(记)由 gull【动】鸥,易受骗之人,笨人;vt. 欺诈,骗,使上当;n. gullibility
(例)The gullible tourist was tricked out of $100.

gymnast [ˈdʒimnæst] n. 体操家(someone who is skilled in gymnastics)
(记)gymn(体操)+ast→体操家
(例)The famous entrepreneur Li Ning used to be famous as a gymnast all over the world.

gynecologist [ˌgainiˈkɔlədʒist] n. 妇科医生(someone who treats the diseases of the female reproductive system, including the breasts)
(记)gynaec(女人)+olog(学科)+ist(人)→妇科医生
同根词:gynaecoid(女性的);gynephobia(恐女症)

gyration [ˌdʒaiəˈreiʃən] n. 旋转,回旋(the act of moving in a circular or spiral path, rotating or revolving on an axis, or whirling)
(记)来自 gyrate,gyr(转)+ate→旋转

H

habitat [ˈhæbitæt] n. 栖息地(a place where a plant or an animal lives or thrives; the home required by a plant or an animal)
(记)habit(住)+at→住的地方→栖息地
同根词:habitant(居民); habitable(可居住的)
(例)The scientist spent two years searching for the

habitats of bats.

habitation [ˌhæbiˈteiʃən] n. 居住;住处(a home; a dwelling; a place where sb. lives);聚居地(a colony or settlement)

(记)对照英文解释和上面的 habitat 区别开来

(例)A foster home is the typical habitation for orphans until they are adopted. / The habitation of many college students is a college dormitory.

hadron [ˈhædrɔn] n.【物】强子(一种基本粒子)

(记)hadr(厚壮)+on→强子

hail [heil] v. 向…欢呼(to greet and honor sb.)

(例)The city hailed the victorious team with a parade.

hallmark [ˈhɔːlmɑːk] n.(伦敦金业公会证明金银纯度的)检验标记;品质证明(an official mark stamped on British gold and silver articles, orig. at Goldsmiths' hall in London, as a guarantee of genuineness);标志,特点(any mark or symbol of genuineness of high quality)

(记)分割记忆:hall－mark

(例)The silver bowl had a famous silversmith's hallmark stamped on the bottom. / The employees worked hard to make the company's name the hallmark of fine clothing.

hamper [ˈhæmpə] v. 阻碍(to hinder or interfere with sb. or sth.);n. 有盖提篮(a covered basket for carrying or containing things)

(例)The fierce storm hampered our efforts to get to town by sunset. / Put your dirty shirt in the clothes hamper.

hamster [ˈhæmstə] n.【动】仓鼠(a small, furry rodent, often kept as a pet)

(例)After his parents said he couldn't have a dog, Bill asked for a hamster.

handicap [ˈhændikæp] n. 障碍,不利条件;残废(a disability; a disadvantage; sth. that hinders sb. from doing sth. in the usual way)

(记)handi + cap→手上套了一个帽子,就形成了障碍

(例)A minor handicap causes her to use a cane when she walks.

hard-edge a./n.(以轮廓分明、色彩强烈的几何形体为特点的)硬边绘画(的)(designating any painting or work of art in which there are hard, or clearly defined, edges to the shapes, as of color, on the surface)

(记)hard(硬的)+edge(边)→硬边绘画

hardy [ˈhɑːdi] a. 耐寒的;强壮的(robust; able to live under difficult conditions;〔of a plant〕able to survive a severe winter freeze)

(记)hard(硬的)+y→强壮的,耐寒的

(例)An evergreen is a hardy tree. / The hardy cattle survived the long journey on the trail.

harness [ˈhɑːnis] n. 马具(a set of straps that is placed on a horse so that it can pull a cart or a carriage);v. 套上马具(to put a set of straps on a horse);利用(to use a natural source of energy to produce power)

(例)The farmer put the harness on the horse and led it out to the carriage. / Tell the servants to harness the horses! We must leave now. / The engineers want to find a way to harness the river's power.

hatchback [ˈhætʃbæk]] n.[美]有可向上开启天窗的汽车背部(the sloping back door of a car hinged to the roof)

(记)hatch(舱口盖)+back(背部)→有可向上开启天窗的汽车背部

(例)The woman unlocked the hatchback, opened it, and placed her packages in the car.

haven [ˈheivn] n.安息所,避难所(a safe place; a shelter; a refuge)

(记)比 heaven(天堂)少一个字母,是活着时的安息所

(例)The little cabin was a safe haven from the furious storm. / The child felt safe in the haven of his mother's arms.

havoc [ˈhævək] n.大破坏,浩劫(destruction; ruin);大混乱,大杂乱(confusion; chaos; disorder)

(记)分割记忆:hav 看作 have, oc 看作 oc－cur(发生)→有事发生→混乱

(例)Tornadoes, severe earthquakes, and plagues create widespread havoc. / Hookworms(钩虫) live a long, long time in the small intestine, creating havoc all the while.

hazardous [ˈhæzədəs] a.危险的(dangerous; risky)

(记)hazard(危险)+ous→危险的

(例)There were three car accidents on the hazardous road today.

hedgehog [ˈhedʒhɔg] n.【动】猬;[美]豪猪

(记)组合词:hedge(树篱)+hog(猪)

(例)In the moonlight, I saw a hedgehog scurry(快跑) across the yard.

hedonist [ˈhiːdənist] n.享乐主义者(someone who believes that pleasure is the most important thing in life)

(记)hedon(愉快)+ist→愉快的人→享乐主义者

hefty [ˈhefti] a.[美口]很重的;健壮的([of sb.] large,

strong, and capable of moving great weight);异常大的(large; bulky; sizable)

(记)heft 本身是一个词,意为"重,重要性,有影响"

(例)The hefty man moved the cupboard easily. / The hungry boy took a hefty helping of mashed potatoes.

hegemony [hiː'dʒeməni] n.霸权;领导权(leadership or dominance, esp. that of one state or nation over others)

(记)hegemo(领导者)+ny→霸权;领导权

(例)hegemony over these islands(对这些岛屿的统治权)

helicopter ['helikɔptə] n.直升机(an aircraft with large, rotating blades)

(例) The presidential helicopter landed on the White House lawn.

hem [hem] n.(衣服等的)折边,卷边(the folded and sewn edge of a piece of cloth)

(记)不要把 hem 当成了 ham(火腿)

(例)The hem of my dress has become unstitched.

hepatitis [ˌhepə'taitis] n.肝炎(an inflammatory disease of the liver)

(记)hepat(肝)+itis(炎症)→肝炎

同根词:hepatic(肝的)

(例)Hepatitis is usually accompanied by a fever.

herbicide ['həːbisaid] n.除草剂(a chemical that kills plants; weedkiller)

(记)herb(草)+i+cide(杀)→除草剂

(例)My mom prefers organic food and refuses to use herbicide in the garden.

hereditary [hi'reditəri] a. 世袭的(having title, right, etc. by inheritance)

(记)heredit(留给后人)+ary→世袭的

(例)William's hereditary title permitted him to attend certain social functions.

heretical [hi'retikəl] a. 异端邪说的(different from accepted beliefs, esp. in religion)

(记)heret(异)+ical→异端邪说的,heretic 本身就是"异教徒"的意思

(例)This church is not tolerant of heretical views.

heritage ['heritidʒ] n. 遗产(property that is or can be inherited)

(记)herit(继承)+age→遗产

(例)Jane's uncle died and left her a substantial heritage.

herring ['heriŋ] n. 鲱鱼(单复数同)(an edible fish with silver scales that swims in large groups)

(记)her+ring,不妨把鲱鱼记为"她的指环"

(例)A herring is a very tiny fish. / Herring are found in huge numbers in Atlantic Ocean.

heterogeneity [ˌhetərəudʒi'ni:iti] n. 异类;不同(being different or opposite in structure, quality, etc.; being dissimilar)

(记)hetero(异)+gene(产生)+ity→产生相异→不同;异类

(例)The variety of his books demonstrated the heterogeneity of his interests. / the cultural heterogeneity of the area

hexagon ['heksəgən] n. 六边形(a shape that has six sides; a polygon that has six sides)

(记)hexa(六)+gon(角)

参考:hexapod(昆虫,有六足的节肢动物)

(例)A stop sign has the shape of a hexagon.

hierarchy ['haiərɑ:ki] n. 分成等级的僧侣统治集团(a sys-

tem of church government by priests or other clergy in graded ranks);统治集团(the group of officials, esp. the highest officials, in such a system);等级制度(a system with levels or ranks)
(记)hier(神圣)+archy(统治)→僧侣统治→等级制度
同根词:hieratic(僧侣的);hieron(圣地)
(例)The military has a rigid hierarchy with numerous ranks. / the governmental hierarchy(政府的等级制)

highlight [ˊhailait] v.使突出;以强烈光线照射(to make sth. visually distinctive or prominent so it gets more attention);集中注意力于(to focus attention on sth.)
(记)high+light→高灯照着的地方→使突出,以强烈光线照射
(例)The singer is highlighted on the stage. / In his speech, the candidate highlighted the financial mess the country was in.

hinder [ˈhində, ˈhaində] vt.阻止;妨碍(to attempt to prevent or block sb. from doing sth.)
(记)hind(后面)+er→拉在后面→阻碍
(例)The tall fence hindered the children from going to the lake. / Her parents hindered her from moving to a new job.

hinterland [ˈhintəlænd] n. 内地;穷乡僻壤(the undeveloped area of a region; the interior of a country away from the shore or away from a river)
(记)hinter(=hinder 后面的)+land(土地)
(例)The pioneers moved westward into the hinterland.

hitherto [ˊhiðəˊtuː] ad.迄今,到目前为止(until this time;

to now)
(记)hither(到…为止)+to→迄今,到目前为止
(例)hitherto unknown(迄今为止未知的)/ The printing press made books available to people hitherto unable to afford them.

hockey [ˈhɔki] n. 冰球(a game played on ice where skaters try to hit a rubber disk into a goal area)
(记)和其他球类如 cricket(垒球),golf(高尔夫球),baseball(棒球),rugby(橄榄球),handball(手球)一起记
(例)Hockey is a fast-moving sport.

holistic [həuˈlistik] a. 全面的,全盘的(of, concerned with, or dealing with wholes or integrated systems rather than with their parts)
(记)来自 holism(【哲】整体论),hol(o)(整个的,完全的)+ism(学说,主义)→整体论
同根词:holoscope(全息照相机);holophone(声音全息记录器)
(例)holistic health care(全面的医疗保健)/ a holistic and accurate view(全面而又准确的观点)

homicide [ˈhɔmisaid] n. 杀人;杀人者(the act of killing a person; a murder)
(记)homi(人)+cide(杀)→杀人,杀人者
(例)The police investigated the homicide.

hominid [ˈhɔminid] n./a. 灵长目动物(的)(primates including all forms of humans, extinct and living)
(记)homi(人)+nid→像人的动物→灵长目动物

hominization [ˌhɔminaiˈzeifən] n. (使)人(性化)(the process of furthering the evolutionary development of [man])
(记)来自 hominize(使人〔性〕化),homi(人)+nize→使人化,使人性化
(例)the progressive hominization of the machine

(机器的逐步人化)

homogeneous [ˌhɔməˈdʒiːnjəs] a. 同类的;同质的(made from the same kinds of things;similar; alike)
(记)homo(相同)+gene(产生)+ous→产生相同→使一致
(例)The population of the small town was homogeneous-mostly merchants and laborers. / The people of this country are homogeneous.(这个国家的人同属一个种族。)

hone [həun] n. 细磨刀石(a fine-grained, hard stone used to sharpen cutting tools);v. 磨刀(to sharpen with or as with a hone)
(记)注意不要和 horn(号角)相混
(例)hone one's artistic skills(磨励技艺)/ Can you hone the knife for me? It is too blunt.

hormone [ˈhɔːməun] n.【生化】荷尔蒙,内分泌(one of the chemicals produced by glands in the body and carried through the body by the bloodstream)
(记)horm(鼓动,冲动)+one→激素
(例)The doctors checked the level of hormones in the patient's blood.

horrendous [hɔˈrendəs] a. 可怕的,令人惊惧的(terrible; awful; horrible)
(记)horr(可怕)+endous→可怕的
同根词:horrible(骇人听闻的); horrify(使恐惧)
(例)The horrendous fire destroyed much of the town. / The family was killed in a horrendous car accident.

hospitable [ˈhɔspitəbl] a. 好客的(welcoming; kind and generous to guests and strangers; friendly);(气候,环境)宜人的(favoring the health, growth, comfort, etc. of new arrivals; not adverse);易接受的(receptive or open, as to new ideas)

(记)hospit(主人和客人)+able→喜欢作主人来迎接客人的→好客的

(例)The hospitable host encouraged the party guests to make themselves at home. / a hospitable climate(宜人的气候)

hostility [hɔs'tiliti] n. 敌意,敌视;敌对状态(the condition of being unfriendly or antagonistic)

(记)来自 hostile(敌意的)

(例)Mary was greeted with hostility when she tried to apologize to Dave.

household ['haushəuld] n. 同住在一家的人(the people who live in a house or apartment);家务(the home affairs);a. 家常普通的(common; ordinary)

(记)house+hold→家庭拥有的→家常普通的

(例)There are five people in the Smith household. / a household word(家喻户晓的名字): The advertisement campaign is designed to make this new product a household word in every Chinese home.

hue [hjuː] n. 形式,样子(general appearance; aspect);颜色,色彩(color; shade, or intensity of a color)

(记)hue 还有"大声叫喊,大声反对"之意(hue and cry);可以和 cue(暗示,提示)一起记

(例)The room was decorated in different hues of blue. / I'm not very fond of that hue of red.(我不怎么喜欢那种红颜色。)

hum [hʌm] n. 嗡嗡声(a long, vibrating sound, like a long "mmmmm"; a low murmur; a quiet buzzing sound);v. 哼(歌)(to sing [a tune, etc.] with the lips closed);忙碌,充满活力

(例)We could hear the hum of the busy bees. /

Unable to remember the words to the song, she just hummed.

humanitarian [hju(:)ˌmæniˈtεəriən] n. 博爱主义者,慈善家(someone who tries to make other people's lives better); a. 博爱的(devoted to promoting the welfare of humanity)

(记)human(人类)+itarian→爱人类的→博爱的;博爱主义者

hydrogen [ˈhaidridʒən] n.【化】氢

(记)hydro(水)+gen(产生)→能合成产生水的→氢

(例)Each water molecule consists of two atoms of hydrogen and one atom of oxygen.

hyperbole [haiˈpə:bəli] n.夸张,夸张的说法(exaggeration for effect and not meant to be taken literally)

(记)hyper(高于)+bole(扔)→扔得比别人高→夸张

(例)Nobody believes his hyperbole.

hypersensitive [ˈhaipəˈsensitiv] a. 过分敏感的(very sensitive to other people's behavior; abnormally or excessively sensitive)

(记)hyper(过分)+sensitive(敏感的)

(例)The hypersensitive child knew his parents had been fighting. / hypersensitive concern(神经过敏的担心)

hypertension [haipəˈtenʃən] n.【医】高血压(high blood pressure);过度紧张(abnormally high tension)

(记)hyper(过分)+tension(拉力,牵力)

(例)The old man takes medicine every day to control his hypertension.

hypnotist [ˈhipnətist] n. 施行催眠术的人(someone who is able to place someone in a sleep-like condition of

semiconsciousness)
(记)hypno(睡眠)+tist(人)→使睡眠的人→施行睡眠术的人
同根词:hypnosis(睡眠状态);hypnopedia(睡眠教学法)
(例)The hypnotist asked the patient to close his eyes and go to sleep.

hypotenuse [haiˊpɔtinjuːz] n.(直角三角形的)斜边(the longest side of a right triangle, located opposite the right angle)
(记)hypo(在…下面)+ten(拉)+use→从下面拉到上面的一条线→斜边

hypothesis [haiˊpɔθisiːz] n.假设,假说(a conjecture; a possible explanation; an idea that has not been proved but that explains the facts about sth.)
(记)hypo(在…下面)+thesis(论点)→非真正论点→假说
(例)The scientists agreed to have their hypothesis tested by other scientists. / raise a hypothesis(提出一个假说)

I

ice-polished a. 冰蚀的
(记)ice-polish(磨光)+ed→被冰磨光的→冰蚀的

iconography [ˌaikɔˊnɔgrəfi] n.肖像画法(the art of representing or illustrating by pictures, figures, images, etc.); 肖像学(the study of symbols, themes, and subject matter in the visual arts);插画,图解(icons collectively)
(记)icon(肖像)+o+graphy(画法)→肖像画法

identical [aiˊdentikəl] a. 同一的;相同的(exactly the same

as sb. or sth. else)
(记)identic(相同)+al→同一的,identic 本身是一个词,"相同的,同一的"
(例)The second printing of this book is identical to the first. / It's the identical watch which was stolen from me.(这正是我被偷走的那块手表。)

identify [ai'dentifai] v. 认明,认出(to state or declare who or what sb. or sth. is; to assert sb. or sth.'s identity)
(记)ident(相同)+ify→使对上号→认明,认出
(例)The doctor identified the disease that made me sick. / He identified the coat as his brother's.

ideographic [ˌidiəu'græfik] a. 表意文字的,表意符号的(of, or having the nature of, a graphic symbol representing an object or idea)
(记)ideo(=idea 思想,意义)+graphic(记录的)→把意义记录下来的→表意文字的
(例)the ideographic stage in the development of writing(文字发展中的表意阶段)

idioglossia ['idiə'glɔsiə] n. 自解语症(只有自己懂的语言)
(记)idio(个人,独特)+glos(glot)(语言)+sia→只有自己懂的语言

idiosyncrasy [ˌidiə'siŋkrəsi] n. 特殊癖性或行为(the temperament or mental constitution peculiar to a person or group; any personal peculiarity, mannerism, etc.)
(记)idio(个人,独特)+syn(共同)+crasy(混合)→混合了个人特性的行为→癖好,特有的习性
同根词:idiom(习语); idiopathy(特发病)
(例)Many talented people have idiosyncrasies.(许多有才能的人有怪癖。)/ One of his idiosyncrasies is eating a hamburger for breakfast.

idle ['aidl] a. 不做事的(not working; unemployed);

懒惰的(habitually lazy; not liking work);v. 浪费光阴(to waste; squander)

(记)同义词:dawdle(游手好闲，混日子),也是以dle结尾

(例)I was idle for three months until I found work in another city. / She idled away the last hour of work talking on the phone.

ignition [igˊniʃən] n. 点火,着火(catching fire; bursting)

(记)来自ignite,ign(点燃)+ite→燃烧,发光

(例)an ignition point(燃点) / The ignition of the forest was caused by lighting.(森林起火是由雷电引起的。)

iguana [iˊgwɑːnə] n.【动】鬣蜥(产于美洲和西印度群岛的一种大蜥蜴)(a lizard found in tropical areas of the Western Hemisphere)

illiterate [iˊlitərit] n. 文盲(unable to write or read)

(记)il(不)+literate(识字的)→不识字的

(例)The rich man established a school to teach illiterate people to read.

illuminate [iˊljuːmineit] v. 照明(to cover sb. or sth. with light);启迪(to make sth. clearer or easier to understand)

(记)il(进入,in在字母"l"前的变体)+lumin(明亮)+ate→进入明亮→照明

同根词:luminant(发光的;杰出人物)

(例)A single candle illuminated the small, empty room. / Could you please illuminate your theory with a little more explanation?

illusionary [iˊljuːʃənəri] a. 幻觉的;错误的(like an illusion; false)

(记)来自illusion(幻觉),il+lus(玩弄)+ion→被玩弄→错觉

(例)The signals that the recession was ending were illusionary. / illusionary stage effects(造成错觉的舞台效果)

illusory [i'ljuːsəri] a. 虚幻的(deceptive; unreal; illusive)

(记)来自 illusion, il + lus(玩弄)→被玩弄→错觉

(例)Most often mist hides the illusory Alps.(云雾常常遮掩了梦幻般的阿尔卑斯山。) / illusory hopes(不切实际的希望)

immaterial [imə'tiəriəl] a. 无关紧要的(not relevant; having nothing to do with sth.);非实体的

(记)im(不) + material(实体)→非实体的,引申为"不重要的"

(例)The judge ordered that the lawyer's immaterial comments be removed from the record. / ghosts and other immaterial entities(鬼魂及其他无形体)

imminent ['iminənt] a. 急迫的;迫近的;危急的(likely to happen without delay; impending; threatening: said of danger, evil, misfortune)

(记)im(进入) + min(突出) + ent→突进来→逼近的

同根词:eminent(出众的);prominent(杰出的)

(例)Black clouds usually mean rain is imminent. / That species is in imminent danger of extinction.(那类动物濒临灭绝的危险。)

immoral [i'mɔːrəl] a. 不道德的(without morals; not moral; breaking moral rules)

(记)im(不) + moral(道德的),和 amoral(不受道德约束的),unmoral(无关道德问题的)区别记忆

(例)Killing is immoral. / Lying and stealing are considered immoral conducts in every human society.

immune [iˈmjuːn] a. 免疫的(not susceptible to some specified disease because of the presence of the specific antibodies);免除惩罚的(protected against sth. disagreeable or harmful)
(记)im(没有)+mune(责任)→没有责任→免除的
(例)You will be immune to measles if you are properly vaccinated. / The culprit cooperated on the condition that he would be immune form prosecution.

immunological [ˌimjuˈnɔlədʒikəl] a.【医】免疫学的
(记)im(没有)+mun(责任)+olog(学科)+ical→免疫学的

immutable [iˈmjuːtəbl] a. 不变的(never changing or varying; unchangeable)
(记)im(不)+mut(变化)+able→不变的
同根词:mutation(变化);commute(交换,改变)
(例)nature's immutable laws(大自然永恒的规律)

impact [ˈimpækt] n. 冲击(the forceful collision of objects striking one another);影响(the influence or effect of sb. or sth.)
(记)im(起强调作用)+pact(压)→使劲压→冲击
(例)The impact of the baseball knocked me to the ground. / Your lectures have had a powerful impact on my thinking.

impart [imˈpɑːt] v. 传授;告知(to give information or advice 〔to sb.〕)
(记)im(进入)+part(部分)→成为(知识)一部分→告知
(例)The witness imparted what she knew to the police. / impart the secret to sb.(向某人透露秘密)

impartiality [ˈimˌpɑːʃiˈæliti] n. 公平;无私(the state or quality of favoring no one side or party more than another; without prejudice or bias; fairness; justness)
(记)来自 impartial(公正的,无私的),im(不)+ partial(有偏见的)
(例)Our math teacher is famous for his strictness and impartiality.

impasse [imˈpæs] n. 僵局;死路(a place where movement or progress is blocked by sth.; a deadlock)
(记)im(不)+passe(通过)→通不过→僵局
(例)The negotiation has reached an impasse.(谈判已陷入僵局。)/ The impasses cannot be broken.(僵局无法打破。)

impede [imˈpiːd] v. 妨碍,阻碍(to obstruct or hinder sb. or sth.)
(记)im(进入)+pede(脚)→把脚放入→妨碍
同根词:centipede(蜈蚣);podiatry(足病学)
(例)Our journey was impeded by a violent snowstorm. / This should not impede normal state relations.

impediment [imˈpedimənt] n. 妨碍,阻碍物(sth. that gets in the way of sb. or sth.; obstacle)
(例)The bad traffic was an impediment to going to work on time. / The new taxes were a major impediment to economic growth.

imperative [imˈperətiv] a. 急需的;必要的(necessary; having to be done; urgent)
(记)imper(命令)+ative→命令的,紧急的
同根词:imperator(绝对统治者)
(例)Wearing a helmet is imperative when riding a motorcycle.

imperial [imˈpiəriəl] a. 帝国的(of or about an empire);最

高权力的(having supreme authority; sovereign);专横的;傲慢的(imperious)
(记)imperia(imperium 帝国)+l→帝国的;最高权力的;专横的
(例)a haughty and imperial manner(高傲专横的态度)

impersonal [im'pəːsənl] a. 非个人的(not personal);不受个人情感影响的(not showing human feelings, esp. sympathy or warmth)
(记)im(非)+person(人,角色)+al→非个人的
(例)The teacher's criticism of the class was impersonal.(老师对班级的评价并非针对哪一个同学的。)/impersonal assessment(客观的评价)

impetus ['impitəs] n. 推动力;刺激(driving force or motive; incentive; impulse)
(记)im(进入)+pet(追求)+us→进入追求→推动力
同根词:competition(竞争,角逐)
(例)The impetus of the car as it struck the wall crushed many of the stones of the wall. / the primary impetus behind the economic recovery(促进经济恢复的推动力)

impinge [im'pindʒ] v. 撞击,冲击(to strike, hit, or dash);侵害(to make inroads and encroach on or upon the property or rights of another)
(记)im(=in)+pinge(打击)→撞击,冲击
(例)Your political opinions will necessarily impinge on your public life.(你的政治观点一定会影响你的社会生活。)

implant [im'plɑːnt] v. 注入,灌输(to put sth. into the body, such as tissue or a medical device; to establish sth. in sb.'s mind)

(记)im(进入)+plant(种植)→种入→灌输

(例)The doctor implanted a pacemaker to regulate my heartbeat. / Listening to the songs over and over again implanted their lyrics in my brain.

implication [ˌimpliˈkeiʃən] n. 牵连(the condition of being found to be involved in something criminal or bad);暗示(a hint; sth. that is implied)

(记)来自 implicate,im(进入)+plic(重叠)+ate→重叠进去→牵连

(例)This guy is suspected of implication in a number of robberies(此人被怀疑与多宗抢劫案有牵连。) / Your implication that I stole the money enraged me.

implicit [imˈplisit] a. 含蓄的(hinted; indirect; implied);不言明的(having no doubt; absolute)

(记)im(进入)+plic(重叠)+it(→)叠在里面→含蓄的

(例)My advisor gave me an implicit warning to study harder. / I have total and implicit confidence that you can do this well.

imposition [ˌimpəˈziʃən] n. 征税(sth. placed or set [tax, fine, etc. on or upon] as by authority);强加(the forcing of oneself, one's presence or will, etc. on another without right or invitation)

(记)来自 impose,im(进入)+pose(放)→放进去→强加

同根词:dispose(布置,处理)

(例)the imposition of heavy taxes(苛捐杂税的征收) / I felt a flash of anger over the imposition on my privacy.

impoverish [imˈpɔvəriʃ] v.使贫困(to reduce or destroy sb.'s wealth)

(记)im(进入)+pover(贫困)+ish→进入贫困
参考:poverty(贫困)
(例)The high taxes on our house almost impoverished us. / His family is impoverished by misfortune and sickness.

impressionable [im'preʃənəbl] a. 易受影响的(easily influenced)
(记)impression(印象)+able→容易对…留下印象的→易受影响的
(例)He is very impressionable and agrees with everyone he talks to. / a highly impressionable age (可塑性极强的年龄)

impunity [im'pju:niti] n. 免除处罚(without risk of punishment)
(记)im(不)+pun(罚)+ity→不罚
同根词:punitive(惩罚性的)
(例)The diplomat parked in illegal parking spaces with impunity)

inadvertent [ˌinəd'və:tənt] a. 不经心的;疏忽的;非故意的(accidental; not intentional)
(记)in(不)+advertent(故意的)→非故意的
(例)Your inadvertent comments reflect what you really think. / I was charged an extra $100 due to an inadvertent computer error.

inalienable [in'eiljənəbl] a. 不可分割的(that may not be taken away or transferred)
(记)in(不)+alien(疏远)+able→不可疏远→不可分割的
(例)inalienable rights(不可剥夺的权力) / an inalienable part of the territory of a country(一国领土不可分割的部分)

incandescent [ˌinkæn'desnt] a. 白热的(glowing or white with heat);热烈的(zestful; ardent)

(记)in(进入)+cand(白热)+escent(开始…的)→开始发热的

(例)The embers of the fire were still incandescent even though the flames had disappeared.(尽管火焰已灭,火的余烬仍然炽热。) / incandescent affection(热烈的爱)

incentive [inˊsentiv] n. 刺激;鼓励(stimulating one to take action, work harder, etc.; encouraging; motivating)

(记)in(进入)+cent(=cant 唱说)+ive→说服人做事→上进心,刺激

(例)As an incentive, the workers were promised a bonus if they finished the project ahead of schedule. / the government's tax incentive for industry to move into depressed areas(政府鼓励工业迁入萧条地区的税收优惠)

incineration [inˌsinəˊreiʃən] n. 焚化;毁灭(the process of burning up or burning sth. into ashes)

(记)来自 incinerate(v. 焚化,火葬),in+ciner(灰)+ate→把…烧成灰→焚化

(例)harness the energy from refuse incineration(利用焚烧垃圾所产生的能量)

incipient [inˊsipiənt] a. 初期的;刚出现的(beginning to be evident; starting to be recognized for what it is)

(记)in+cip(拿)+ient→拿进来的→刚出现的

同根词:precipitate(加速,促进)

(例)The project we are working on is an incipient disaster. / The medicine stopped the boy's incipient cough from becoming worse.

incisive [inˊsaisiv] a. 一针见血的(sharp; keen; penetrating; acute)

(记)来自 incise,in(进入)+cise(切)→切入

(例)an incisive mind(敏锐的头脑) / an incisive criticism

incompatible [ˌinkəmˈpætəbl] a. 不相容的(not able to exist in harmony or agreement)

(记)in(不)+compatible(和谐的)

(例)Dogs and cats aru usually incompatible. / Discrimination is incompatible with democratic principles.(歧视不符合民主原则。)

incongruity [ˌinkɔŋˈgruiti] n. 不一致(the condition, quality, or fact of being out of place or not fitting in)

(记)来自 incongruous, in(不)+congruous(全等的,一致的)→不一致的

(例)the incongruity of the clerk's apparel(那位职员衣着不协调)

inconsequential [inˌkɔnsiˈkwenʃəl] a. 不重要的,微不足道的(of no consequence; unimportant; trivial)

(记)in(不)+consequential(重要的)

(例)He considered the sum inconsequential.(他认为这笔款子微不足道。)/ The details are inconsequential.

incorporate [inˈkɔːpəreit] v. 合并,并入(to make sb. or sth. part of a whole or a group);组成公司(to form a corporation)

(记)in(进入)+corpor(团体)→进入团体→合并

(例)The school's curriculum incorporates the study of art and music. / They incorporated his proposals into their plan.

increment [ˈinkrimənt] n. 增值,增加(an increase; the amount that sth. increases; a step in a series of increases)

(记)in(进入)+cre(增加)+ment→使增加→增加

同根词:accretion(自然增大);incretion(内分泌)
(例)Each unit on this chart corresponds to a $ 1,000 increment. / Every day the patient felt tiny new increments of strength come to him.

incriminate [in'krimi'neit] vt. 控告;显示…有罪(to charge with a crime);连累(某人),归罪于(to involve in, or make appear guilty of, a crime or fault)
(记)in(进入)+crimin(罪行)+ate→被牵连到罪行中
(例)The fact that he ran away seemed to incriminate the boy.(他得以逃跑似乎与那个男孩有牵连。)/ He incriminated several people in front of the grand jury.

inculcation [ˌinkʌl'keiʃən] n. 灌输;谆谆教诲(the act of impressing upon the mind by frequent repetition or persistent urging)
(记)来自 inculcate(灌输,谆谆教诲),in(进入)+culc(=cult 培养,种植)+ate→种进去→灌输

incumbent [in'kʌmbənt] n. 在职者,现任者(the person currently holding the elected office)
(记)in+cumb(躺)+ent→躺在(职位)上的人
同根词:encumber(妨碍);recumbent(斜躺的);cumbersome(笨重的)
(例)The incumbent senator decided to retire at the end of her term.

incursion [in'kəːʃən] n. 侵犯,入侵(a sudden, brief invasion or raid)
(记)in(进入)+curs(跑)+ion→跑进来→入侵
(例)They strengthened their northern border against any possible incursions by guerrillas.

indelible [in'delibl] a. 擦拭不掉的;不可磨灭的(that cannot be erased, blotted out, eliminated, etc.; per-

manent; lasting)
(记)in + del(= delete 擦掉) + ible→不能擦掉的
(例)The scene of horror left an indelible impression on his memory. / indelible strawberry stains on a tablecloth

indenture [inˈdentʃə] n. 契约,合同(a written contract or agreement)
(记)in(进入) + dent(牙齿) + ure(状态),原指古代师徒间分割成锯齿状的契约

indices [ˈindisiːz] n. (index 的复数)(物价,工资,就业,生产的)指数(a scale where prices or amounts of certain things are compared with the prices or amounts of those same things at an earlier date)
(例)According to the consumer price index, the price of food doubled between 1960 and 1975.

indigenous [inˈdidʒinəs] a. 土产的,本地的(existing or growing naturally in a region; native)
(例)The indigenous people of the area know which plants are safe to eat and which are poisonous.

indigent [ˈindidʒənt] a. 贫穷的,贫困的(very poor; very needy)
(记)indi(内部) + gen(= egent 缺乏)内部缺乏,贫困的;分割记忆:in(没有) - dig(挖) - ent,挖不出东西→贫困的
(例)The indigent family lived under a bridge.

indignation [ˌindigˈneiʃən] n. 愤慨(anger or resentment)
(记)in(不) + dign(礼貌) + ation→不礼貌→愤慨
同根词:dignity(尊贵,礼貌);indign(不得体的)
(例)His indignation over your casual comments cannot be justified.

indiscriminate [ˌindisˈkriminit] a. 不加选择的(not choosing carefully; random)

(记)in(不)+discriminate(区别)
(例)Her husband is quite indiscriminate in his choice of clothing.

inducement [inˈdjuːsmənt] n. 引诱;劝诱;诱因,动机(sth. that is used to persuade or encourage sb. to do sth.)
(记)来自 induce(诱导,引起),in(进入)+duce(引导)→引入,引起
(例)As an inducement for me to buy the car, the salesman lowered the price.

indulge [inˈdʌldʒ] vt. 使自己沉迷;放纵(to gratify a desire; to give in to a craving; to yield to a passion); 允许(某人)延期付款(to allow a debtor to defer payment without penalty)
(例)I indulged myself in a long, relaxing shower after a hard day.

inept [iˈnept] a. 不适当的,不合场面的(not suitable to the purpose; unfit);无能的(awkward; clumsy)
(记)in(无)+ept(熟练的)→不熟练的→无能的
(例)The inept dancer tripped and fell over his partner's feet.

inertia [iˈnəːʃjə] n. 惰性;懒惰(a tendency to remain in a fixed condition without change; disinclination to move or act)
(记)来自 inert(惰性的),in(不)+ert(动)→不动的→惰性的
(例)Due to bureaucratic inertia, the project did not take off in time.

inevitable [inˈevitəbl] a. 不可避免的([of sth.] certain to happen)
(记)in(不)+evitable(可以避免的)→不可避免的
(例)Death is the inevitable ending of life.

inexorable [inˈeksərəbl] a. 不为所动的,坚决不变的(that

cannot be moved or influenced by persuasion or entreaty; unrelenting)

(记)in(不)+exorable(可说服的)→不可说服的; ex(出)+ora(演说)+able→能够说服

同根词:oration(演讲)

(例) Try as you may, but you cannot possibly change your inexorable fate.

inexplicable [in'eksplikəbl] a. 无法解释的(not able to be explained; unexplainable)

(记)in(不)+explicable(可以解释的)

(例)The young man's death was sudden and inexplicable.

inextricable [in'ekstrikəbl] a. 无法拯救的(that one cannot set oneself free from);无法脱开的;复杂的(that cannot be disentangled or untied; so complicated or involved as to be insolvable)

(记)in(不)+extric(摆脱)+able→不能摆脱的

参考:extricate(拯救,摆脱)

(例)The poor woman was caught in an inextricable dilemma.

infancy ['infənsi] n. 婴儿期,幼年期(the state or period of being a baby);初期(the earliest stage of anything)

(记)来自 infant(婴儿)

(例) In its feeble infancy, the tiny state was not match to its giant neighbor.

infectious [in'fekʃəs] a. 传染的([of disease] able to spread from organism to organism);感染性的,易传播的([of certain activities] spreading from one person to another)

(记)来自 infect(传染,感染),in(进入)+fect(放)+ious→放进去→使感染

(例) The highly infectious flu can easily spread

across the densely populated city.

infest [in'fest] v. 侵害，扰乱(to invade sth. in large numbers)

(记)in(进入)+fest(匆忙)→匆忙起来→骚扰

同根词:festinate(赶快,加速)

(例)Cockroaches have infested our kitchen and dining room.

infield ['infi:ld] n.(棒球,垒球球场的)内场(the area enclosed by the four base lines of a baseball field)

(记)和 outfield(外场)一起记

infirmary [in'fə:məri] n. 医院,医务室(尤指学校等附设的病房或配药处)(a place for the care of the sick, injured, or infirm; esp., a building or room, as in a school, that serves as a hospital or dispensary)

(记)in(不)+firm(结实的)+ary→柔弱的人常去的地方→医院,医务室

(例)My teacher helped me walk to the infirmary.

inflammatory [in'flæmətəri] a. 使激怒的,煽动性的(rousing or likely to rouse excitement, anger, violence, rioting, etc.);【医】发炎的,炎症的(caused by, or characterized by varied combination of redness, pain, heat, swelling and loss of function)

(记)in(进入)+flam(e)(火)+matory→进火的→煽动性的

(例)The racist made a highly inflammatory speech. / inflammatory diseases

inflection [in'flekʃən] n. 弯曲;向内弯曲(a turning, bending or curving);变音,转调(any change in tone or pitch of the voice; modulation)

(记)in(向内)+flect(弯曲)+ion→向内弯曲,变音,转调

(例)to signal a question by a rising inflection(用升

调表示一个疑问句)

influx [ˈinflʌks] n. 流入,汇集(the sudden arrival of many things or people);河口(the point where a body of water, such as a river, joins another body of water)

(记)in(向内)+flux(流)→流入;河口

(例)The recent influx of immigrants caused a housing shortage in the small town.

infrared [ˈinfrəˈred] a. 红外线的,红外区的(designating those invisible rays just beyond the red end of the visible spectrum)

ingenious [inˈdʒiːnjəs] a. 聪明的,有发明天才的(inventive; showing cleverness)

(记)in(内在)+gen(产生)+ious→聪明产生于内→聪慧的,注意不要和 ingenuous(坦率的,天真的)相混

(例)Your ingenious ideas have saved the company millions of dollars.

ingenuity [ˌindʒiˈnju(ː)iti] n. 巧思,聪敏(the cleverness used in planning or inventing sth.)

(例)We have electricity because of Thomas Edison's ingenuity.

ingest [ˌinˈdʒest] v. 咽下,吞下(to eat or drink sth; to swallow sth.)

(记)in(进入)+gest(带)→带进去→咽下去

同根词:congestion(拥挤),digest(消化)

(例)Do not ingest this medicine! It is to be rubbed on the skin.

ingrained [ˌinˈgreind] a. 根深蒂固的(inveterate; thoroughgoing)

(记)in(进入)+grain(木头的纹理)→进入纹理之内→根深蒂固的

(例)He's got some ingrained bad habits, such as smoking and gambling.

inhalation [ˌinhəˈleiʃən] n.【医】吸入(the act of breathing in or drawing in〔air, vapor, etc.〕into the lungs)

(记)来自 inhale(吸入),in(进)+hale(呼吸)→吸气

同根词:exhale(呼气),halitus(气息,蒸气)

inherent [ˌinˈhiərənt] a.天生的;固有的

(记)in(内在)+her(继承)+ent→天生继承下来的

(例)Her personality has an inherent charm.

inherited [ˌinˈheritid] a.(病等)遗传的(received by heritage)

(记)inherit(继承)+ed

(例)Afflicted with inherited myopia(近视), she cannot see very far.

in-house [inˈhaus] a.起源于机构内部的;机构内部的(originating within an organization, company, etc., rather than brought in from outside)

(记)in-house→房子内的→起源于机构内部的;机构内部的

(例)The lawyer is an in-house counsel for a large corporation.

inhumane [ˌinhjuːˈmein] a.不近人情的(not human, unmoved by the suffering of others; cruel, brutal, unkind)

(记)注意不要和 inhuman(残忍的)混淆

(例)It's really inhumane of you to say such cruel words to a little child.

iniquitous [iˈnikwitəs] a. 邪恶的,不公正的(lack of righteousness or justice; wicked)

(记)in(不)+iquit(=equit 公正)+ous→不公正

的

(例) The emperor's iniquitous rule enraged his subjects.

initial [ˌiˈniʃəl] a. 最初的,初始的(first; occurring or appearing at the beginning of sth.)

(例)The initial uncertainty over the newborn's life was very troubling to his parents.

injunction [ˌinˈdʒʌŋkʃən] n. 命令,责戒(an enjoining, bidding command);【律】指令,禁令(an order from a court that one must do or not do sth.)

(记)in(进入)+junct(连接)+ion→和(法令)相连接→命令

参考:enjoin(命令)

(例) The court issued an injunction that prevents our company from selling our products without the proper labels.

innate [ˈiˈneit] a. 生来的,天赋的(present in sb. since birth; inborn; instinctive)

(记)in(内生)+nate(出生)→出生时带来的

同根词:natality(出生率)

(例)The ability to learn language is an innate human ability.

inoculate [iˈnɔkjuleit] v. 预防注射(to inject a serum, vaccine, etc. into a living organism, esp. in order to create immunity)

(记)in(不)+ocul(萌芽,眼睛)+ate→不让萌芽成长→预防注射

(例)Have you been inoculated for measles yet?

inordinate [iˈnɔːdinit] a. 过度的,过分的(lacking restraint or moderation, too great or too many; immoderate)

(记)in(不)+ordin(正常)→ate→(生活)不正常的,无节制的

(例)The company's inordinate debt load has been stifling its growth.

inpatient [ˈinˌpeiʃənt] n. 住院病人(a hospital patient who stays one or more nights in the hospital getting treatment)

(记)in(进入)+patient(病人)→进住医院的病人→住院病人;注意与impatient(不耐烦的)的区别

(例)I checked into the hospital as an inpatient for my surgery.

input [ˈin-put] n.【经】投入(the amount of money, material, effort, etc. put into a project or process; investment);输入(电路,电压或功率)(an electronic signal that is fed into a circuit)

(记)in(入)+put(投放)→投入,输入

(例)The input was cut off when the wire snapped.

inquisitorial [inˌkwiziˈtɔːriəl] a. 审问官似的(of or like an inquisitor or inquisition);爱打听别人事情的(inquisitive; prying)

(记)in(进入)+quisit(询问)+orial→深入询问→爱打听别人事情的

同根词:prerequisite(先决条件);inquisition(调查)

(例)The tax authorities were endowed with plenty of inquisitorial power.

insatiable [inˈseiʃiəbl] a. 不能满足的,贪得无厌的(constantly wanting more; that cannot be satisfied or appeased; very greedy)

(记)in(不能)+sati(足够)+able→怎么也不能足够的→不能满足的,贪得无厌的

(例)The hungry child had an insatiable appetite.

inscribe [inˈskraib] v. 内切或内接(to draw [a figure] inside another figure so that their boundaries touch at as many points as possible)

(记)in + scribe(切)→内切

(例)a regular polygon inscribed in a circle(圆的内接正多边形)

inscribe [in'skraib] v. 铭刻,题献(to write, mark or engrave〔words, symbols, etc.〕on some surface)

(记)in + scribe(写,刻)→刻上去→铭刻,题献

(例)He inscribed the greeting card with his signature.

insidious [in'sidiəs] a. 祸害隐伏的(operating in a slow or not easily apparent manner; more dangerous than seems evident)

(记)in(里面) + sid(坐) + ious→(祸害)坐在里面的

同根词:assiduous(勤勉的);preside(主持)

(例)an insidious disease(隐伏的疾病)/ The politician's insidious speech failed to generate any interest among the audience for his extremist views.

insight ['insait] n. 洞察力,洞悉,见识(the ability to make pertinent observations);【心】顿悟(awareness of one's own mental attitude and behavior)

(例)The old man helped us with his insights and perspectives.

insomnia [in'sɔmniə] n. 失眠,失眠症(the inability to fall asleep or remain asleep)

(记)in(不) + somn(睡眠) + ia→不能睡眠→失眠症

同根词:somniferous(催眠的);somnolent(想睡的)

(例)Drinking a lot of coffee at night can cause insomnia.

installation [ˌinstɔ'leiʃən] n. 就职(putting sb. in a position or office);安装(setting up equipment; putting equipment in place so that it will work)

(记)in(进入) + stall(停止) + ation→停在里面→就职

(例)The installation of the new president was a simple ceremony. / The installation of the dishwasher took the plumber only a few hours.

instantaneous [ˌinstən'teinjəs] a. 即时的,立刻的(immediate; without delay; at once)

(记)instant(马上的,立即的) + aneous→立即的

参考:instantize(把食品等预先配制好)

(例)My instantaneous reply to his nosy question was "No!"

instigate ['instigeit] v. 激起,煽动(to cause by inciting; foment)

(记)in(进入) + stig(=sting 刺激) + ate→刺激起来→煽动

(例)to instigate a rebellion(煽动叛乱)

instil(l) [in'stil] v. 滴注(to put in drop by drop);逐渐灌输(to put 〔an idea, principle, feeling, etc.〕 into little by little; impart gradually)

(记)in(进入) + still(水滴)→像水滴一样进入→滴注

同根词:distill(蒸馏)

(例)Years of working as a waitress instilled a lot of patience in Anne.

insulate ['insjuleit] v. 使绝缘(to cover sth. with a material that prevents the passage of electricity, heat, or sound);使隔离(from)(to separate sb. or sth. from other things or people by distance or a barrier)

(记)insul(岛) + ate→成为岛一样→隔离

(例)The woman insulated the recording studio with material that made it soundproof.

insulin [ˊinsjulin] n.【生】胰岛素(a hormone made by the pancreas, which regulates glucose in the body)
(记)insul(岛)+in(素)→胰岛素
(例)People with diabetes must inject insulin on a regular basis.

intact [inˊtækt] a. 完整的,未动过的(not damaged; whole)
(记)in(不)+tact(接触)→未接触过→完整的
同根词:contact(接触);tactile(接触的)
(例)All the parts of the old radio were still intact.

intake [ˊinteik] n.吸入,收纳(the act or process of taking in);纳入(数量)(the amount or thing taken in)
(记)in+take→往里收→吸入,收纳
(例)The intake of air was blocked by a rubber stopper.

intangible [inˊtændʒəbl] a. 不可捉摸的(that cannot be easily defined, formulated, or grasped; vague)
(记)in(不)+tangible(可触摸的)
(例)Thoughts and ideas are intangible things on which it is impossible to place a value.

integral [ˊintigrəl] n.整体(a whole)
(记)in(不,没有)+tegr(动)+al→没动的→整体

integrate [ˊintigreit] v.使结合,使完整(to make whole or complete by adding or bringing together parts; unify)
(记)integr(完整)+ate→完整化→成为整体
同根词:integrity(完整,正直);integrant(不可分割的)
(例)The district integrated the schools by busing the children in from different neighborhoods.

intercept [ˌintəːˊsept] v.拦截,截击(to stop or seize sth. as it is moved from one place to another)

(记)inter(在中间)+cept(拿)→从中间拿→拦截
(例)I tried to hand a note to my friend, but the teacher intercepted it.

interdependency [ˌintədiˈpendənsi] n. 相互依赖(dependence on each other or one another; mutual dependence)
(记)inter(相互)+dependen(t)(依赖)+cy→相互依赖
(例)The interdependency between husband and wife is the hallmark of a good marriage.

interest rate 利率(payment made by a borrower for a loan, expressed as a percentage)

interior [inˈtiəriə] n. interior angle 内角(the angle formed inside a polygon by adjacent sides)
(记)和 exterior angle(外角)一起记

interlude [ˈintə(ː)luːd] n.(两个事件中的)穿插事件;间隔的时间或空间(an interval; the period of time between two things)
(记)inter(在中间)+lude(玩耍)→在玩闹之间→休息
(例)I took a short interlude between the conference and dinner.

intermediary [ˌintə(ː)ˈmiːdjəri] a. 媒介的(acting between two persons; acting as mediator);n. 中间人,媒介物(a go-between; mediator; any medium, means, or agency)
(记)inter(在中间)+medi(中间)+ary→进入中间状态→媒介的
参考:intermediate(中间的,中等程度的)
(例)A cocoon is an intermediary between caterpillar and butterfly.

intermittent [ˌintə(ː)ˈmitənt] a. 断断续续的,间歇的(off and on; stopping and starting; not continuous)

(记)来自 intermit(暂停,中断)

(例)We had intermittent rain all day long. / The old man suffers from intermittent headaches.

internecine [ˌintə(:)ˈniːsain] a. 内讧的,两败俱伤的(deadly or harmful to both sides of a group involved in a conflict, as a civil war; mutually destructive or harmful)

(记)inter(相互)+nec(杀)+ine→互相杀→自相残杀

(例)This internecine struggle would hasten the demise of the empire.

interpolation [inˌtəːpəuˈleiʃən] n. 插入,窜改;【数】内推法

(记)来自 interpolate(插入,窜改),inter(在中间)+pol(=polish 修饰)+ate→在中间修饰→插入,窜改

(例)The editor put all his interpolations into brackets.

interrelated [ˌintəriˈleitid] a. 相互关联的(mutually related)

(记)inter+relate(相关)+d→相互关联的

(例)Many urban problems, such as drugs, poverty, and crime, are interrelated.

interrogate [inˈterəgeit] v. 审问,审讯(to ask questions of sb. about sth., esp. a crime)

(记)inter+rog(问)+ate→在中间问→审问

同根词:arrogate(冒称)

(例)The investigator interrogated everyone present during the incident.

intersect [ˌintə(:)ˈsekt] v. 相交([for two things, such as roads, paths, or lines] to touch or cross each other)

(记)inter+sect(切,割)→从中间切→横截

同根词:dissect(解剖);section(部分)

(例)There is smoke coming from where the wires intersect.

intersection [ˌintə(ː)ˈsekʃən] n. 横断,十字路口(the junction of two or more roads, streets, highways, etc.; the place where roads or streets intersect)
(例)Can you wait for me at the intersection, okay?

intestinal [inˈtestinl] a. 肠的(of, in, or affecting the intestines)

intestine [inˈtestin] n. 肠
(记)in(内)+test(外壳)+ine→在外壳之内→内脏
参考:test(虫的外壳)

intricate [ˈintrikit] a. 复杂,难懂的(complex; involving many parts)
(记)in(进)+tric(琐碎,复杂)+ate→错综复杂的
同根词:extricate(解救)
(例)The human eye is a very intricate part of the body.

intricacy [ˈintrikəsi] n. 复杂的事物(something intricate)
(例)to delve into the intricacies of business management

intrigue [inˈtriːg] v. 密谋(to plot or scheme secretly or underhandedly);引起极大兴趣(to excite the interest or curiosity of)
(记)in(使)+trigue(引出,引发)→引发(兴趣)
(例)The news intrigued all of us.

intriguing [inˈtriːgiŋ] a. 引起极大兴趣的(interesting; causing curiosity or interest)
(例)The reporter wrote an intriguing story about the moon.

intrinsic [inˈtrinsik] a. 固有的,内在的([of sth. abstract] essential and inherent)

(记)intr(= intro 向内) + insic(可能来自 inside)→内在的

(例)Paying careful attention and responding quickly are intrinsic parts of good driving.

intrinsically [in'trinsikəli] ad. 内在地(being located within, or exclusively of, a part)

Inuit ['injuːit] n. 因纽特人(a member or group of native people of northern North America, inhabiting areas from Greenland and E Canada to Alaska)

(记)音译

invalidate [in'vælideit] vt. 使无效力,证明无效(to make invalid; deprive of legal force)

(记)in(无) + valid(有效的) + ate→无效的

(例)A contract is invalidated if only one party signs it.

inventory ['invəntri] n. 存货清单(a list showing the number of each item that has been packed, received, shipped, etc.)

(记)in(进入) + vent(来) + ory→对库存货物清查

注意:invention(发明),inventive(发明的)

(例)The clerk checked the inventory to see if large paper clips were available.

invertebrate [in'vəːtibrit] n. 无脊椎动物(a type of animal that does not have a spine)

(记)in(无) + vertebrate(脊椎的)

(例)Worms and flies are examples of invertebrate.

inveterate [in' vetərit] a. 积习已深的(settled in a habit, practice, prejudice, etc.; habitual)

(记)in(进入) + veter(老) + ate→变老了→积习已深的

同根词:veteran(老兵)

(例)Cats have an inveterate dislike of dogs.

invigorate [in'vigəreit] v. 使精力充沛,使活跃(to give new strength and vigor to sb. or sth.)
(记)in(使)+vigor(活力)+ate→使有活力→鼓励
(例)A quick breath of fresh air invigorated me and I went back to study for GMAT with more energy.

invoke [in'vəuk] vt. 祈求(神灵)保佑(to call on 〔God etc.〕 for blessing, help, inspiration, support);行使(法权等),实行(to resort or put into use 〔a law, ruling, penalty, etc.〕 as pertinent)
(记)in(进入)+voke(喊,唤)→唤起来→祈求
(例)to invoke an article of the U.N. charter(援引联合国宪章的条款)

irate [ai'reit] a. 发怒的,愤怒的,激怒的(very angry, mad, or upset)
(记)ira(生气,发怒)+te→发怒的,激怒的
(例)The irate teacher demanded to know who broke the window

irrational [i'ræʃənl] n. 无理数(a real number not expressible as an integer or as a quotient of two integers)
(记)ir(非,无)+rational(有理数)→无理数

irrelevant [i'relivənt] a. 不相关的(not relevant; having nothing to do with what is being discussed)
(记)ir(不)+relevant(相关)→不相关的
(例)It is rude to interrupt with irrelevant comments.

irritant ['iritənt] n. 刺激物(sb. or sth. that causes irritation or inflammation); a. 刺激的,引起发炎的(causing irritation or inflammation)
(记)ir+rit(刺激)+ant→刺激物
(例)Smoke is an irritant that causes my eyes to water.

Islamic [iz'læmik] a. 伊斯兰教的,穆斯林的(of the reli-

gion of Muslims)
(记)由 Islam(伊斯兰教)而来
(例)There are a few Islamic temples in Beijing.

isolation [ˌaisəˈleiʃən] n. 隔离,隔绝(keeping sb. or sth. away from other things or people)
(例)The prisoner was kept in isolation.

J

jacket [ˈdʒækit] n.(书籍的)护封,公文套,唱片套(a cover for a book or a record album)
(记)jacket 主要是套在…的东西,另如夹克
(例)The novel's plot is summarized on the inside of the book jacket.

jawbone [ˈdʒɔːbəun] n. 颚骨,牙床骨(the upper or lower bone that forms the mouth and supports the teeth)
(记)jaw(颚,颌)+bone(骨头)
(例)The suspect's face has a prominent lower jawbone.

jeopardize [ˈdʒepədaiz] v. 危及,危害(to endanger)
(记)jeopard(危险)+ize→使处于危险中→危及,危害;n. jeopardy
(例)Wear a life jacket. Don't jeopardize your safety.

jettison [ˈdʒetisn] v. 向外抛弃(to throw sth. overboard, esp. to make an aircraft or a ship lighter);n. 抛弃的货物(goods thrown overboard to lighten a ship, airplane, etc. in an emergency)
(记)来自 jet(喷出),分割记忆:jetti(扔)-son(儿子)→抛弃
(例)The pilot jettisoned the heavy cargo from the plane.

jolt [dʒəult] vt. 使颠簸，振摇(to shake up or jar, as with a bumpy ride or sharp blow)
(记)该词原先写作"jot"，为拟声词
(例)The old bus jolted us as it went over the stony road.

judicious [dʒu(:)ˊdiʃəs] a. 有判断力的，明智的([formal] showing or having good sense)
(记)judic(判断)+ious→有判断力的
(例)He got rich by making judicious investments.

jumbo [ˊdʒʌmbəu] n. 体大而笨拙的人；庞然大物；显赫的人(a very large person, animal, or thing)；a. 巨大的(extra large; larger than regular)
(记)本是一头大象的名字，代指"体大而笨拙的人"，或作形容词用时指"巨大的"
(例)I ordered jumbo shrimps at the seafood restaurant.

jurisdiction [dʒuərisˊdikʃən] n. 司法(权)；裁判权；管辖权，管辖(the legal authority of a judge or government official)
(记)juris(=jury，法律)+diction(措词)
(例)The city cop has no jurisdiction in the matter that happened outside the city limits.

juvenile [ˊdʒuːvənail] a. 青少年的(young or youthful)；幼稚的(immature or childish)
(记)juven(年青)+ile→年青的，少年的
同根词：rejuvenate(返老还童)
(例)His juvenile voice on the phone made people think that he is still a teenager.

juxtapose [ˊdʒʌkstəpəuz] v. 并排，并置(to put side by side or close together)
(记)juxta(接近)+pose(放)→并放，并排
(例)When two similar objects are juxtaposed, they

will show their differences distinctly.

K

Keynesian [ˊkeinziən] a.(英国经济学家)凯恩斯(Keynes)的;凯恩斯主义的(of or about the economic theories of Keynes and his followers)

kidnap [ˊkidnæp] v.绑架(to take sb. away by force, esp. in order to make a demand for sth.; to abduct sb.)
(记)联想:kid(小孩)+nap(小睡,疏忽)→趁小孩睡觉时抱走→绑架
(例)The criminal tried to kidnap the rich family's children.

kinetic [kəˊnetik] a. 运动的(of or resulting from motion)
(记)kinet(动)+ic→运动的
同根词:kinescope(显像管);kinematics(运动学)
(例)Through vigorous exercises, he developed his kinetic forces./human kinetics 人体运动学

kinship [ˊkinʃip] n.(家属或亲属)关系,类似家属的密切关系(family relationship; close connection)
(记)kin(亲属)+ship(性质,状态)→(家属或亲属)关系
(例)The woman said she could prove her kinship with the movie star.

knack [næk] n. 特殊能力(ability to do something easily; particular skill; dexterity);窍门(a clever expedient or way of doing something)
(记)knock 的变体,意为敲开脑袋→开窍
(例)Getting this box open requires special knack.

L

lactic [ˊlæktik] a. 乳汁的(of or obtained from milk)

(记)lact(乳)+ic→乳汁的
同根词:lactate(哺乳),lactogenic(催乳的)

landfill [ˈlændfil] n. 垃圾堆(a place where trash and other waste is dumped)
(记)land(地)+fill(满)→堆得满地的地方→垃圾堆
(例)I took the old refrigerator to the landfill.

larvae [ˈlɑːviː] n.(larva 的复数)幼虫,幼体(the first stage of the life of an insect after it leaves the egg)
(例)Most larvae look somewhat like worms.

latch [lætʃ] n. 闩,碰锁,弹簧锁(a lock for a door or window that can be locked and unlocked with a key);vt. 用闩把…闩上(to fasten or close with a latch)
(记)可以和 lock 一起记
(例)I shut the window and slid the latch into place. / I latched the front door before I went to bed.

lateral [ˈlætərəl] a. 边的(of or about the side of sth.)
(记)组合词如:bilateral(双边的),quadrilateral(四条边的)
(例)My lateral movement was restricted by the narrow walls of the passageway.

latitude [ˈlætitjuːd] n. 纬度(the distance north or south of the equator measured in degrees);自由(freedom)
(记)lati(阔)+tude→纬度
同根词:latifoliate(阔叶的)
(例)The South Pole is at latitude 90 degrees south.

laudable [ˈlɔːdəbl] a. 值得称赞的(worthy of praise; deserving praise or honor)
(记)laud 是动词,为"称赞"之意

(例) The company rewarded its workers with bonuses for their laudable efforts. / Your desire to help the poor is laudable.

laudatory [ˈlɔːdətəri] a. 赞扬的,表扬的(expressing praise; commendatory)

(记)比较该词与 laudable 的区别

(例) His laudatory words lifted the spirit of the tired soldiers.

laurel [ˈlɔrəl] n. 月桂树(a shrub with leaves that are a shiny green all year round); 光荣,荣誉(fame; honor)

参考:laureate(戴桂冠的,获奖者)

(例) I made a wreath out of laurel. / The older members of the team will have to look to their laurels when young people join.

lease [liːs] n. 租约,租期(a rental contract); v. 出租(to rent a property to sb.)

(记)分割记忆:l - ease(安心), 有了租约安心

(例)I signed a lease to rent a truck for a week. / My landlord leases apartment units to renters around the city.

leery [ˈliəri] a. 机警的,狡猾的(on one's guard; wary; suspicious)

(记)leer(斜眼看,睨视) + y→斜眼看的样子→狡猾的样子→机警的,狡猾的

(例)He was leery about making too many promises.

leeway [ˈliːwei] n. 余地(margin of time, money, etc.; room for freedom of action)

(记)lee(庇荫,背风处) + way→余地

(例)There isn't enough leeway to turn the piano to move it into the living room. / Teenagers should be given enough leeway to let them enjoy life, but not enough to let them get into trouble.

legislature [ˈledʒisleitʃə] n. 立法机关(the body of people who are elected or appointed to make laws)

(记)legis(法律)+lat(放)+ure→放出法律→立法

(例)The state legislature lowered the speed limit.

legitimacy [liˈdʒitiməsi] n. 合法性,正统性(the quality of being lawful or justified)

(记)legitim(合法)+acy→合法的

参考:legitimize(使合法,正式批准)

(例)The royal scandal has perhaps weakened the legitimacy of the monarchy.

legitimate [liˈdʒitimit] a. 合法的(sanctioned by law or custom, lawful);正当的(justifiable or justified)

(记)legitim(合法)+ate→合法的

(例)It was impossible for the illegal alien to find a legitimate job. / Illness is the only legitimate excuse for missing football practice.

lethal [ˈli:θəl] a. 致命的(causing death; fatal)

(记)leth(死,僵)+al→致死的

同根词:lethality(致死性);lethargy(昏睡)

(例)The farmer's wife died when she swallowed some lethal poison.

letup [ˈletʌp] n. 放松,停顿(a pause; a reduction in or stopping of an activity)

(记)let+up→站起来放松放松→放松,停顿

(例)There was no letup in the heavy rainfall all day. / We can only hope for a letup in the spoiled little girl's requests.

lever [ˈlevə] n.【物】杠杆(a bar of metal or wood, resting on a pivot, used to increase one's power in lift-

ing or moving heavy objects)
(记)比较 lever(杠杆)和 level(水平)
(例)I pushed down on the lever to lift the rock on the other end.

levy [ˈlevi] v./n. 征税,罚款(to impose or collect [a tax, tribute, fine, etc.]; an imposing and collecting of a tax or other payment);征兵(to enlist [troops] for military service, usually by force)
(记)lev(升起)+y→把税收起来→征税
(例)A strict levy was imposed on all imported goods. /The state legislature levied a tax on alcohol.

lexicographer [ˌleksiˈkɔgrəfə] n. 词典编纂人(a person who writes or complies a dictionary)
(记)lexico(词汇)+graph(写)+er→写词汇的人→词典编纂人
(例)The author of this book is an experienced lexicographer.

liability [ˌlaiəˈbiliti] n. 债务(the debts of a person or business);责任(the state of being bound or obliged)
(记)来自 lier(约束),lia+ble+ity→债务
(例)With sizable income rolling in from his stock investment, he has been able to discharge all his liabilities.

liken [ˈlaikən] vt. 把…比作;把…比拟(to)(to compare)
(记)like(像)+n→把…比作
(例)He likened the computer game to a real game for children.

limestone [ˈlaimstəun] n.【建】石灰石(rock made of calcium compounds used as a building material)
(记)lime(石灰)+stone(石头)→石灰石

(例)The lobby floor was done in limestone.

lingo [ˈliŋgəu] n. 外国话(贬义);行话;方言;隐语(strange or incomprehensible language or speech)

(记)ling(u)(语言)+o→外国话,行话

(例)If you want to be a good lawyer, you have to learn the lingo of the legal profession.

linguist [ˈliŋgwist] n. 语言学家(a person accomplished in languages, esp. one who speaks several languages)

(记)lingu(语言)+ist(人)→研究语言的人

(例)The former president of the university is a very famous linguist in our country.

linguistics [ˈliŋgwistiks] n. 语言学(the study of human speech including the units, nature, structure, and modification of language)

(记)lingu(语言)+istics(学科)→语言学

lionize [ˈlaiənaiz] v. 崇拜,看重(to treat as an object of great interest or importance)

(记)lion(狮子)+ize→看作狮子→崇拜

(例)The media have lionized a lousy singer who passed himself off as a great performer.

liquidation [ˌlikwiˈdeiʃən] n.(债务的)了结;(企业的)清理;资产的变现(the sale of assets; selling goods, stocks, bonds, real estate, etc.)

(记)来自 liquidate,liquid(清澈的)+ate→弄清澈→清除,清偿

(例)The court ordered the liquidation of the bankrupt firm.

liquidator [ˈlikwideitə] n. 清算人(a person, often a court appointed official, who divides up the assets of a failed business)

参考:liquidation

listless [ˈlistlis] a. 无精打采的(characterized by lack of

interest, energy or spirit)
(记)list(渴望) + less→无渴望的→没精打采的
(例)The listless dog slept under the tree. / I feel so listless. I think I need a nap.

litigant [ˈlitigənt] a.(人)在诉讼中的(being engaged in a lawsuit);n.诉讼当事人(one engaged in a lawsuit)
(记)litig(打官司) + ant→打官司的人→诉讼当事人

live [laiv] a. 实况(broadcast directly at the time of production)
(例)The major TV networks all broadcast live the unprecedented trial of the country's president.

livelihood [ˈlaivlihud] n.生活,生计(the way of earning a living; employment; the source of money needed for living)
(记)live(生活) + li + hood
(例)What do you do for your livelihood? / Being a private tutor was my livelihood when I was in college.

livestock [ˈlaivstɔk] n.(总称)家畜,牲畜(animals that are kept on a farm or ranch, usually for the production of food)
(记)live(活的) + stock(一群种畜;家畜)
(例)The farmer lost all of his livestock in the flood.

loaf [ləuf] vi.游荡,无所事事(to waste time)
(记)和 loiter(闲荡, 虚度, 徘徊),idle(不做事;闲置),dawdle(闲荡;懒散地工作)一起记;另外,loaf 还有"一条面包"的意思,如谚语曰:Half a loaf is better than none.(聊胜于无)
(例)I loafed all day Saturday.

lobbyist [ˈlɔbiist] n.游说立法者的人,说客(someone who

is paid to try to influence the vote of a lawmaker)
(记)lobby(大厅)+ist(人)→院外活动集团的成员
(例)The representative refused all gifts from lobbyists.

lobe [ləub] n.耳垂;(脑,肺,肝等的)叶;【植】裂片
(记)lob(叶)+e→叶状物
(例)a lobe of the brain/ lung/ liver(〔脑,肺,肝等的〕叶)

locale [ləu'kɑːl] n.(事情发生的)场所,地点(a location, esp. where a certain event happens)
(记)local(地方)+e→地点
同根词:locality(地点,地区);collocate(排列,组合)
(例)I visited the locale where my father had been born.

locomotion [ˌləukə'məuʃən] n.运动,移位(moving from one place to another; the ability to move from one place to another)
(记)loco(地方)+mot(动)+ion→从一地方动到另一地方→移位
(例)The biologist studied the locomotion of snakes.

longevity [lɔn'dʒeviti] n.长寿(a long life)
(记)long(长)+ev(时间)+ity→活得时间长→长寿
同根词:medieval(中世纪的);primeval(原始的)
(例)Longevity is a characteristic of my family. All my ancestors lived longer than 80 years.

loom [luːm] vi.赫然耸现,逼近(to appear in an impressively great or exaggerated form)
(记)loom 还有"织布机"之意

参考:loop(圈,环);loot(战利物);loon(愚人,懒人)
(例)A terrible thought loomed up in his mind.

lore [lɔː] n.知识(knowledge gained through study or experience);全部传说(legends and stories among a particular people or in a particular community)
(记)the lore of herbs(草木植物知识)
参考:folklore(民间传说)

luminescence [ˌluːmiˈnesns] n.【物】发冷光(the low temperature emission of light [as by a chemical or physiological process])
(记)lumin(光)+escence(状态,过程)→有光的样子→发冷光;联系记忆:其他以escence结尾的词如:convalescence(逐渐康复);fluorescence(荧光,荧光性)

luminosity [ˌluːmiˈnɔsiti] n.光明,光辉(the quality or state of emitting or reflecting usu. steady, suffused, or glowing light);发光体(sth. giving off light);【物】发光度(brightness)
(记)lumin(光)+osity→光明;发光体
(例)the luminosity curve(发光度曲线)

lunar [ˈluːnə] a.月球的,有关月球的(of or relating to the moon)
(记)lun(月亮)+ar→月亮的
(例)The astronauts brought back some lunar rocks to the earth.

lush [lʌʃ] a.草木茂盛的(covered with plants and thick vegetation);豪华的(luxurious; comfortable)
(记)本是个拟声词,形容草木长得茂盛,发出滋滋的声音
(例)The explorer walked through the lush jungle./I couldn't afford to stay at the lush hotel a

second night.

M

magnetic [mæg'netik] a. 磁的;有吸引力的(able to draw or attract iron or steel in the way that a magnet does)
(记)来自 magnet(吸铁石)+ic→磁的
(例)The magnetic attraction of the north pole is evident in the movement of the needle of a compass.

magnitude ['mægnitjuːd] n. 重要性([of sth.] importance);星球的光亮度(a degree of measurement of the brightness of a star)
(记)magn(大)+itude(状态)→大的状态→巨大,重大
(例)The president deals with problems of great magnitude. / Some stars have a variable magnitude and appear much brighter now and then.

maim [meim] vt. 使残废(to injure a part of the body so that it can no longer be used)
(记)和 main(主要的)一起记
(例)His hand was maimed by a piece of heavy machinery.

mainstream ['meinstriːm] n. 主流,主要倾向(a prevailing current or direction of activity or influence)
(记)main(主要的)+stream(流)→主流,主要倾向
(例)the mainstream of a river/ the mainstream of history

maize [meiz] n.【植】玉米(corn)
(记)maize 还可作形容词,"玉米色的,黄色的"
(例)a field planted with maize(一片种玉米的地)

maladaptive [ˊmæləˊdæptiv] a. 不适应的(marked by poor or inadequate adjustment)
(记)mal(坏)+adapt(适应)+ive→适应得差→不适应的
(例)The maladaptive tree grows only in the south of the country.

malady [ˊmælədi] n.疾病,弊病(a sickness; an illness)
(记)mal(坏)+ady(习惯)→不好的习惯引起疾病→疾病,弊病
(例)My frail neighbor suffers from an incurable malady.

malaria [məˊlɛəriə] n.疟疾(a parasitic disease carried by infected mosquitoes in tropical areas, causing chills and fever);潮湿的空气,瘴气(unwholesome or poisonous air, as from marshy ground; miasma)
(记)mala(坏)+aria(空气)→不好的空气→瘴气;疟疾
(例)The tourists took medication to protect themselves from malaria.

malfunction [ˊmælˊfʌŋʃən] v.失灵,发生故障(to fail to work properly);n.故障(a failure to work properly)
(记)mal(坏)+function(功能)→功能不好→故障
(例)When my computer malfunctioned, my term paper was deleted. / I used the stairs because of a malfunction with the elevator.

malpractice [ˊmælˊpræktis] n.不法行为,玩忽职守;治疗失当(injurious or unprofessional treatment or culpable neglect of a patient by a physician)
(记)mal(坏)+practice→实行得不好→不法行为,治疗不当

mammalian [mæˊmeiljən] a. 哺乳动物的,哺乳纲的(of mammals)

(记)mamma(乳房)+lian→哺乳动物的
参考:mammilla(乳头);mammalogy(哺乳动物学)

mandatory [ˈmændətəri] a. 强制的,命令的(obligatory; not optional; required)
(记)来自 mandate,mand(命令)+ate→命令
(例)Many primary schools have mandatory foreign language requirements.

maneuver [məˈnuːvə] v./n.(军队等)调遣,策略,操纵(to manage or plan skillfully or shrewdly; manipulate or scheme)
(记)man(手)+euvre→用手来做→操纵,调动
(例)At the last moment, the basketball player made a clever maneuver that allowed a goal to be made.

manipulate [məˈnipjuleit] vt. 操纵(to control or handle sth. with skill; to control or handle sb. or sth. for one's own benefit)
(记)来自 manipulate(熟练地操作,使用); manipul(用手做)
(例)The artist manipulates his painting brush deftly. / Anne manipulated the meeting to further her own agenda.

mannerism [ˈmænərizəm] n. 个人惯用的格调;(说话举止)癖性,习气(a gesture or movement of a certain person; a habit or trait of a certain person; a peculiarity of manner in behavior, speech, etc. that has become a habit)
(记)manner(方式)+ism→个人惯用的格调,癖性
(例)One of his mannerisms is raising his eyebrows. / The stranger's quick, jerky mannerisms frightened me.

manufacture [ˌmænjuˈfæktʃə] v. 生产(to make sth. in large

amounts in a factory or by using machine)
(记)manu(手)+facture(制作)→用手做→生产
(例)These shoes were manufactured in China.

margin [ˈmɑːdʒin] n.【商】成本与售价的差额,赚头(the difference between the cost and the selling price of goods produced, sold, etc.)
(记)margin通常是"边缘"之意→赚头
(例)Our company had very large profit margins this year.

marginal [ˈmɑːdʒinəl] a. 边上的(at an edge);勉强够格的(close to a limit, esp. a lower limit);很少的(slight; not much; not very important)
(记)来自margin(边缘)+al
(例)Marginal annotations made it easy to read the text. / a marginal standard of living / I only have a marginal interest in classical music.

marijuana [ˌmærəˈwɑːnə] n. 大麻(hemp);大麻中的毒质(dried hemp leaves and stems used as an illegal drug that is usually smoked)
(记)由人名组成的土族语言:Maria Juana, Mary Jane
(例)The police arrested the student for selling marijuana.

marine [məˈriːn] a. 海的,与海有关的(of or concerning the sea)
(记)mar(海)+ine(海的)
同根词:submarine(潜水艇);mariculture(水产养殖)
(例)The marine biologist studied lobsters and crabs.

marrow [ˈmærəu] n. 骨髓,精华(soft, fatty tissue inside bones)

(记)可以和 narrow(狭窄的)一起记
(例)The dog ate the marrow from the bone it was chewing on. / The cancer has spread to the patient's bone marrow.

martial [ˈmɑːʃəl] n. 军事的(of military life; military)
(记)Martial 罗马战神
(例)The army imposed martial law after overthrowing the government.

masculinity [ˌmæskjuˈliniti] n. 男性(气质)(the condition of being manly; maleness)
(记)masculin(男性的)+ity→男性(气质)
(例)The actor's subtle masculinity made him a popular star.

mask [mɑːsk] vt. 戴面具(to wear a covering that disguises the face);掩饰(to conceal sth.);伪装(to disguise)
(例)Your medicine has masked the symptoms of a serious disease. / The spy masked the message in a secret code.

mason [ˈmeisn] n. 石匠(someone who makes walls of stones or bricks for a living)
(记)另记住 masonry(石工技术)
(例)The mason completed the brick wall in only two days.

mass [mæs] n.【物】质量(the scientific term for the amount of matter in an object)
(记)mass 还有"群众"之意
(例)The astronomers examined a dense mass deep in the universe. / mass culture (大众文化)

maternal [məˈtəːnl] a. 母亲的(of or about mothers or motherhood);母方的,母系的(related through the mother's side of the family)

(记)mater(母亲)+nal→母亲的;母系的

(例)Her maternal instinct led her to check on her baby./That man is not my father's brother;he's my maternal uncle.

mature [mə'tjuə] v. 成熟(to become adult or grown up);到期([for a payment] to be due)

(例)The girls matured into a young woman. / These bonds will mature in 10 years.

maximum ['mæksiməm] n. 最大值(the highest amount or degree possible; the upper limit or boundary)

(记)maxim(大)+um→最大值

(例)I turned the volume on my stereo up to the maximum.

meander [mi'ændə] v. 蜿蜒曲折([of a stream]to take a winding or tortuous course);闲谈,漫步(to wander aimlessly or idly; ramble)

(记)来自 the Meander(米安德河),以其蜿蜒曲折而著名

measles ['mi:zlz] n.(单复数同)【医】麻疹(an easily spread disease common in children)

(记)measle(点)+s→麻疹

(例)The measles cause a high fever and a skin rash of small red dots.

mechanism ['mekənizəm] n. 机械装置(a machine; a moving part of a machine);机制(a system whose components work together like the parts of a machine)

(记)mechan(机械)+ism→机械装置,机制

(例)An automobile engine is a complicated mechanism./The television program detailed the mechanism of birth. / The mechanism of chewing is more complicated than it might seem.

median ['mi:djən] a. 中间的(middle; intermediate);n.

(三角形)中线(designating a line extending from a vertex of a triangle to the middle of the opposite side),中数(把数字按大小排列,中间一项为中数)

(记)medi(中间)+an→中间的或中间的数

(例) The report listed the median age of each state's population.

medieval [ˌmediˈiːvəl] a. 中世纪的,中古的(of or about the Middle Ages in Europe, from about 500 to about 1450)

(记)medi(中间)+ev(时代)+al→中世纪的,中古的

(例)Countless people died of the plague in medieval times.

medium [ˈmiːdjəm] a.中等的

(记)medi(中间)+um→中间的→中等的

(例)Her husband is a man of medium size./ medium blue

medium [ˈmiːdjəm] n.(常用复数 media)媒介(any means, agency, or instrumentality; a means of communication that reaches the general public and carries advertising)

(例)Language is the most important medium of communication./ The story has been widely reported in the mass media.

meek [miːk] a. 逆来顺受的,缺少勇气和胆量的(too submissive; easily imposed on; spineless; spiritless);适中的,柔和的(gentle or kind)

(记)和 submissive(顺从的),tame(没精打采的;顺从的),obedient(服从的,顺从的),mild(温和的,温柔的)一起记

(例)You're too meek. You need to stand up for

yourself. / The meek old man waited quietly in line.

megalithic [ˌmegəˈliθik] a. 巨石制的，有巨石特征的(made of, about, or characteristic of a huge stone)
(记)mega(巨大的) + lith(石) + ic→巨石的，巨石制的；n. megalith(巨石)

melancholy [ˈmelənkəli] a. 忧郁的，令人悲伤的(sad; unhappy)
(记)melan(黑色) + chol(=bile 胆汁) + y→胆汁发黑→忧郁的
(例)The melancholy song made me cry. / I tried to cheer up my melancholy friend.

membrane [ˈmembrein] n. 薄膜，细胞膜(a very thin layer found in plants and animals)
(记)分割记忆：membr 看作 member，brane 看作 brain(头脑)
(例)The biologist examined the membrane under a microscope.

memento [miˈmentəu] n. 纪念品(a souvenir; sth. that reminds one of sb. else or of a place that one has visited)
(记)mem(记忆) + ento→纪念品
同根词：memoir(传记，回忆录)；memorable(难忘的)
(例)My host gave me a small gift as memento of my trip to France. / He keeps this small lock of hair as a memento of his former girlfriend who died in an accident.

memoir [ˈmemwɑː] n. (复)回忆录，自传；传略(a written story about sth. that happened in one's life; a written recollection; a written remembrance)
(例) The former president wrote his memoirs

shortly before he died. / The actress's agent urged her to write her memoir.

merchant [ˈməːtʃənt] n. 商人(someone who buys and sells products in order to make money)

(例)My great grandfather was a grain merchant in the south of China.

metabolize [meˈtæbəlaiz] v. (使)产生代谢变化(to change by, or subject to, the chemical and physical processes continuously going on in living organisms and cells)

(记)meta(变化) + bol(= throw 扔) + ize→产生变化→使新陈代谢

metamorphose [metəˈmɔːfəuz] vt. 使变形,使变质(to change in form or nature;undergo change in character)

(记)meta(变化) + morph(形状) + ose→使变形,使变质

(例)The spoiled child metamorphosed into a responsible adult at the university.

meteorite [ˈmiːtjərait] n.【天】流星,陨石(a rock from space that did not completely burn up when it entered the atmosphere)

(记)meteor(流星) + ite→流星,陨石

(例)The meteorite was examined to see if it was radioactive.

meteorologist [ˌmiːtiəˈrɔlədʒist] n. 气象学家(one specializes in the science and study of the atmosphere and weather conditions)

(记)meteor(流星) + olog(学科) + ist(人)→气象学家

methodology [ˌmeθəˈdɔlədʒi] n. 方法论,方法学(the science or study of method);(某一学科的)一套方法(a system of methods, as in any particular science)

(记)method(方法)+ology(学科)→方法论,方法学

(例)Your results are wrong because your methodology was faulty. / The researcher explained her methodology at the conference.

metropolitan [ˌmetrəˈpɔlitən] a. 大都市的,都市生活的(urban; characteristic of a large or important city)

(记)metro(mother)+polit(城市)+an→大都市的

(例) The company was headquartered in a metropolitan business center.

migrant [ˈmaigrənt] n. 候鸟;移居者(a person or an animal that moves from place to place);农业季节工人(a farm laborer who moves from place to place to harvest seasonal crops)

(记)migr(移动)+ant→移动的人或物→移民

参考:immigrant(移入民);emigrant(移出)

(例)The migrants traveled from city to city. / The geese flying overhead are migrants. They fly south every winter.

milieu [ˈmiːljəː] n. 周围环境,社会环境,背景(environment, esp. social and cultural setting)

(记)mid(中间)+lieu(地方)→在一个地方之中

(例)A child's character is greatly influenced by his milieu.

millennia [miˈleniə] n.(millennium[miˈleniəm]的复数)一千年(a period of 1,000 years);千年纪念(the thousandth anniversary of sth.)

(记)mill(千)+ennium(年)→一千年,千年纪念

同根词:biennium(二年期间)

(例)The powerful kingdom lasted for over a millennium. / The ancient city celebrated its second millennium with a large parade.

mimic [ˈmimik] v. 模仿,效仿(to copy the way other people act or speak)

(记)mim(动作) + ic→模仿,效仿

(例)The comedian mimicked the president's voice.

mingle [ˈmiŋgl] v. 混合(to blend or mix)

(记)和同义词 blend 和 mix 一起记

(例)You must chill the sauce overnight so the flavors can mingle. / The dense smoke and dangerous fumes mingled in the air.

miniature [ˈminjətʃə] n. 小画像(a small painting, esp. a portrait); 缩样(a copy or model on a very small scale)

(记)mini(极小的) + ature→极小的画像等

同根词:minikin(娇小的动物或人);minimal(最小的)

(例)This model car is a miniature of a real one.

minimum [ˈminiməm] n. 最小值(the least amount or degree possible; the smallest amount or degree possible)

(记)mini(极小的) + mum→最小值

(例)At a minimum, you will be working 40 hours a week.

minus [ˈmainəs] prep. / a. 减(less; reduced by; decreased by)

(记)minu(小) + s→使…减小

(例)My weekly wage minus taxes is 500 yuan. / Five minus three is two.

minute [maiˈnjuːt] a. 微小的,极小的(very small)

(记)minu(小) + te→微小的,极小的

(例)There was a minute hair floating in my soup.

mishap [misˈhæp] n. 不幸,坏运气(an unlucky event or accident; bad luck; an unfortunate accident)

(记)mis(坏) + hap(运气)→运气不好

同根词:happiness(幸福)

(例)The fisherman drowned in a boating mishap.

missile [ˊmisail] n. 投射出的物体或武器(sth. that is thrown, shot or fired at a target);导弹(a rocket carrying bombs or weapons that can be shot at a target very far away)

(记)miss(发送)+ile(物体)→发送出去的东西→投射物

同根词:dismiss(开除,解散);emissary(使者,间谍)

(例)The principal banned all missiles at school. / Long-range missiles were aimed at the enemy's capital.

mite [mait] n. 极小量;小虫(tiny insects or other microscopic organisms)

(记)mite 原意"螨虫",词组:a mite on an elephant(大象身上一小虫),引申为"小量,一点点"

(例)The money offered a mite of comfort to the unlucky woman.

mitigate [ˊmitigeit] v. 减轻(to make or become milder, less severe, less rigorous, or less painful)

(记)miti(小,轻)+gate(=ag 做)→弄轻→减轻

(例)Nothing could mitigate her disappointment. / The criminal mitigated his punishment by cooperating with the police in their investigation.

mob [mɔb] v. 成群结队袭击,聚众生事([for a large group of people] to crowd around sb. or sth.)

(记)不要和 mop(拖把;拖地)相混

(例)Hundreds of fans mobbed the movie star. / The reporters mobbed the mayor after the press conference.

mobility [məuˊbiliti] n. 能动性(the ability to move)

(记)mobil(可以动的)+ity→能动性

(例)An electricity-powered wheelchair gave the disabled man increased mobility.

modest [ˈmɔdist] a.(希望,要求)有节制的,不过分的(not excessive; moderate; not large)

(记)mode(测量)+st→有限量的,有节制的→(希望,要求)有节制的,不过分的

(例)I live in a modest home in a middle-class neighborhood. / My family survives on a modest income.

modification [ˌmɔdifiˈkeiʃən] n.修正,改正(a slight change; an alternation; the act of changing sth.)

(记)来自 modify(修改)

(例)My boss accepted my proposal with some minor modifications.

modify [ˈmɔdifai] v.修改(to change or alter, esp. slightly or partially);缓和,减轻(to limit or reduce slightly; to moderate)

(记)mod(=mode 方式,时髦)+ify→使改变方式→修改

(例)Sensing anger in the audience, the politician quickly modified his statement.

mold [məuld] vt.用模子做,浇铸(to make or shape with a special hollow container);对…产生影响(to have a strong or important influence on public opinion, thought, etc.)

(记)比较记忆:cold(冷的); bold(大胆的); fold(折叠); gold(金子); hold(抓住);mold(模子)

(例)The sculptor molded a flowerpot out of clay.

molten [ˈməultən] a.熔融的,熔化的(melted, made into liquid)

(记)曾是古语中 melt 的过去分词,现用作形容词

(例)The center of the earth is molten rock.

momentous [məu'mentəs] a. 极重要的,严重的(very important, serious, significant)

(记)moment(时刻)+ous→刻不容缓的→重要的

(例)I celebrated the momentous occasion by giving a short speech.

monarch ['mɔnək] n. 君主,最高统治者(a king or a queen; the ruler of a monarchy)

(记)mon(单个)+arch(统治者)→个人统治→君主

(例)The evil prince killed the reigning monarch.

monitor ['mɔnitə] v. 监听,监控(to listen in on [a foreign broadcast, telephone conversation, etc.] as for gathering political or military information);追踪;检验(to watch or check on [a person or thing])

(记)monitor 作为"班长"讲大家都知道(虽然 class representative 更常用);计算机显示器也叫 monitor

(例)The police monitored the criminal's every move. / My supervisor closely monitored my experimentation in the lab.

monochrome ['mɔnəkrəum] n. 单色,单色照片(a painting, drawing, design or photograph in one color or shades of one color);a. 单色的(of or done in one color or shades of one color)

(记)mono(单一)+chrome(色)→单色;单色的

(例)The monitor for my computer used to be monochrome, but I have updated it into SVGA.

monopoly [mə'nɔpəli] n. 垄断,专利权(a business that is the only provider of a service or product)

(记)mono(单个)+poly(运用)→一个人用→垄断

同根词:employ(雇用);deploy(调度,部署)

(例) The government tries to make sure that no company develops a monopoly without its permission. / The breakup of monopoly resulted in lower prices.

monotonous [mə'nɔtənəs] a. 单调的,无聊的(unchanging in tone; staying on the same note; boring; tedious)
(记) mono(单个) + ton(声音) + ous → 一个声音的 → 单调的
(例) My professor's monotonous voice put me to sleep. / I quit my monotonous job after one year.

monsoon [mɔn'suːn] n. 季风,季雨,大风(the rainy season in South Asia)
(记)联想记忆:mon + soon(马上)→马上要到了→季风,季雨
(例) The monsoon caused flood in many Indian villages. / We left India before the monsoon began.

morale [mɔ'rɑːl] n. 士气,精神力量(confidence; the amount of confidence felt by a person or a group of people)
(记)和 moral(道德的)一起记
(例) The losing team's morale was low. / The soldiers sang songs to boost their morale.

morphine ['mɔːfiːn] n. 吗啡(a bitter, white or colorless narcotic alkaloid, derived from opium)
(记)汉语的"吗啡"为音译

mortality [mɔː'tæliti] n. 死亡率(the proportion of deaths to the population of a region, nation, etc.; death rate);失败率(the number or proportion that fail);人类(human beings collectively; mankind)
(记)mort(死) + ality→死亡率
(例) The scientists tried to slow the rate of mortality from cancer. / the mortality of the first-year

students

mortgage [ˈmɔːgidʒ] n. 抵押贷款，抵押证书(an agreement by which a borrower grants a lender the ownership of an asset in exchange for a loan of money)；v. 抵押(to use an asset to secure a loan)
(记)mort(死亡)+gage(抵押品)
(例)We had a party when we made the last payment on our home mortgage. / I mortgaged the house so my children could go to college.

mosaic [məuˈzeiik] n. 镶嵌，马赛克(a design made from many pieces of colored substances, esp. glass or stone)
(记)"马赛克"为音译
(例)The church window was a mosaic made of colored glass.

mosque [mɔsk] n. 清真寺(an Islamic building of worship)
(记)和"莫斯科"发音颇像
(例)There was a mosque at the center of the small Arab village.

mosquito [məsˈkiːtəu] n. 蚊子
(例)I became sick when I was bitten by an infected mosquito.

moth [mɔθ] n. 蛾
(例)Moths had eaten a hole in my sweater.

motion [ˈməuʃən] n. 提议，动议，尤指会议提案(a formal proposal that sth. be done, made during a meeting)
(记)mot(动)+ion→动议
(例)The council voted on the motion to cut taxes.

mound [maund] n. 土丘(a small hill or pile)
(记)和 ground 一起记：mound on the ground
(例)The dog made a mound of dirt when it dug up

a bone.

movement [ˈmuːvmənt] n.【音】乐章(a division of a symphony or other classical music work)

(记)movement 作为"运动"的意思大家都熟悉,但"乐章"一意不可忘

(例)The first movement of this symphony is better than the other two.

multiple [ˈmʌltipl] n.倍数(a number that can be divided by another number without a remainder);

(记)和 multiply(乘),multiplier(乘数),multiplicand(被乘数)一起记

(例)Twelve is a multiple of six.

multiply [ˈmʌltiplai] v.乘

(例)You have to multiply the length by the width to get the size of the area.

mundane [mʌnˈdein] a. 现世的,世俗的(of the world, esp., worldly, as distinguished from heavenly, spiritual, etc.)

(例)He resented returning to this kind of mundane routine. / nothing but a mundane businessman(不过是个俗气的商人)

municipal [mjuːˈnisipəl] a. 市政的(of, or having to do with a city, town, etc. or its local government);地方自治的(having self-government)

(记)muni(官方职责)+cipal→市政的

(例)The municipal workers went on strike today.

mural [ˈmjuərəl] a. 墙壁的;n.壁画(a picture or scene that is painted on the surface of a wall)

(记)mur(墙)+al→墙上的画→壁画

同根词:demur(反对);immure(监禁)

(例)The students painted a mural on the side of the school. / This mural depicts the first moon landing.

mutation [mjuː'teiʃən] n. 突变,变异(random and unpredictable genetic change)
(记)mut(变)+ation→变化
同根词:immutable(不可变的)
(例)The tomato's perfect shape was brought about by mutation. / Mutation can be caused by radiation.

mute [mjuːt] a. 沉默的(quiet; silent);n.【音】弱音器(devices used to soften or muffle the tone of an instrument)
(例)My roommate was mute as usual at the dinner table.

mutiny ['mjuːtini] n./v. 叛变,反抗(against)(revolt against, often by force to legitimate authorities; esp. rebellion of soldiers or sailors against their officers)
(记)mut(变化)+iny→叛变,反抗
(例)Mutiny is a poor way to show disagreement with the captain. / The unprepared soldiers mutinied rather than die in battle.

mutual ['mjuː tjuəl] a. 相互的(shared by two or more people);共同的(common to two or more people; known to two or more people)
(例)My friend and I have mutual respect for each other. / He and I share a lot of mutual interests, so we are together often.

myopic [mai'ɔpik] a. 近视的(unable to see far away; nearsighted);缺乏远见的(narrow-minded; not able to foresee situations)
(记)my(坏)+op(光,眼)+ic→眼病的→近视的
同根词:optometrist(验光师)

(例)I wear glasses because I'm myopic. / My myopic supervisor is not suited for management.

mystic [ˊmistik] a. 神秘的,神秘主义的(obscure and mysterious; unclear or confusing);n. 神秘主义者(someone who communicates with the spiritual world)

(记)myst(神秘)+ic→神秘的;神秘主义的

(例)The mystic writing on the wall could not be understood by anyone. / The mystic told me that she had a message from my dead grandmother.

mythological [ˌmiθəˊlɔdʒikl] a. 神话学的(of the science or study of myths);虚构的(imaginary, fictitious, or not based on facts or scientists)

(记)myth(神话)+olog(学科)+ical→神话的,神话学的

(例)The phoenix is a mythological bird.

N

nadir [ˊneidiə] n. 最低点(the lowest point)

(记)反义词:zenith(最高点)

(例)After he lost the election, his spirits sank to their nadir.

narcissistic [ˌnɑːsiˊsistik] a. 自我陶醉的,自恋的(loving oneself; excessively interested in one's own appearance, comfort, importance, abilities, etc.)

(记)来自 Narcissus, 希腊神话中的美少年,因爱恋自己水中的影子而淹死,化为水仙花

(例)The narcissistic girl has very few friends.

narrator [nəˊreitə] n. 讲述者,叙述者 (one who tells a story)

(记)narrat(讲述)+or→讲述者,叙述者

natal [ˊneitl]a. 出生的，诞生时的(connected with one's birth; dating from birth)
(记)nat(出生)+al→出生的
同根词：nativity(出生)；natural(自然的)
(例)natal day(生日)

NATO [ˊneitəu] North Atlantic Treaty Organization 北大西洋公约组织

naval [ˊneivəl] a. 海军的；船的(of or about a navy)
(记)nav(海军；船)+al→海军的；船的
(例)The port city was under enemy naval attack./a naval force(海军部队)

navigation [ˌnæviˊgeiʃən] n. 航行，航海，航空(the act or process of steering a ship, plane, or other vehicle in some direction)
(记)nav(航行)+igat(做)+ion→航行，航海，航空
(例)The accident at sea was blamed on the captain's poor navigation.

neologism [ni(ː)ˊɔlədʒizəm] n. 新字，新义(a new word or a new meaning for an established word)
(记)neo(新)+log(话语)+ism→新话语→新字
(例)After a few years abroad, I cannot really understand some of the neologisms now popular among Beijing residents.

neonate [ˊniːəneit] n. 出生婴儿(a newly-born infant during its first month of life)
(记)neo(新)+nate(出生)

neoorthodoxy [niːəˊɔːθədɔːks]n. 新正统教(20世纪强调宗教传统教规改革的新教运动)(a movement in 20th-century protestantism, stressing traditional doctrine of the Reformation in reaction to theological liberation)

(记)neo(新)+orthodoxy(正统)→新正统

neutral [ˈnjuːtrəl] a. 中间的,中立的(not aligned with either side in a war, conflict, or argument)
(记)neut(e)r(中性的,无性的)+al→中间的,中立的
(例)Switzerland remained neutral during World War II. / The conflict was resolved with the help of a neutral mediator.

neutrino [njuːˈtriːnəu] n. 中微子(any of three leptons having a mass approaching zero and no charge)
(记)neutri(中性的,无性的)+no→中微子

neutron star 【天】中子星

nexus [ˈneksəs] n. 联系,连结(a connection, tie, or link between individuals of a group, members of series, etc.)
(记)nex(=nect 连系)+us→连结
(例)There is only a cash nexus between the estranged brothers.

niche [nitʃ] n.(放艺术品等的)壁龛(a recess or hollow in a wall, as for a statue, bust, or vase);合适的位置(a place or position particularly suitable to the person or thing in it)
(例)I placed a small vase of flowers in the niche in the hallway. / She found her niche in radio broadcasting. / have a niche in the temple of fame (流芳百世)/ a niche market(特殊市场)

nickel [ˈnikl] n.【化】镍(a metallic element that does not rust easily);v. 把…镀镍(to plate with nickel)
(记)美国和加拿大的五分镍币也叫 nickel
(例)Nickel is often mixed with other metals to make them stronger.

nicotine [ˈnikətiːn] n. 尼古丁(a toxic substance found in tobacco)

(记)来自人名 Nicot，1560 年将烟草引入法国

(例)It's hard to stop smoking because nicotine is addictive.

nitrogen [ˈnaitridʒən] n.【化】氮(a gaseous element that is the main component of air)

(记)nitro(含氮的)+gen(产生)→氮

(例)Most fertilizers are very rich in nitrogen. / nitrogen oxide(氧化氮)

nomad [ˈnɔməd] n. 流浪者(any wanderer who has no fixed home)；游牧部落的人(a member of a tribe or people having no permanent home, but moving about constantly in search of food, pasture, etc.)

(记)分割记忆：no－mad→不疯也狂的人→流浪者

(例)The nomads stopped at an oasis in the desert.

nostalgia [nɔsˈtældʒiə] n. 怀旧之情(a longing for sth. far away or long ago or for former happy circumstances)；思乡病(a longing to go back to one's home；homesickness)

(记)nost(家)+alg(痛)+ia→想家病

参考：nostomania(怀乡狂)

(例)The old man remembered his college days with nostalgia.

notorious [nəuˈtɔːriəs] a. 臭名昭彰的(well known for sth. bad)

(记)not(知道)+orious(多的)→人所共知的→臭名昭著的

(例)He is a notorious liar.

nova [ˈnəuvə] n.【天】新星＝newstar(a type of variable star)

novelty [ˈnɔvəlti] n. 新奇(的事物)(the quality of being

new, original; sth. that is new, or original)
(记)novel(新的)+ty→新奇
(例)When I first started working here, I enjoyed the novelty of the job. / Seeing how other people live is a novelty that the children enjoyed.

novice [ˈnɔvis] n. 新手(someone who is new at a job or responsibility)
参考:neophyte(新手)
(例)I helped my boss train the novices.

noxious [ˈnɔkʃəs] a. 有害的,有毒的(harmful; poisonous);使道德败坏的,讨厌的(morally injurious; corrupting; unwholesome)
(记)nox(毒)+ious→有毒的
参考:nocuous(有害的)
(例)The rats were poisoned by noxious fumes.

nuance [nju(ː)ˈɑːns] n. 细微的差异(a subtle difference, usually in meaning)
(例)He doesn't understand the nuance between "childish" and "childlike".

nuclear [ˈnjuːkliə] a. 核心的,中心的(of or about the nucleus of an atom or the energy created by splitting or fusing the nuclei of atoms)
(记)nucle(核的)+ar→核心的,中心的
(例)nuclear weapons/ nuclear families

nucleon [ˈnjuːkliːɔn] n. 核子(neutron and the proton that are the fundamental particles making up the atomic nucleus)
(记)nucle(核的)+on→核子

nucleus [ˈnjuːkliəs] n.(复数为 nuclei)核,中心(a thing or part forming the center around which other things or parts are grouped or collected; core);【生】细胞核;【天】慧核;原子核

(记)nucle(核)+us→核

(例)The management problems stemmed from the nucleus of the company. / Energy is created by splitting an atom's nucleus.

null [nʌl] a. 无效的(without legal force;invalid),不存在的(amounting to naught, nil);n.零(zero)

(记)和 dull(迟钝的;无趣的)一起记

(例)At the end of the first inning(回合), our team's score was null. / The judge declared the law to be null and void.

numerator [ˈnjuːməreitə] n.分子(the number above the line in a fraction)

(记)numer(数)+ator 变化了产生新的数→分子,和 denominator(分母)一起记

(例)If a fraction's numerator is 0, then the fraction is equal to 0.

nutritious [njuːˈtriʃəs] a. 有营养的,富含营养的(very nourishing)

(记)nutri(营养)+tious→有营养的

(例)I ate a nutritious meal after exercising at the gym.

nylon [ˈnailən] n.【纺】尼龙(a very strong, stretchy, lightweight, synthetic fiber);尼龙制品(any of the materials made from nylon)

(记)注意读音和汉译并不一样

(例)My water-resistant tent is made from nylon.

O

oatmeal [ˈəutmiːl] n.燕麦片(crushed grains of a kind of cereal, usually eaten with milk and sugar);燕麦粥(a porridge made from such oats)

(记)oat(燕麦)+meal(餐)→燕麦粥

(例)Many westners eat oatmeal for breakfast.

obedience [ə'biːdjəns] n. 服从,顺从(the condition of being obeying or submissive)

(记)来自obey,obe(服从)+dience→服从的

(例)The unruly children showed no obedience to their parents.

obeisance [əu'beisəns] n. 鞠躬,敬礼(a gesture of respect or reverence, such as a bow)

(记)obei(=obey服从)+sance→服从的态度→鞠躬

(例)The Prime Minister made the traditional obeisance to the King.

obesity [əu'biːsiti] n. 肥胖(the state of being very fat, stout, or corpulent)

(记)来自obese(肥胖的),ob(完全)+ese(吃)→都吃了→肥胖

(例)Child obesity is now becoming a serious problem in China.

obituary [ə'bitjuəri] n. 讣告,讣闻(a notice of sb.'s death, as in a newspaper, usually with a brief biography); a. 报告死亡的(of or recording a death)

(记)obit(忌辰)+uary→告知死亡日期的→讣告;报告死亡的

(例)The newspaper printed the bishop's obituary the day after he died.

obligatory [ɔ'bligətəri] a. 强制性的,义务的(legally or morally binding; required)

(记)来自oblig(e)(强迫,迫使)+atory→迫使做的→强制性的,义务的

(例)Wearing seat belts while driving is obligatory in Canada.

obnoxious [əb'nɔkʃəs] a. 令人不愉快的，可憎的（very unpleasant; objectionable; offensive）
（记）ob（坏）+ nox（毒）+ ious→有毒的，令人不快的
（例）She ignored the obnoxious man and went into a store.

obscure [əb'skjuə] a. 模糊的（not clear or distinct; faint or undefined），晦涩的（lacking light; dim; dark; murky）；v. 隐藏（to conceal from view; hide），使…模糊（to darken; make dim）
（记）ob（离开）+ scure（跑）→跑掉→使…模糊
参考：scurry（急跑的）
（例）My classmate mumbled some obscure reason for being late. / The polluted air in Beijing obscures the stars at night.

obsess [əb'ses] vt. 迷住；使困窘，使烦扰（to haunt or trouble in mind, esp. to an abnormal degree; preoccupy greatly）
（记）ob + sess（= sit 坐）→坐着不走→迷住
（例）I am obsessed with keeping my apartment clean.

obsidian [ɔb'sidiən] n.【矿】黑岩（a hard volcanic glass）
（记）分割记忆：ob - si - dian

obsolescence [ˌɔbsə'lesns] n. 过时（the state of being in the process of becoming obsolete）
（记）来自 obsolete（废弃的），obsol（废弃）+ escence（开始…的）→开始被废弃→过时
（例）Technology has caused the obsolescence of many mechanical devices.

obtrusive [əb'tru:siv] a. 突出的（inclined to push out or thrush forward）；炫耀的（calling attention to itself in a displeasing way）

(记)来自 obtrude(突出),ob(向外)+trude(伸出)→向外伸→突出
(例)His obtrusive behavior is annoying.

obviate [ˈɔbvieit] v. 排除(困难)(to do away with or prevent by effective measures)
(记) ob(离开) + via(路) + ate → 使障碍离开道路 → 排除
同根词:viable(可行的,能活的)
(例)The culprit's confession obviated the need for a trial.

occupy [ˈɔkjupai] v. 占领;战胜(to take possession of, possess);忙于某事(to keep sb. busy by doing sth.)
(例)The war began after Iraq occupied Kuwait. / The manager occupied himself by preparing the monthly budget.

octagon [ˈɔktəgən] n. 八边形(a flat figure or shape with eight sides)
(记)octa(八)+gon(角)→八个角的→八边形
(例) Stop signs are made in the shape of an octagon.

odds [ɔdz] n. 机会,成败的可能性(the chance of gain or loss,success or failure);差异(difference or amount of difference)
(例)It makes no odds whether she comes or not.

odor [ˈəudə] n. 气味(a smell, whether pleasant or unpleasant; fragrance, stench, etc.)
(记)od(闻)+or→气味
(例)The odor of freshly baked apple pie came from the kitchen.

offset [ˈɔːfset] v. 抵销;补偿(to balance, complement, counteract, compensate for, etc.)

(记)off + set(放)→放掉→抵销

(例)She has to offset her husband's small salary by living economically. / Their wage increases would be offset by higher prices.

offshoot [ˈɔ(:)fʃuːt] n. 分枝;支脉,支流(anything that branches off, or derives from, a main source)

(记)off + shoot(急流)→流到一边→支脉,支流

(例)His work is an offshoot of an earlier project. / The cafe is an offshoot from the successful bakery.

off-the-shelf a. (货品)现成常备的;非定制的([commercial products] that are ready for use without modification)

(记)off-the-shelf→直接从货架上取下的→现成常备的;非定制的

(例)off-the-shelf instruments(现成仪表)

olfactory [ɔlˈfæktəri] a. 嗅觉的(of the sense of smell)

(记)ol(= smell 味) + fact(做) + ory→做出味道来→闻到→嗅觉的

(例)an olfactory experiment(嗅觉实验)

omen [ˈəumen] n. 征兆,预兆(a thing or happening supposed to foretell a future event, either good or evil; augury)

(例)Some people think black cats are an omen of bad luck. / Black rain clouds are an omen of heavy rainstorms.

omnipotent [ɔmˈnipətənt] a. 全能的;万能的(having unlimited power or authority; all-powerful)

(记)omni(全部) + potent(有力的)→全能的

同根词:omnifaceted(全面的);omnipresent(无所不在的)

(例)The omnipotent king killed his political enemies.

onset [ˊɔnset] n.攻击,袭击(an attack; assault);突然开始(a beginning; start)

(记)on+set(放)→放在…上→攻击,袭击

(例)You'd better take the tablets at the very onset of a cold. / I knew my sneezing was the onset of a major cold.

opaque [əuˊpeik] a.不透明的(not letting light pass through; not transparent or translucent);难懂的(hard to understand; obscure)

(记)来自 opacus(遮蔽阳光的),opa(不透明)+que

(例)The room was dark because all of the windows were opaque. / I couldn't understand my professor's opaque lecturer.

optical [ˊɔptikəl] a. 眼的,视觉的;光学的(connected with the sense of sight; visual; ocular)

(记)optic(眼的)+al→眼的,视觉的

(例)Mirages and hallucinations are optical illusions. / I was given an optical exam to determine my range of vision.

optimal [ˊɔptiməl] a. 最佳的(most favorable or desirable; best; optimum)

(记)optim(最好)+al→最佳的

(例)This is the optimal time for harvesting apples.

opulent [ˊɔpjulənt] a.富裕的(very wealthy or rich); 充足的(characterized by abundance or profusion; luxuriant)

(记)opul(财富)+ent→富裕的

(例)She wore an evening dress to the opulent dinner party. / The owner of the company owned two opulent houses.

orchestra [ˊɔːkistrə] n.管弦乐队(a group of musicians and

the instruments they play)
(例)He plays the violin in the city's orchestra.

ordinance [ˈɔːdinəns] n. 法令,条例(a local rule or regulation)
(记)ordin(命令) + ance;注意不要和 ordnance(大炮)相混
(例)Some cities now have ordinance against smoking in public places.

ordinate [ˈɔːdinit] n. 纵坐标(the vertical Cartesian coordinate on a plane, measured from the x-axis along a line parallel with the y-axis to point P)
(记)ord(顺序) + inate→使数在上面按顺序排列→纵坐标

ore [ɔː] n. 矿,矿砂,矿石(any natural combination of minerals, esp. one from which a metal or metals can be profitably extracted)
(记)就比 or 多一个字母 e
(例)The prospector studied the ore, looking for gold. / ore body(矿体)

orientation [ɔːrienˈteiʃən] n. 定向(the position or direction that someone or sth. is in; the way that sb. or sth. is positioned)
(记)来自 orient(v. 确定方向),ori(升起) + ent→依(太阳)升起确定方向→定向
(例)That street has a north-south orientation. / The company's business strategy has no clear orientation.

orthodox [ˈɔːθədɔks] a. 正统的,正派的(having the usual, customary or accepted beliefs and attributes; traditional and usual)
(记)ortho(正) + dox(观点)→正统观点的
同根词: heterodox(异端邪说的), paradox(矛盾的)

(例)Mary is very modern and liberal, but John is more orthodox in his behavior.

ostensible [ɔs'tensəbl] a. 表面上的;伪装的(apparent, seeming or pretended)

(记)ostens(显现)+ible→显现出来的→表面上的

(例)His ostensible reason for quitting smoking is his health, but the real reason is he can't afford it.

ostentation [ɔsten'teiʃən] n. 夸示,炫耀(showy display, as of wealth, knowledge, etc.; pretentiousness)

(记)ostent(显现)+ation→显现出来→炫耀

(例)the ostentation of a rich man(富人的摆阔)

oust [aust] v. 驱逐,放逐(to force or drive out; expel, dispossess)

(记)out 本身就表示"出来",把"s"从"out"中"驱逐,放逐"

(例)The city council ousted the crooked mayor. / The landlord ousted the tenant who never paid rent.

outdated [aut'deitid] a. 过时的(no longer current or popular;antiquated)

(记)out(超过)+date(日期)+d→过了日期的→过时的

(例)The children made fun of the old woman's outdated clothing. / Our outdated computer works very slowly.

outdistance ['autdistəns] vt.(指赛跑或竞争中)把…远远抛在后面;大大超越(to leave behind or get ahead of, as in a race)

(记)out(超过)+distance(距离)→超过一段距离→把…远远抛在后面;大大超越

(例)You outdistanced me because you left an hour before I did.

outfield [ˊautfi:ld] n.(棒球或垒球等)外场(the playing area of a baseball field beyond the infield)
(记)和 infield(内场)一起记

outgrowth [ˊautgrəuθ] n.长出,派生出(the act of growing out);旁枝;支派(that which grows out; offshoot or excrescence);副产品;结果(a result; consequence; development)
(记)out(超出)+growth(生长)→长出来了→长出,派生出
(例)a woody outgrowth on a tree trunk / Inflation is an outgrowth of war. / He sees teaching as an outgrowth of his poetry-writing.

outlay [ˊautlei] n.支出,费用(a spending [of money, energy, etc.])
(记)out+lay(放)→放出来的→支出,费用
(例)The state expended a huge outlay of money on the new stadium. / During the war, the outlay of energy and resources was rationed.

outlet [ˊautlet] n.(河流等)出口(a steam, river, etc. that flows out from a lake);通风口(a passage or vent for letting sth. out);发泄(感情或精力)的方法(a means of expression);销路(a market for goods)
(记)out+let(让)→出口;发泄
(例)A chimney is an outlet for smoke from a fireplace. / an outlet for the emotions / Boxing is an outlet for his aggressiveness.

outmoded [autˊməudid] a.(式样等)过时了的,废弃了的(no longer in fashion or accepted; obsolete)
(记)out(出)+mode(时髦)+d→不再时髦的
(例)I wish we could get rid of that old, outmoded sofa and buy a new, stylish one.

outmost [ˈautməust] a. 最外面的,远离中心的(most remote; outermost)
(记)out(外面)+most(最)→最外面的,远离中心的
(例)The Pluto(冥王星) is the outmost planet in the solar system.

outnumber [autˈnʌmbə] vt.在数量上超过(to exceed in number)
(记)out(超过)+number(数量)→在数量上超过
(例)Our army outnumbered the enemy's meager troops. / The winning votes outnumbered the losing ones by a 2-1 margin.

outpatient [ˈautpeiʃənt] n.门诊病人(a patient who is treated at a hospital, clinic, etc. and leaves without becoming an inpatient)
(记)和 inpatient(住院病人)一起记
(例)The woman with a minor infection was treated as an outpatient. / an outpatient department(门诊部)

output [ˈautput] n.产量(the amount of sth. that is made or produced; production);输出功率(the useful voltage, current, or power delivered by amplifiers, generators, receivers, etc. or by a circuit)
(记)out+put(放)→往外放的→产量;输出功率
(例)the annul output of steel

outrageous [autˈreidʒəs] a.无礼的,蛮横的(shocking; insulting; causing great danger or indignation)
(记)来自 outrage(n.残暴,暴行),out(出)+rage(狂怒,狂暴)→过分狂暴→暴行
(例)The mayor apologized for his outrageous remarks.

outright [ˈautrait] a. 直率的,无保留的(direct);彻底的,

全部的(complete)
(记)out + right(直接)→直接出来→直率的，无保留的
(例)The witness accused the defendant of being an outright liar.

oval [ˊəuvəl] a. 卵形的(having the form of an egg; ellipsoid)
(记)美国总统经常在白宫的 the oval office(椭圆办公室)发布消息
(例)That planet's move follows an oval orbit. / I served the fish on an oval platter.

ovarian [əuˊvεəriən] a.【解】卵巢的(of the female reproductive gland producing eggs and, in vertebrates, sex hormones)
(记)来自 ovary(卵巢)，ovari(卵巢) + an→卵巢的

overarch [əuvəˊɑːtʃ] vt. 在…上方成拱形(to form an arch over〔sth.〕)
(记)over + arch(拱形)→在…上方成拱形
(例)The street was overarched by elm trees.(街道两旁榆树成荫。)/ the stones that overarch the ditch

overextend [əuvərikˊstend] vt. 使伸延过长，过分扩张；使承担过多义务；使冒过多风险(to extend beyond reasonable limits or beyond one's capacity to meet obligations or commitments)
(记)over + extend(延伸)→过分延伸→使承担过多义务
(例)We pulled back from positions of weakness where we were overextended.(我们从战线拉得过长的薄弱阵地上撤回来。)

overlie [ˊəuvəˊlai] vt. 躺在…上面；压在…上面(to lie on or over)；盖得使窒息(to stifle or smother by lying on)

(记)over + lie(躺)→在…上面躺/压得过分要窒息

(例)sows that overlie one's piglets(压死自己生养的小猪的母猪)

overlord [ˈəuvəlɔːd] n.最高领主(a lord ranking above other lords, esp. in the feudal system)

(记)over + lord(领主)→领主上的领主→最高领主

overrefine [əuvəriˈfain] vt.对…做过分的精炼;过分优雅(refine too much)

(记)over(过分) + refine(精炼)

overriding [əuvəˈraiːdiŋ] a. 最重要的(the most important)

(记)over + rid(骑) + ing→骑在一切上的→最重要的

(例)an overriding concern / an overriding need

overrun [əuvəˈrʌn] vt.溢出,泛滥(to overflow);(侵略军)横行(to run over or beyond certain limits)

(记)over + run→跑出来了→溢出/(侵略军)横行

(例)During the flood season, the river overruns its banks for several miles. / The invading army overran a few scattered guerrilla outposts.(入侵军占领了游击队若干分散的前哨阵地。)

overt [əuˈvəːt] a. 公开的,非秘密的(not hidden; open; observable; apparent; manifest)

(记)o(出) + vert(转)→转出来→公开的

参考:covert(秘密的)

(例)Some overt displays of affections are inappropriate in public.

overtone [ˈəuvətəun] n.【音】泛音;弦外之音,暗示(an implication; nuance)

(记)over + tone(音调)→多出来的音→暗示

(例)a reply full of overtones(话里有话的回答)

overuse [ˈəuvəˈjuːz] vt.把…使用过度;把…使用过久(to use too much or too often)

(记)over + use→用得过多→把…使用过度

(例)Don't overuse this kind of medication. It may be dangerous to your health.

overweening [ˈəuvəˈwiːniŋ] a. 自负的,过于自信的(arrogant; excessively proud)

(记)over(过分) + ween(想象,得意) + ing→过分想象自己的伟大

(例)an overweening attitude

oxide [ˈɔksaid] n.氧化物(a binary compound of oxygen with some other element or with a radical)

(记)oxidize(v. 氧化,生锈),hydroxide(氢氧化物),carbon dioxide(二氧化碳),nitrogen oxide(氮氧化物),monoxide(一氧化物)

ozone [ˈəuzəun] n.臭氧

(例)Ozone in the upper atmosphere absorbs ultraviolet rays.

P

pagination [pædʒiˈneiʃən] n.标记页数(the act of numbering the pages of a book, etc.);页码(page)

(记)pag(页) + ination→标页

(例)The pagination is wrong. There's no page 21.

painstaking [ˈpeinzteikiŋ] a. 苦干的,辛勤的;费力的(take pains; very careful; diligent);刻苦的;极小心的(characteristic of great care)

(记)pains(劳苦) + taking(接受)→苦干的,辛勤的

(例)The artist copied the painting with painstaking accuracy. / The diners gave the waitress a large tip for her painstaking service.

pair [pεə] vi. 合作,配合(to form a pair; match);vt. 组成对,把人(或物)组成对(form a pair of 〔two persons or things〕 by matching, joining, mating, etc.)

(记)pair 作名词用时是一对的意思,作动词也是组成对之意

(例)I paired the socks together. / The dance instructor paired the two remaining students.

palatable [ˈpælətəbl] a. 美味的,愉快的(being pleasant or acceptable to the taste;tasty)

(记)来自 palat(e)(上腭,爱好)+able→好吃的; n. palatability

(例)This soup isn't excellent, but it's palatable.

paleolithic [pæliəˈliθik] a. 旧石器时代的(of an Old World cultural period characterized by the use of flint, stone, and bone tools)

(记)paleo(古)+lith(石头)+ic→旧石器的

参考:neolithic(新石器时代的)

pallid [ˈpælid] a. 苍白的,没血色的(faint in color; pale; wan)

(记)pall(=pale 苍白)+id→苍白的,没血色的

(例)The sick woman covered her pallid skin with makeup. / People who work by night and sleep by day often look pallid.

palm [pɑːm] n. 手掌,手心(the inner part or surface of the hand between the fingers and wrist);棕榈(树/叶)(a tropical tree);胜利(victory; triumph)

(记)这儿的"胜利"一意是由"棕榈叶"而来的

(例)I placed my ticket in the palm of the usher's hand. / Coconuts grow on palms. / She carried off the palm by sheer perseverance.(她全靠坚韧不拔才取得了胜利。)

paltry [ˊpɔːltri] a. 无价值的,微不足道的(practically worthless; trifling; insignificant; contemptible; petty)

(记)分割记忆:pal = pale - try(努力)→白努力

(例)The rich old man willed his family only a paltry sum of money. / The diner's paltry tip was an insult to the waiter.

pamphlet [ˊpæmflit] n.小册子(a small, thin, unbound book made up of sheets of paper stapled or stitched together and usually having a paper cover)

(记)来自拉丁文 pamphilus,是一首爱情名诗;pam = pan(全部),phil(爱) + us→表达爱情

(例)The charity's goals are described in this pamphlet.

panacea [pænəˊsiə] n.万灵药(a supposed remedy, cure or medicine for all diseases or ills; cure-all)

(记)pan(全部) + acea(治疗)→灵丹妙药

(例)The medicine was promoted as a panacea for all ashes and pains.

panel [ˊpænl] n.专门小组;讨论小组(a group of people who are selected to talk about sth. or judge sb. or sth.);仪表板(a surface that has controls, gauges, or instruments on it, used to control and monitor sth.)

(记)pan 本身就有"面板"之意,加上"el"还是板;需特别注意"专门小组"一意

(例)A panel of experts discussed the epidemic on the news program. / The pilot flipped a few switches on the control panel.

pang [pæŋ] n.剧痛;痛苦(a sudden, sharp, and brief

pain, physical or emotional; spasm of distress)
(记)bang(重击)一下就造成了 pang;不过,pang 更常指精神情感上的痛苦
(例)After working all morning without eating, I felt pangs of hunger. / Pangs of guilt caused me to confess what I had done.

paperwork [ˈpeipəwəːk] n. 日常文书工作(the keeping of records, filing of reports, etc.)
(记)paper(文件) + work→整理文件的工作→日常文书工作
(例)She thinks her job is boring because all she does is paperwork.

paradigm [ˈpærədaim] n. 范例,示范(a pattern, example or model)
(记) para (旁边) + digm (显示) → 显示给旁边的看 → 榜样,示范
(例)This episode may serve as a paradigm of industry's problems.(这一插曲可以称作工业界各种问题的典型例子。)

parallel lines [ˈpærəlelˈlainz]平行线

parallel [ˈpærəlel] a. 平行的(extending in the same direction so as never to meet, as lines, planes, etc.);类似的(closely similar or corresponding, as in purpose, tendency, time or essential parts)
(记) para (旁) + allel (另一个) → 总在另一个旁边→平行
(例) A pair of parallel lines will never meet. / When I was in a parallel situation, I called the police.

paramount [ˈpærəmaunt] a. 最高权力的,决定性的(ranking higher than any other, as in power or importance; supreme)

(记)para(超过) + mount(登上)→登上并超过→最重要的

(例)Cutting waste was a paramount goal in the senator's tax plan. / For the mayor, crime is an issue of paramount importance.

paranormal [pærəˈnɔːməl] a. 超自然的,异常的(phenomena outside the range of the normal)

(记)para(超过) + normal(正常的)→异常的,超自然的

(例)paranormal phenomena(超自然现象)

paraphrase [ˈpærəfreiz] n. 释义,意译(a rewording of the meaning expressed in sth. spoken or written);vt. 将…释义(to express in a rewording of the meaning expressed in sth. spoken or written)

(记)para(旁边) + phrase(措词)→旁边的措辞→释义,意译

(例)The newspaper's paraphrase of the senator's speech was misleading. / Could you paraphrase your question? I don't understand you.

parapsychology [pærəsaiˈkɔlədʒi] n.【心】灵学(the branch of psychology that investigates psychic phenomena)

(记)para(旁边) + psychology(心理学)→心理学旁边的学问→灵学

parasite [ˈpærəsait] n. 寄生虫;食客

(记)para(旁边) + site(食物)→在…旁边攫取食物→寄生虫

(例)The sick cow was infested with parasites. / Her husband had become a real parasite and did nothing to share the cost of food or rent.

pare [pɛə] vt. 削(果)皮;剪;修(to cut or trim away [the rind, skin, covering, rough surface, etc.] of [anything]; peel);逐渐消减(reduce or diminish

〔costs, etc.〕gradually)

(记)pare 按词源来说是"准备"的意思,削果皮就是准备吃吧;不要混淆 pare 和 pair(一对)

(例)The cook pared the pears before cutting them up for the fruit salad. / The school board pared down the budget by 5%. / My work load was pared when my boss hired another worker.

parenthetical [ˌpærənˈθetikəl] a. 作为插入语的(of or having the nature of a parenthesis);放在括号里的(placed within parentheses)

(记)来自 parenthesis(插入语),分割记忆:parent(父,母) - thesis(论文),源自 paren(= para) - thesis(放)→放在旁边的话→插入语

(例)John, who is usually an excellent public speaker, made so many parenthetical remarks that I could hardly follow his thoughts.

parish [ˈpæriʃ] n. 教区(an administrative district of various churches);教区全体居民(the members of the congregation of any church)

(记)比较 perish(死亡)和 parish(教区,教区全体居民)

(例)The new priest introduced himself to each family in the parish.

parochial [pəˈrəukjəl] a. 教区的(of or in a parish or parishes);思想狭隘的(restricted to a small area or scope; narrow; limited; provincial)

(记)来自 parish(教区)

(例)The parochial school doesn't hold classes on religious holidays. / The people of the small town were very parochial in their interests.

parole [pəˈrəul] n. 特别口令(a special password used only by certain authorized persons);假释(the release of

a prisoner whose sentence has not expired, on condition of future good behavior)
(记)联想记忆:pa(particular)(特别的)+role(角色)→特别的角色→假释
(例)His parole does not permit him to leave the state, carry a weapon, use drugs or commit a crime.

particular [pə'tikjulə] n. 细节(a detail; item of information; point);(复)详细情况(specific details about sth.)
(记)particular 作形容词用时表示"特殊的,特别的",和 particle(微粒)同词源,所以作名词用时可指细节
(例)My boss stressed the important particulars of the project. / What are the particulars of your request?

particulate [pə'tikjulit] n. 微粒,粒子(a very minute particle);a. 微粒的(consisting of very small, separate particles)
(记)来自 particle(微粒)

partisan [pɑːti'zæn] n. 党派支持者(someone who supports a political party);a. 有(政治)偏见的(strongly supporting a political party)
(记)party(党)+san(人)→党人,信徒,党的支持者
(例)Since he is a partisan, you know exactly what his opinion will be.

pass [pɑːs] n. 飞机或人造卫星等的一次掠过(a flight over a specified point or at a target)
(记)此意少见,但好理解

passbook ['pæsbuk] n. 存折(bankbook)
(记)pass(通过)+book(账簿)→让通过去拿钱的东西→存折

(例)The teller stamped my passbook every time I made a deposit. / We use electronic banking and therefore do not have a passbook.

pasta [peist] n. 意大利面食

(记)谐音:怕死它,很多人不习惯意大利人喜爱的面食,所以 pasta(怕死它)

(例)Spaghetti is a long, thin type of pasta.

pasture [ˈpɑːstʃə] n. 牧场,牧草(a field of grass, esp. one where animals graze);v. 放牧(to put 〔cattle, etc.〕 out to graze in a pasture)

(例)Sheep are grazing in the pasture.

patent [ˈpeitənt] a. 显而易见的(obvious; plain; evident);n. 专利权(证书)(the exclusive right, registered with the government, to exploit the ownership of an invention)

(记)pat(公开)+ent→公开的→显然的

参考:patency(明白,开放)

(例)a patent lie / The inventor held the patents on dozens of devices.

paternalism [pəˈtəːnlizəm] n. 家长式统治,家长作风;家长主义(the principle or system of controlling like a father)

(记)来自 paternal 父亲的

(例)a philosophy flavored with paternalism

pathogenic [pæθəˈdʒenik] a.【医】病原的,致病的,发病的(able to cause disease)

(记)path(病)+gen(产生)+ic→病原的,致病的

(例)A scientist found two new pathogenic bacteria. / The researcher found a vaccine for the pathogenic virus.

pathology [pəˈθɔlədʒi] n. 病理学(the branch of medicine that deals with the nature of disease, esp. with the

structural and functional changes caused by disease)
(记)path(病)+ology(学科)→病理学
(例)internal pathology(内科病理学)

patron [ˈpeitrən] n. 赞助者;顾客(a benefactor; someone who gives money to an institution or an organization)
(例)The patron of the museum donated a large sum of money for the art exhibition. / The store informed all of its regular patrons of the upcoming sale.

patronage [ˈpeitrənidʒ] n. 赞助,惠顾(the business provided [to a store] by a customer)
(记)patron(赞助人)+age→赞助
(例)The store manager thanked the loyal customers for their patronage.

patronize [ˈpeitrənaiz] v. 赞助;光顾(to be a regular customer of a store, restaurant, hotel or other business)
(记)patron(赞助人)+ize→赞助;光顾
(例)Customers prefer to patronize stores that provide good service.

peak [piːk] n. 山峰,顶峰(the top of a mountain);v. 憔悴,消瘦(to become thin and drawn or weak and wan, as from illness)
(记)peak 作为"山峰"一意大家都熟悉
(例)The explorer climbed to the peak of the mountain. / peak and pine(变得消瘦憔悴)

pecuniary [piˈkjuːnjəri] a. 金钱上的,金钱的(of or involving money)
(记)pecuni(钱财)+ary
(例)Under Louis XVI, the pecuniary situation of

France became more and more serious. / Mr Lu received some pecuniary compensation for the loss he sustained in the accident.

pedagogical [pedəˊgɔdʒikəl] a. 教育的,教学法的(of or characteristic of teachers or of teaching)

(记)来自 pedagogy,ped(儿童)+agog(引导)+y →引导儿童之学→教学

同根词:demagogue(煽动者)

(例)pedagogical techniques(教学技巧)

pedantic [piˊdæntik] a. 迂腐的,呆的(of or about a person who puts unnecessary stress on minor or trivial points of learning)

(记)pedant(书呆子)+ic→引申为受过教育的人的样子→书呆子样,迂腐的

(例)Pedantic as it may sound, the word choices he emphasizes is by no means irrelevant or superfluous.

peddler [ˊpedlə] n. 小贩(a person who goes from place to place selling small articles)

(记)ped(篮子)+dler→拎着篮子到处卖→小贩

(例)I didn't open the door when the peddler came to my house.

pedestrian [piˊdestriən] n. 行人(one who goes on foot; walker);a. 缺乏想象力的(lacking interest or imagination; prosaic; ordinary and dull)

(记)ped(脚)+estrian→用脚走的→徒步的

(例)Drivers must stop for pedestrians who are in the street. / This novel has a rather pedestrian plot, involving love, marriage, and life in a small village.

peer [piə] n. 同等之人,同辈(a person or thing of the same rank, value, quality, ability); v. 仔细看(to look closely)

(例)Bill calls most of his peers by their first names. / The doctor peered at the patient's x-rays for over a minute.

pelvis ['pelvis] n. 骨盆(the hip bones and the bottom of the backbone)

(记)pel(容器)+vis→骨盆

(例)Men's and women's pelvises are shaped differently.

penalty ['penlti] n. 处罚(a punishment for breaking a rule or law);罚款(a fine or forfeit);(行为等造成的)困难,障碍(the disadvantage, suffering, handicap, etc. imposed upon an offender)

(记)penal(惩罚)+ty→惩罚

(例)In this city, the penalty for speeding is a $50 fine.

pendant ['pendənt] a. 吊着的,悬挂的(hanging; suspended; overhanging; undecided; pending)

(记)pend(挂)+ant→挂着的,吊着的;与 pendent(悬而未决的)不同

(例)a pendant lamp(吊灯)

penetrate ['penətreit] v. 刺穿,渗入(to make a way into or through sth.; pierce);了解(to gain insight into something)

(记)pen(全部)+etr(=enter 进入)+ate→全部进入→刺穿

(例)The bullets penetrated the wall. / His research penetrated into the essence of the complicated matter.

peninsula [pə'ninsjulə] n. 半岛(a land area almost entirely surrounded by water and connected with the mainland by an isthmus)

(记)pen(几乎)+insula(小岛)→几乎是个小岛→半岛

(例)The tourist traveled all over the Italian peninsula.

penitence [ˈpenətəns] n.后悔;忏悔(the state of being truly sorry for having sinned or done other wrongs and willing to atone; repentance)

(记)与 penitentiary(感化、悔改的地方即监狱)一起记

(例)The thief expressed penitence for all his past actions.

penitentiary [peniˈtenʃəri] n.监狱,感化院(a prison for persons convicted of serious crimes)

(记)penitent(后悔)+iary→让人感化的地方→监狱,教养所

(例)The criminal was sentenced to the penitentiary for 20 years. / The lawyer went to the penitentiary to speak to his client.

penny-pinch [ˈpeniˈpintʃ] vt.对…吝啬(to be extremely frugal or stingy)

(记)pinch(捏),花每个 penny(美分/便士)都要捏一下→吝啬

pension [ˈpenʃən] n.养老金,退休金(money that is paid to a former employee, from retirement until death)

(例)The city raised taxes to maintain its employee's pensions.

pentagon [ˈpentəgən] n.五边形(a geometric figure having five sides)

(记)penta(五)+gon(角)→五个角的多边形→五边形;美国的五角大楼也叫 pentagon

(例)The sum of the interior angles of a pentagon equals 540 degrees.

per capita [pə'kæpitə] ad. 每人(for each person)
(记)per(每)+capita(头,脑袋)→按头来计算→每人
(例)The amount of energy used per capita has increased greatly. / per capita income

perceive [pə'siːv] v. 察觉,发觉(to be aware of sb. or sth. with one's mind)
(记)per(全部)+ceive(拿住)→全部拿住→发觉
同根词:conceive(设计,想象)
(例)The eyes perceive color and the ears perceive sound.

perception [pə'sepʃən] n. 察觉,发觉(the ability to see, hear, taste, touch or smell)
(记)由 perceive 而来
(例)The blind man's perception of sound was very precise.

perennial [pə'renjəl] a. 终年的;永久的(〔of a plant〕 living for two or more years)
(记)per+enn(年)+ial→一年到头的→永久的
(例)I prefer perennial plants to those that last only a single year.

perfunctory [pə'fʌŋktəri] a. 草率的,敷衍的(done without interest or care)
(记)per(表面)+funct(做)+ory→表面做→马马虎虎的
(例)Whoever was supposed to clean this room did a very perfunctory job.

perimeter [pə'remitə] n. 周长(the entire outside edge of sth.; the length of the outside edge of sth.)
(记)peri(周围)+meter(测量)→周长
(例)Guards watched the perimeter of the prison yard.

periodicity [piriə'disiti] n. 周期性,周期数,间发性(the tendency, quality or fact of recurring at regular intervals)

(记)period(周期)+icity→周期性

peripheral [pə'rifərəl] a. 不重要的(not as important as other things; incidental);外围的(at the distant border or edge of sth.; not in the center)

(记)来自下面的 periphery 一词

(例)The city's transit system even reached several neighborhoods in peripheral parts of the county. / The extensive report also addressed peripheral concerns.

periphery [pə'rifəri] n. 外围(a boundary line, esp. that of a rounded figure; perimeter);不重要的部分(parts or aspects that are less important)

(记)peri(周围)+pher(带)+y→带到周围→外围

perish ['periʃ] v. 死,暴卒(to die, esp. in a violent or untimely manner)

(记)per(通过)+ish(去)→去通过→死

(例)The stray dog perished during the harsh winter.

perk [pəːk] v. 昂首,意气洋洋(to raise [the head, ears, etc.] briskly or spiritedly);振作,活跃起来(to become lively or animated; to recover one's spirits)

(记)perk 作名词用时有个常用的意思:额外津贴,不过作此意讲时为口语,且用复数

(例)The good news perked him up.(好消息使他精神振奋。)/ He perked up noticeably when the letter arrived. / Although the salary is not impressive, I like the perks this job offers.

permeate ['pəːmieit] v. 扩散,渗透(to spread or diffuse; penetrate)

(记)per(全部)+mea(通过)+ate→通过→渗透
(例)Nasty water from the flood permeated our carpeting.

permutation [pəːmjuˊteiʃən] n.【数】排列(顺序)改变
(记)per(全部)+mut(改变)+ation→全部改变
(例)The permutations of A, B, and C taken two at a time are AB, BA, AC, CA, BC, CB

pernicious [pəːˊniʃəs] a. 有害的,致命的(causing great injury, destruction, or ruin; fatal; deadly)
(记)per(全部)+nic(毒、死)+ious→有毒的→有害的
同根词:innocent(无罪的,天真的)
(例)The pernicious gossip destroyed the actor's career.

perpendicular [pəːpənˊdikjulə] n.垂直(an upright position)
(记)per(全部)+pend(挂)+icular→全部挂的状态→垂直

perpetrator [ˊpəːpitreitə] n.作恶者,犯罪者,行凶者(someone who does or performs [sth. evil, criminal, or offensive], who is guilty of sth.)
(记)来自 perpetrate,per(全部)+petr(石头)+ate→成为石头→做坏事不悔改
同根词:petrify(石化,僵化)
(例)The police caught the perpetrator near the crime scene.

persecute [ˊpəːsikjuːt] v.迫害(to afflict or harass constantly so as to injure or distress; oppress cruelly)
(记)per(全部)+secu(跟随)+te→从头到尾跟随→迫害
参考:prosecute(控告)
(例)Millions of Jews were persecuted during World War II.

perspiration [pə:spə'reiʃen] n. 出汗(the act of sweating)
(记)per(全部) + spir(呼吸) + ation 全身都呼吸，出汗
同根词：inspiration(灵感)
(例)be bathed in / wet with perspiration(大汗淋漓) / The perspiration broke out on his forehead.

pertinent ['pə:tinənt] a. 恰当的，贴切的(having some connection with the matter at hand; relevant; to the point)
(记) per (始终) + tin (拿住) + ent → 始终拿在手里→有关系的
(例) My supervisor's criticisms about my paper were quite pertinent.

pervasive [pə'veisiv] a. 遍及的，弥漫的(tending to spread throughout)
(记)per(遍及) + vade(走)→走遍；弥漫
(例) A pervasive feeling of anger was evident throughout the jail.

perversion [pə'və:ʃən] n. 堕落；曲解(sth. that has been changed to become abnormal or unnatural)
(记)来自 perverse, per(始终) + verse(转)→始终反着转→不正常的→堕落了
同根词：adversary(对手)；reverse(颠倒，倒退)
(例) The movie is a perversion of the author's book.

pesticide ['pestisaid] n. 杀虫剂(a chemical that kills animals or insects that destroy crops, spread disease, and intrude into people's homes)
(记)pest(害虫) + i + cide(杀)→杀虫剂
(例)The farmer sprayed his crops with pesticide.

petition [pi'tiʃən] n. 请愿，请愿书(a solemn, earnest supplication or request to authority)

(记)pet(寻求) + ition→寻求(帮助)→请愿
(例)I signed a petition to install a stop sign at the dangerous corner. / The workers signed a petition demanding better working conditions.

pharmaceutical [ˌfɑːməˈsjuːtəkl] a. 药学的,药用的(of or about drugs and medicines)
(记)pharmac(药) + eutical→药用的,药学的
(例)The pharmaceutical company researched the new drug's effects. / The researcher studied the pharmaceutical benefits of herbs.

pharmacologist [fɑːməˈkɔlədʒist] n. 药理学家,药物学家(someone who specializes in drugs and medicine)
(记)pharmac(药) + olog(学科) + ist→药理学家,药物学家

phase [feiz] n. 阶段,状态(a stage in the development of sb. or sth.; a stage in a sequence of events);方面,侧面(any of the ways in which sth. may be observed, considered, or presented; aspect)
(记)月亮的"月相"(新月,上弦,满月,下弦)也叫phase
(例)The doctor explained the different phases of the disease.

phonograph [ˈfəunəgrɑːf] n. 留声机,唱机(a record player)
(记)phono(声) + graph(记录)→能把声音记录下的→留声机,唱机
(例)My phonograph's needle needs to be replaced.

phony [ˈfəuni] a. 假的,伪造的(fake; not real; counterfeit; not genuine)
(记)由英国小偷的黑话"fawney"演变而来,意指偷来的戒指是镀金的,不是真金的
(例)The phony diamond shattered because it was really glass. / The phony doctor had no training at

all.

photosynthesis [fəutəˊsinθəsis] n.【生】光合作用

(记)photo(光)+synthesis(综合)→光合作用

同根词:photics(光学);photography(照相)

physiological [fiziəˊlɔdʒikəl] a. 生理学的,生理的(of or about the science and study of the properties of and relationships between matter and energy)

(记)physi(生理)+olog(学科)+ical→生理学的

pigment [ˊpigmənt] n.天然色素(a substance in a plant or animal that causes it to have a certain color);干粉颜料(a colored substance that is mixed with a liquid to make paint or ink)

(记)联想记忆:pigmeat(猪肉,肉感女人),pigment(色素)

(例)People who have little pigment in their skin get sunburns easily. / The dye contains green pigment.

pinnacle [ˊpinəkl] n.尖塔;山峰(the highest point of sth.)

(记)来自 pin(针)+(n)acle→像针一样尖的东西→山峰

(例)reach the pinnacle of power

pint [paint] n.品脱(英美干量或液量名=1/2 夸脱或1/8 加仑

(记)汉语的"品脱"是音译

(例)I bought a pint of milk at the store.

pinto [ˊpintəu] a.杂色的(marked with patches of white and black or another dark color); n.杂色马(a pinto horse or pony);斑豆(pinto bean)

(记)按谐音记 pinto;拼的,拼凑的→杂色的

plague [pleig] n.瘟疫(an epidemic; a disease that kills people and is quickly spread),讨厌的人物(a nuisance);v.烦扰(to annoy sb. with repeated ques-

tions, problems, etc.)
(记)plag(击,打)+ue→能打倒人的→瘟疫;烦扰
(例)The plague has killed millions through the centuries. / The customer plagued the clerk with petty concerns.

plaintiff [ˈpleintif] n.【律】原告(someone who sues sb. else; someone who brings a lawsuit against sb. else)
(记)plaint(哀诉,抱怨)+tiff→哀诉的一方→原告
同根词:plaint(哀诉,起诉)
(例)The judge instructed the plaintiff to speak loudly so the jury could hear.

plane [plein] n.平面(a flat surface)
(记)plane(飞机)总是要飞得平稳,像飞在一个plane(平面)上一样
(例)The intersection of two planes is a line.

plaque [plɑːk] n.(用金属,象牙,陶瓷等制的)匾,饰(a decorative panel with a message or a list of people's names printed on it);【医】血小板(a deposit of fatty or fibrous material in a blood vessel wall)
(记)注意和上面的plague(瘟疫)分清,读时也要仔细辨别
(例)Each employee is given a small plaque upon retirement.

platform [ˈplætfɔːm] n.纲领(a formal statement of the ideas and politics of a political party)
(记)该词另一常用义为"平台",plat(flat)(平的)+form(外形)→平台
(例)The Republicans and the Democrats have different platforms. / Mary was upset with the philosophy of her party's platform.

plausible [ˈplɔːzəbl] a. 似乎合理的；嘴巧的（believable; seeming to be true or right）

（记）plaus（鼓掌）+ible→值得鼓掌的→可行的

同根词：plaudits（称赞）；applause（鼓掌）

（例）The jury believed the witness's plausible testimony.

plead [pliːd] vt. 为…（案件）辩护（to declare in court that one is guilty or not guilty before the trial actually begins）；以…为理由／借口（to claim sth. as an excuse）

（记）来自 plea（恳求，辩护）

（例）The defendant pled not guilty. / He pled that he did not have enough time to be as careful as she should.

pleiotropic [ˌplaiəuˈtrɔpik] a. 多效性的，多向性的（exerting simultaneous effects on more than one characteristics in the offspring）

（记）pleio（更多，较多）+ trop（tropy）（向…性）+ ic →多向性的

（例）The mutation was pleiotropic.（这突变是多向性的。）

pliant [ˈplaiənt] a. 易弯的；柔软的（easily bent; pliable）

（记）pli（＝ply 弯，折）+able→能弯曲的

（例）pliant leather（柔韧的皮革）

pliers [ˈplaiəz] n.（用作单数或复数）钳子，老虎钳（a tool with rough jaws, used to grasp objects）

（记）pli（＝ply 弯曲）+ers→使东西弯曲的东西→钳子

（例）The carpenter kept two pairs of pliers in his toolbox.

plumb [plʌm] ad. 精确地，完全地（entirely; wholly; absolutely）；v. 了解意义（to try to determine what

sth. means);测水深(to determine how deep water is)
(记)由 plumb(铅锤)意义转化而来
(例)I was plumb tired out. / She plumbed the meaning of the confusing article.

plummet [ˈplʌmit] v. 垂直或突然地坠下(to plunge; to drop quickly and suddenly)
(记)plummet 原意为"测深锤"
(例)The company's stock prices plummeted after it declared bankruptcy.

pluralistic [pluərəˈlistik] a. 兼职的(holding more than one office or church benefice at the same time);【哲】多元论的(of or about the theory that reality is made of a multiplicity of ultimate beings, principles or substances)
(记)plura(多个的)+listic→兼职的;多元论的

plywood [ˈplaiwud] n. 胶合板,层压木板(a wooden panel made of several thin sheets of wood that are glued together)
(记)ply(一层;一层厚)+wood(木)→层压木板,胶合板
(例)Plywood is often sold in pieces that are eight feet long and four feet wide.

pneumonia [njuːˈməunjə] n.【医】肺炎(an infection of the lungs involving fluid in the lungs)
(记)pneumon(肺,元气)+ia→肺炎
同根词:pneuma(元气,精神);pneumatic(元气的,精神的)
(例)Elderly people are prone to pneumonia.

poacher [pəutʃə] n. 偷猎者(someone who hunts for animals or fish illegally)
(记)poach 本身是个动词,"侵入偷猎,偷捕"

(例)These poachers of elephants want to get tusks to sell for money.

pointed [ˈpɔintid] a. 尖的(having a point; sharp; sharpened to a point);犀利的(sharp; incisive; to the point, as an epigram);显然的,突出的(very evident; emphasized; conspicuous)

(记)point(尖端)+ed→尖的;突出的

(例)pointed fingernails

poke [pəuk] v. 刺,戳(to push sb. or sth. with one's finger, fist or elbow, or with a blunt object);poke and pry 管闲事,打听消息(to intrude; meddle)

(记)和 joke 一起记;poke fun at 嘲笑(某人)

(例)The little boy poked his brother in the ribs with his finger.

polarity [pəuˈlæriti] n. 极端,(性质,特点等)正好相反(having or showing contrary qualities, powers, tendencies, forms, etc. as the roots and stems of a plant, the two electrodes of a battery, etc.)

(记)polar(地极的)+ity→走两极→极端

(例)In electrical wiring, polarity is shown by the different colors of the wire.

pollen [ˈpɔlən] n. 花粉(a yellow powder made by flowers that is part of the process of causing flowers to make seeds)

(记)pol(灰尘)+len→灰尘状的东西→花粉

(例)The bee transported pollen from flower to flower.

pollinate [ˈpɔləneit] v. 授粉,传粉(to transfer pollen from a stamen to the upper tip of the pistil of [a flower])

(记)pollin(花粉)+ate→授粉

(例)Insects or wind pollinate the majority of plants.

pollination [pɔlə'neiʃən] n. 授粉

polyarchy ['pɔliɑːki] n. 多头政治

(记)poly(多,众)+archy(统治)→多头政治

polygon ['pɔligən] n. 多边形(a closed plane figure, esp. one with more than four sides and angles)

(记)poly(多,众)+gon(角)→多角→多边形

polygraph ['pɔligrɑːf] n. 测谎器(an instrument for recording simultaneously changes in blood pressure, respiration, pulse rate, etc; lie detector)

(记)poly(多,众)+graph(写,记录)→写得多的或从多方面记录的→多产作家;测谎器

pompous ['pɔmpəs] a. 自大的(arrogant; overly dignified; stuffy)

(记) pomp (盛大;排场;炫耀) + ous → 讲究排场的→自大的

(例) The pompous explorer bragged about his achievements.

pop [pɔp] v. 突然爆开(to cause sth. to explode or burst);突然提出(to put suddenly quickly or unexpectedly);(眼睛)张大(to open wide suddenly or protrude, as with amazement: said of the eyes)

(记)popcorn(爆米花)大家都知道,其中的 pop 就是用的"突然爆开"一意

(例)The children popped the balloons during the party. /I was surprised when he popped the question.

porcelain ['pɔːslin] n. 瓷(a thin, strong ceramic material);瓷器(laneous dishes or ornaments, collectively)

(记)为法语词

(例)My coffee cup is made of fine porcelain.

pornography [pɔː'nɔgrəfi]n. 色情描写,色情文学,色情画(erotic pictures, movies or books meant to cause sb. to be-

come sexually excited)
(记)porno(色情)+graphy(写)→色情描写,色情文学,色情画
(例)The police asked the store owner to stop selling pornography.

portage [ˈpɔːtidʒ] n.两条水路间(货物,小船等的)陆上运输(the carrying of boats and supplies overland from one lake or river to another, as during a canoe trip)
(记)port(持)+age→持着走→运输

portend [pɔːˈtend] v.预兆,预示(to be omen or warning of; foreshadow; presage)
(记)por(=pro 在前面)+tend(倾向)→预示,预兆
(例)He doesn't know what the situation portends for his country.

portrayal [pɔːˈtreiəl] n.描绘,描写(the act of making a picture or portrait of; depicting; delineation);画像,肖像(a portrait)
(记)portray(画)+al→描绘,描写;n. portrait(肖像,画像);v. portray(画,表现)
(例)an eye-catching portrayal of the graceful Madam Sun Yat-sen / specialize in the portrayal of heroism

posterity [pɔsˈteriti] n.子孙,后代(the people of the future; the people who will live in the future)
(记)post(后)+erity→后面的人→后代
(例)The author hoped her poems would survive for posterity.

poststructuralism [pəustˈstrʌktʃərəlizəm] n.后结构主义
(记)post(后)+structura(结构)+lism(主义)→后结构主义

potent [ˈpəutənt] a.强有力的(powerful; having a strong

effect)
(记)poten(力量)+t→强有力的
(例)The potent drug knocked me unconscious.

potpourri [pəupə'riː] n. 混杂文集(a medley, miscellany or anthology)
(记)分割记忆:pot(锅)+pour(倾倒)-ri→倒在一锅里→混杂
参考:miscellany(混杂)

pottery ['pɔtəri] n.(总称)陶器(dishes, bowls, vases, and other objects that are made from baked clay);陶器制造术(the act of making objects out of clay and baking them so that the clay hardens; ceramics)
(记)pot(壶,罐)+tory→制造壶、罐等的技术→陶器制造术
(例)The artist sold her pottery at the country fair./My art teacher taught pottery for an entire semester.

practitioner [præk'tiʃənə] n. 开业者(医生,律师等)(someone who works at a certain profession, esp. in medicine or law);实践者
(记)practi(实践)+tion+er→实践者→开业者
(例)The legal practitioner agreed to take my case.

pragmatic [præg'mætik] a. 实用主义的(practical; capable of dealing with the real world)
(记)pragm(实际)+atic→实际的
同根词:practical(实际的,pract=prag)
(例)The pragmatic social worker understood her client's situations.

prairie ['prεəri] n. 大草原(a very large area of land that is covered with different kinds of grasses but which has no trees)
(记)不妨和 pasture(牧场)一起记

(例) The fox chased the rabbit through the tall grass of the prairie.

precaution [priˊkɔːʃən] n. 预防措施(an act that is done to prevent sth. bad from occurring)

(记)pre(预先)+caution(措施)→预防措施

(例)Many diseases can be prevented if you take a few simple precautions.

precipitation [prisipiˊteiʃən] n.【化】沉淀作用(the separation of a solid substance from a liquid);降雨量(rain, snow, sleet, drizzle or other moisture that is made by the atmosphere);仓促;猛然落下(the hurried beginning of a bad situation)

(记)来自 precipitate, pre(提前)+cipit(落下)+ate→提前落下→加速

(例) The precipitation of the substance was achieved by filtering it. /If it gets cold, the precipitation will take the form of snow. /The expiration of the contract was the precipitation of the long strike.

precipitous [priˊsipitəs] a. 陡峭的;仓促的(steep; like the side of a cliff or mountain that is almost straight up and down)

(记)pre(提前)+cipit(落下)+ous→仓促的

(例) He drove carefully down the precipitous mountainside.

precipitously [priˊsipitəsli] ad. 仓促地;突然地(abruptly; suddenly)

precursor [priˊkəːsə] n. 先驱,先行者(someone that is an indication of sb. that will follow)

(记)pre(前面)+curs(跑)+or→跑在前面的人→先驱

(例)Sturm und Drang was a precursor of Romanticism.(狂飙运动是浪漫主义的先驱。)

predator [ˊpreditə] n. 食肉动物(a creature that preys on other creatures)

(记)predat(破坏,掠夺)+or→掠夺者,食肉动物

同根词:predation(捕食,掠夺)

(例)Cats are natural predators of birds.

predecessor [ˊpriːdisesə] n. 前辈,前任者(someone who lived before someone else; someone who held a certain position before someone else);(被取代的)原有事物(a thing replaced by another thing, as in use)

(记)pre(先)+decessor(退休的官员)→前辈,前任者;[转](被取代的)原有事物

(例)The company's president's immediate predecessor was considered a weak leader.

predicament [priˊdikəmənt] n. 困境,穷境(a difficult situation where one must make a difficult choice)

(记)pre(预先)+dica(命令)+ment→被预先命令的状态→不灵活→困境;注意:比较 predication(断言,肯定);prediction(预言)

(例)I was in the predicament of competing against the best runner.

predicate [ˊpredikit] v. 论断,断言(to affirm as a quality, attribute or property of a person or thing)

(记)pre(预先)+dica(命令)+te→论断,断言

(例)be predicated on(使基于,使取决于) / It has been predicated that a seismic shock was the cause of these phenomena.

predisposition [ˊpriːdispəˊziʃən] n. 事先安排,倾向(the condition of being predisposed; inclination or tendency; predilection)

(记)pre(预先)+disposition(性情,倾向)

(例)an ideological predisposition in favour of reform(一种支持改革的思想倾向)

preeminence [pri:'eminəns] n. 杰出,卓越(the quality of being superior to other things or people, outstanding or very distinguished)

(记)来自 preeminent, pre(前面)+eminent(著名的)→在著名的人前面→出类拔萃的

(例)the preeminence of Einstein among the scientists of his day

preface ['prefis] n. 序言,开端(an introduction to a speech or to sth. that is written)

(记)pre(前面)+face(脸面)→前面的脸→开端

(例)The author wrote a new preface for the second edition of her book.

preferential [prefə'renʃəl] a. 优先的,特惠的(of or about getting or giving special treatment or consideration)

(记)prefer(情愿,更喜欢)+ential→优先的,特惠的

(例)The judge's preferential considerations were very biased.

prejudicial [ˌpredʒu'diʃəl] a. 有害的,引起偏见的(causing prejudice or harm; injurious; detrimental)

(记)pre(预先)+judic(判断)+ial→预先判断→有偏见的

(例)Smoking is prejudicial to health.

premature [pri:mə'tjuə] a. 早熟的,过早的(happening, done, arriving or existing before the proper or usual time; too early)

(记)pre(提前)+mature(成熟)→早熟的

(例)Your present is premature. My birthday isn't until next week.

premium ['pri:mjəm] n. 保险金(a regular payment to an insurance company for some kind of protection)

(记)pre(提前)+em(=empt 买)+ium→提前买下的东西→保险费

(例)My insurance premiums are due on the first of each month.

preoccupied [pri'ɔkjupaid] a. 心事重重的,出神的(having all of one's time or attention taken up with sb. or sth.)

(记)pre(预先)+occupied(专心的)→十分专心的

(例)The preoccupied driver crashed into a tree.

preponderance [pri'pɔndərəns] n. 压倒性优势(being greater in amount, weight, power, influence, importance, etc.)

(记)pre(前面)+ponder(重量)+ate→重量超过别的→压倒

(例)The preponderance of public sentiment is with the victim.

prerequisite [pri:'rekwizit] n. 先决条件(sth. that must be done before sth. else is done)

(记)pre(预先)+requisite(要求)→预先要求→先决条件

(例)Passing the test is a prerequisite for graduating.

preservative [pri'zə:vətiv] n. 防腐剂(a substance that keeps sth., such as food, from decaying)

(记)来自 preserve,pre(预先)+serve(保存)

(例)Morticians use preservatives to keep bodies from decaying.

pressboard ['presbɔ:d] n. 压制板(a smooth, stiff, heavy, often glazed, paper used in presses for finishing paper, etc.)

(记)press(压)+board(板)→压出的板→压制板

prestige [pres'ti:ʒ] n. 威信,声望;显赫(good reputation and

high distinction earned through success)
(记)pre(前面)+stige(拉近,拉紧)→把人拉到前面的力量→威望
(例)The influential researcher has a lot of prestige in his field.

prevalence [ˊprevələns] n.盛行(being widespread, predominant or common)
(记)来自 prevalent(普遍的,盛行的),pre(前面)+val(力量)+ent
(例)the prevalence of rumors / the prevalence of automobiles

previous [ˊpriːvjəs] a.前面的,在前的(earlier; happening before sth. else; coming before)
(例)For the previous ten hours, I had been sleeping.

prey [prei] n.被捕食的动物(an animal that is hunted, killed or eaten by another animal);牺牲品;战利品(plunder; booty)
(记)和 pray(祈祷)区分记忆
(例)The eagle swooped down on its prey.

primate [ˊpraimeit] n.灵长类(动物)(a member of advanced group of mammals, including humans, apes and monkeys)
(记)prim(最早的)+ate→最早的动物→灵长类
(例)The archaeologist found the bones of a prehistoric primate.

primer [ˊprimə] n.启蒙书,识字课本(a book that is written to teach children how to read)
(记)prim(最早)+er→最早用的书→启蒙书
(例)The little girl said aloud the words that were written in her primer.

primitive [ˊprimitiv] a.原始的,简单的(very simple; not

complicated)

(记)prim(最早的)+itive→原始的

(例)The sociologist studies primitive cultures in the tropics. / His old computer is a primitive version of the latest model.

principal [ˊprinsəpəl] a. 主要的,负责人的(main; chief; primary; most important);n. 本金(the amount of a debt, investment, etc. minus the interest or on which interest is computed)

(例)Security is the principal reason that we bought an alarm system. / She has paid off both principal and interest of the loan.

probate [ˊprəubeit] n.【律】遗嘱检验(the legal validation of a testamentary document);v. 处(犯人)以缓刑(to postpone the punishment for a wrongdoer)

(记)prob(证明)+ate→去证明→遗嘱检验

(例)They should be probated for first offenses.

probe [prəub] v. 探索,探测(to explore; to examine)

(记)prob(测试,证明)+e→探索,探测

(例)The dentist probed my teeth for cavities. / The detective probed into the circumstances of the murder.

problematic [ˊprɔbləˊmætik] a. 成问题的,有疑问的,未定的(causing doubt; hard to solve; causing problems)

(记)problem(问题)+atic→成问题的,有疑问的

(例)He needed to decide what to do about his problematic job.

proceeds [prəuˊsi:dz] n.【复】收入(款项)(money that is collected or received from sb. or sth.)

(记)proceed 用作单数是"继续做…"的意思→不断地收钱→收入(款项)

(例)The proceeds from the auction were donated to

charity. / All proceeds from the charity concert will support this station.

proctor [ˊprɔktə] n. 代理人(a person employed to manage the affairs of another; agent; attorney);学监,监考人(a person who supervises or monitors students, as at an examination)

(例)The proctor caught several students cheating on the exam.

prodigious [prəˊdidʒəs] a. 很大的,巨大的(large; enormous; vast)

(记)prodig(奇大的)+ious→很大的,巨大的

(例)I have a prodigious amount of work to do before I leave.

prodigy [ˊprɔdidʒi] n. 奇事,非凡之人,天才(a person, thing or act so extraordinary as to inspire wonder)

(记)prodig(奇大的)+y→奇事,非凡之人,天才

(例)The prodigy began college when he was only 9.

produce [ˊprɔdjuːs] n. 农产品(food or food products that are farmed or grown; fruits and vegetables)

(记)和 product(产品,产量)区别开来

(例)They buy produce fresh from the farmers' market.

proficient [prəˊfiʃənt] a. 熟练的,精通的(able to do sth. properly and skillfully; skillful)

(记)pro(在前)+ficient(做的)→做在别人前面→熟练的

参考:sufficient(足够的),deficient(缺乏的)

(例)The proficient pianist played for the city orchestra. / The linguist is proficient in five languages.

profile [ˊprəufail] n. 侧面像(a side view of the face);外

形，轮廓(a view of anything in contour; outline)；传略(a short, vivid biographical and character sketch)；
(记)pro(前面)+file(=fili 线条)→前部的线条→外形，轮廓
(例)I prefer my right profile to my left. / The man's profile stated that he spent four years in the Navy.

profitability [prɔfitə'biliti] n. 盈利率(the rate of the profit to cost or investment)
(记)profit(利润)+ability(能力)→盈利的能力→盈利率

profound [prə'faund] a. 深奥的(showing deep thought or understanding)
(记)pro(向前)+found(底部)→向前到底部→深奥的
(例)It is hard to understand the philosopher's profound statements.

progressive [prə'gresiv] a. 逐渐的(continuing by successive steps)
(记)progress(进步)+ive→一点一点进步的→逐渐的
(例)There is often a progressive loss of sight in old age. / progressive taxation(累进税)

prohibitive [prə'hibitiv] a. 禁止性的；起阻止作用的(preventing or prohibiting sth.)
(记)pro(提前)+hibit(拿住)+ive→提前拿住→抑制的，禁止的
(例)The school's prohibitive atmosphere stifled all creativity.

project [prə'dʒekt, 'prɔdʒekt] vt. 设计，规划(to propose [an act or plan of action])；突出(to stick out; to

extend from a surface)
(记)pro(在…之前)+ject(扔)→在…前扔出来→突出;设计,规划
(例)project a new bridge / The coat hooks project from the wall.

proliferate [prəu'lifəreit] v. 激增,繁殖(to multiply rapidly; increase profusely)
(记)pro(向前)+lifer(后代)+ate→后代增加→繁殖
(例)Tropical vegetation proliferates. / Bicycles proliferated when gasoline prices rose.

prominent ['prɔminənt] a. 突起的,凸出的(sticking out; projecting); 显著的(noticeable); 杰出的(famous; renowned)
(记)pro(向前)+minent(突出)→凸出的→显著的
(例)He's got a prominent chin. / Huge bushes are the prominent feature of our yard. / The reporter interviewed many prominent celebrities.

promulgate ['prɔməlgeit] v. 颁布,传播(to spread the news of sth.; to spread information)
(记)pro(前面)+mulg(人民)+ate→放到人民前面的→颁布
(例)The news of the layoff was quickly promulgated throughout the factory.

prone to ['prəun tuː] 易于…的(likely to 〔do〕 sth.; apt to have sth.)
(例)My sister is prone to sneezing because of her allergies.

pronounced [prə'naunst] a. 明显的(evident; prominent; noticeable);(观点等)强硬的(clearly marked; decided)

(记)来自 pronounce(宣称,发音) + d→ 被宣布的→明显的

(例) There's a pronounced bump on your head where you were hit.

propagation [prɔpə'geiʃən] n. 繁殖(the breeding and raising of plants and animals);传播(spreading sth., such as news or information)

(记)来自 propagate, pro + pag(砍,切) + ate→原义是把树的旁枝剪掉,使主干成长→引申为繁殖

(例)A botanist worked on the propagation of a new species of rose. / The propagation of news is easy with the help of television.

propensity [prə'pensiti] n. 嗜好,习性(a tendency to do sth. or behave a certain way)

(记)pro(向前) + pens(挂) + ity→预先挂好了→癖好

(例)I had a propensity for eating when I was nervous. / Her friends are aware of her propensity for gossiping.

property ['prɔpəti] n. 性质,特征(any trait or attribute proper to a thing);财产,资产(sth. regarded as being possessed by a person or a group of persons)

(例)Jealousy is one property that I don't like in people. / The farmer sold some property to pay for his taxes.

propitious [prə'piʃəs] a. 吉利的,顺利的(favorable; being a good sign or omen)

(记)pro(向前) + pit(= pet 寻求) + ious→所寻求的→吉利的

(例)The propitious sky means it will be a nice day at the beach.

proportion [prə'pɔːʃən] n. 比例(the relationship between the

sizes of different parts of sb. or sth.)
(记)pro(对于)+portion(部分)→相对于每个部分→比例
(例)The worker's bonus is paid in proportion to his productivity.

proportional [prəˈpɔːʃənəl] a. 成比例的,均衡的(having a suitable size, degree or amount as compared with sth. else)
(例)In the cartoon, the cat's head was not proportional to its body.

propound [prəˈpaund] vt. 提出(问题,计划)供考虑;建议(to put forward for consideration; propose);【律】提出(遗嘱等)(to present a will to the proper authority for certification)
(记)pro(向前)+pound(提出,陈述)→提出(问题,计划)供考虑;建议
(例)to propound a question to sb. / propound a riddle

proprietary [prəˈpraiətəri] a. 财产的,私有的,所有权的(ownership)
(记)来自 property(财产,所有物,所有权)

prosaic [prəuˈseiik] a. 单调的,无趣的(commonplace, dull and ordinary)
(记)来自 prose(散文)+aic→散文一般的→单调的
(例)prosaic details of everyday life

prose [prəuz] n. 散文(the ordinary form of written or spoken language, without rhyme or meter);平凡,单调,无聊(dull, commonplace talk, expression, quality, etc)
(例)There were long sections of prose between the poems.

prospect [ˈprɔspekt] n. 展望，视野(a broad view; scene)；指望(anticipation)；前景(sth. hoped for or expected; anticipated outcome)

(记)pro(向…前)+spect(看)→展望；前景

(例) My interview yielded a few interesting prospects for the future. / My company's prospect for success is good.

prospectus [prəsˈpektəs] n. 说明书，简介(a written statement that gives the official details about an event, school or business)

(记)参考 prospect

(例)The prospective client asked to see my company's prospectus. / The school's prospectus presented a statement of its goals.

prosper [ˈprɔspə] v. 繁荣，昌盛；成功(to become successful; to earn enough money so that one can live well; thrive)

(记)pro(前面)+sper(希望)→希望在前→繁荣，昌盛，成功

(例) The banker prospered during the housing boom. / The new toy store prospered at the mall.

protagonist [prəuˈtægənist] n. 提倡者，倡导者(a leader, proponent or supporter of a cause; champion)

(记)prot(首先)+agon(打，行动)+ist→首先行动者→支持者

同根词：antagonist(对抗者)

(例)the chief protagonists of women's rights

protege [ˈprəutiʒei] n. 被保护人，门徒(someone who is under the guidance of someone important, powerful or knowledgeable)

(记)法语词，一般两个 e 上都有点

(例)The director's protege studied all of his films

closely. / The pianist helped his protege perfect her technique.

protein [ˊprəutiːn] n. 蛋白质

(记) prote (首要) + in → 含有动植物体内最主要的→蛋白质

(例) The vegetarian ate beans to get protein. / Meat, fish and poultry are good sources of protein.

protocol [ˊprəutəkɔl] n. 外交礼节(the system of etiquette, rules, and behavior in business, military, or social situations); 协议(an original draft or record of a document, negotiation, etc.)

(记)proto(首要) + col→首要的东西→礼节

(例)The junior officer was reprimanded for not following proper protocol.

proton [ˊprəutɔn] n. 质子(a particle in the center of an atom that carries a positive electrical charge)

(记)proto(首要) + n→首要的东西→质子

(例)The nucleus of a hydrogen atom has one proton.

prototype [ˊprəutətaip] n. 原形(the original example of sth. from which later examples are developed); 典型,标准(a perfect example of a particular type)

(记)proto(首先) + type(形状)→首先的形状→原型

(例)The architect's novel design was the prototype on which more buildings were based.

provenance [ˊprɔvinəns] n. 出处,起源(origin; derivation; source)

(记) pro (前面) + ven (来) + ance → 前面来的东西 → 起源

(例)a word of French provenance

provision [prəˊviʒən] n. 供应(〔pl〕food and supplies needed for everyday living);(法律等)条款(a legal rule; a statement that stipulates sth.; a stipulation)

(记)provide(提供)的名词:pro(向前)+vide(看)

(例)The hikers carried their provisions on their backs. / This provision deals with your royalties (版税) after the third printing.

provocative [prə'vɔkətiv] a.激怒人的,挑战的(causing anger; interest or desire)

(记)来自 provoke(激怒),pro(前面)+voke(喊)→在别人前面喊→ 激怒,挑衅

同根词:invoke(恳求);revoke(取消)

(例)The author's provocative book was also quite controversial.

prowl [praul] v.野兽等四处觅食;【喻】暗中来回寻觅(to sneak around quietly, like an animal hunting for food or a thief looking for sth. to steal)

(例)Many wild animals prowl at night. / The thief prowled in the dark room, looking for valuables.

proximity [prɔk'simiti] n.接近,附近(nearness; how close sth. to sth. else)

(记)proxim(近处)+ity→接近,附近

(例)Due to his proximity to the microphone, his words were clearly recorded.

prudent ['pruːdənt] a.谨慎的,深谋远虑的(wise; thinking carefully before one does sth.)

(记)prud(小心)+ent→小心算计→谨慎的

(例)It would be prudent to think carefully before you choose.

prudery ['pruːdəri] n.过分拘谨,装作正经(the characteristic quality or state of a prude)

(记)法语词,由 prude(过分拘谨的人)而来

(例)This is no time for prudery.(现在可不是故作正经的时候。)

pry [prai] v. 刺探，打听(into)(to make a nosy inquiry);撬开(open up)(to open or raise sth. with a tool by using force)
(记)由 prize(捕获;发现物)演变而来
(例)I resent my parents for prying into my personal life. / The thief pried open the door with a crowbar.

pseudoscience [ˈsjuːdəusains] n. 伪科学(any system of methods, theories, etc. that presumes without warrant to have a scientific basis or application)
(记)pseudo(假的) + science(科学)→伪科学

psyche [saiki] n. 心智，精神(the mind, soul or spirit of a person)
(记)psych(心理) + e→心智，精神
(例)After years of abuse, her psyche is deeply scarred. / The support she got from her friends was good for her psyche.

psychiatric [saikiˈætrik] a. 精神病学的(of the science of treating people who have sickness of the mind)
(记)由 psychiatry 而来，psychi(精神) + atry(病学科)→精神病学
(例)That doctor specializes in psychiatric medicine. / The depressed woman decided to seek psychiatric treatment.

psychoactive [saikəuˈæktiv] a. (药剂)对神经起显著(或特殊)作用(designating or of a drug, chemical, etc. that has a specific effect on the mind)
(记)psycho(精神) + active(积极的)→促进精神积极起来的→对神经起显著作用
(例)This kind of medicine is psychoactive.

psychological [saikə'lɔdʒikəl] a. 心理上的(of the mind; mental); 心理学的(of or about the study and science of the mind)

(记)psych(心理)+olog(学科)+ical→心理学的

(例)Is there a psychological explanation for my depression? / He was paid to participate in a psychological study.

psychopath ['saikəupæθ] n. 精神变态者(sb. who has a serious mental illness, causing criminal actions)

(记)psycho(精神)+path(病患者)→精神变态者

(例)The psychopath was imprisoned in a private cell. / The psychopath tortured his victims before killing them.

psychosis [sai'kəusis] n. 精神病,变态心理(a serious mental illness that alters a person's sense of reality)

(记)psych(精神)+osis(病)→精神病

(例)She took medication to treat her psychosis. / His psychosis were so severe that he never left his house.

publicity [pʌb'lisiti] n. 公开(性)(the state of being public commonly known or observed); 宣传,广告(information that is brought to everyone's attention)

(记)public(公开的)+ity→公开;宣传

(例)Bad publicity hurt the mayor's chances for reelection. / There was a lot of publicity surrounding the sensational trial.

pulp [pʌlp] n. (动,植物体中的)肉质部分;果肉(the soft part inside a fruit, vegetable or plant); 浆状物(any soft, wet substance)

(记)比较记忆:pulp(果肉);bulb(球形物;鳞茎)

(例)I strained the pulp from the orange juice. / The newspaper that landed in the puddle turned into pulp.

pulsation [pʌl'seiʃən] n.【物】脉动(the act of beating or throbbing rhythmically, as the heart);跳动,有节奏的鼓动(a beat; throb; vibration)

(记)来自 pulsate(脉动),puls(脉搏)+ate→脉跳

punctuation [pʌŋktju'eiʃen] n.标点;全部标点符号

(记)来自 punctuate(加标点),punctu(点)+ate→打上点→加标点

(例)The teacher circled mistakes in punctuation with a red pen. / I made sure my essay had proper punctuation before I turned it in.

punitive ['pju:nitiv] a.给予惩罚的,刑罚的(used as a punishment; acting as punishment)

(记)puni(惩罚)+tive→给予惩罚的

同根词:impunity(不受惩罚)

(例)The woman sought punitive damages from the firm that illegally fired her.

pup [pʌp] n.小狗,幼犬,幼兽(a young dog; a puppy; the young of certain animals)

(记)别和 pub(小酒馆)混淆了

(例)He trained the pup to bring him his sleepers.

pupation [pju:'peiʃn] n.【动】化蛹(the process of becoming an insect called pupa)

(记)pupa(蛹)+tion→化蛹

purge [pə:dʒ] v.清洗,洗涤(to make sth. clean by getting rid of what is dirty; to clean sth. out)

(记)pure(纯)+ge→弄干净

(例)The plumber purged the dirty water from the tank. / The cleaning crew purged the basin of its messy contents.

puritan ['pjuəritən] n.清教徒(one of the members of the Church of England in the 1500s and 1600s who

wanted to simplify or purify the Church doctrines and worship practices);极端拘谨的人(a person regarded as excessively strict in morals and religion)
(记)purit(使净化)+an→清教徒
(例)Some Puritans fled England for America.

pursue [pə'sju:] v.追赶,追求(to chase sb. or sth.;to seek sth.)
(记)pur(向前)+sue(求)→追求,追赶
(例)The police pursued the thief down the alley. / Mary pursued a career in law.

putty ['pʌti] n.【建】腻子(a soft, oily substance used to seal pipe connections, to seal the edges of glass in window frames, and to fill uneven surfaces);易于被人摆弄的人(sb. easily influenced by sb. else)
(记)和 party 读音近似
(例)The old putty around the panes of glass started to flake. / His wife is putty in his hands. She never thinks for herself.

pyramid ['pirəmid] n.角锥(a four-sided structure with triangular sides that meet at one point on top)
(记)埃及的金字塔墓也叫 pyramid,因为它们都是角锥形
(例)I set the base of the pyramid on top of a cube.

Q

quadrant ['kwɔdrənt] n.象限【几何】(a quarter of a circleor its circumference)
(记)quadr(四)+ant→由四个部分组成的→象限

quadrilateral [kwɔdri'lætərəl] n.四边形(a plane figure having four sides and four angles)
(记)quadri(四)+lateral(边)→四边形

quadruple [ˈkwɔdrupl] v. 四倍于(to make sth. four times as large; to multiply sth. by four)

(记)quadru(四)+ple(加)→加四次→四倍于

(例)If you quadruple five, you get twenty. / My insurance rates quadrupled after my second accident.

quail [kweil] n. 鹌鹑(a small bird that is often hunted for sport and eaten as food);v. 畏缩,沮丧(to draw back in fear; lose heart or courage; cower)

(记)quail 的"畏缩"一意常考

(例)They frightened some quail from the deep grass.

Quaker [ˈkweikə] n. 公谊会教徒;夸克党(a member of a Christian denomination called the Society of Friends, whose followers oppose war and violence)

(记)音译

(例)Quakers do not support wars or violence.

qualify [ˈkwɔlifai] vt. 使合格,使具有资格(to make someone meet the requirements for sth.);限制(to limit sth.; to restrict sth.; to narrow the meaning of sth.)

(例)Your excellent grades qualify you for a scholarship. / The mayor qualified his statement to clear up an ambiguity. / Most of the flood victims qualified for low-interest loans.

quandary [ˈkwɔndəri] n. 困惑,进退两难(a state of uncertainty; a feeling of not knowing what one should do)

(记)quand(数量)+ary→不知是多少→困惑,进退两难

(例)After I lost my job, I found myself in a real quandary.

quanta [ˈkwɔntə] n.(quantum 的复数)量子(a fixed, elemental unit, as of energy, angular momentum, etc.);量(quantity, or amount);份额(a specified quantity; portion)

(记)quant(数量)+um→量子

(例)quantum chemistry(量子化学)/ quantum number(量子数)

quarantine [ˈkwɔrəntiːn] n.隔离检疫期,隔离(a period of isolation of living things that have an illness or have been exposed to an illness)

(记)quarant(四十)+ine,原意指隔开 40 天

(例)During the quarantine, no one could leave the afflicted village.

quarry [ˈkwɔri] n.猎物;追求物(the object of a hunt or search);采石场(a place where marble, granite, and other kinds of stone are removed from the earth);v.采石(to remove stone from the earth)

(例)The hunter shot his quarry. / The sculptor went to the quarry to get a block of marble. / They have been quarrying granite here for hundreds of years.

quasar [ˈkweizɑː] n.【天】类星体(a kind of starlike celestial objects emitting immense quantities of light and radio waves)

quiescent [kwaiˈesnt] a.静止的,沉寂的(marked by inactivity or repose; tranquilly at rest)

(记)qui(=quiet 安静的)+escent(状态)→静止的

同根词:quietus(债务清偿;寂灭)

(例)His thinking became quiescent as he slept. / The patient's illness was quiescent for the moment.

quintessential [kwintiˈsenʃəl] a.精华的;典型的(most representative of sth. ; being the best example of sth.)

(记)来自 quintessence(精华,完美的典范),quint(五)+ essence(精华)→原指组成世界的五大精华物质

(例)My boss is firm but fair. He's the quintessential supervisor. / This building is the quintessential example of the architect's work.

R

rabble [ˈræbl] n. 乌合之众,暴民(a disorganized or disorderly crowd of people; mob);下等人(the lowest class of people)

(记)注意区别 babble (牙牙学语)

(例)The police tried to disperse the rabble in front of the park.

rabies [ˈreibiːz] n.(单复数同)狂犬病

(记)来自拉丁语 rabidus(疯狂),和 rabid(狂暴的)一起记

raccoon [ræˈkuːn] n. 浣熊(北美住宅区中常见);浣熊毛皮(the skin and fur of raccoon)

(记)来自印第安语,coon 是一种对黑人的蔑称

(例)A raccoon pawed through the garbage can in the alley. / Anne bought a coat made of raccoon.

racist [ˈreisist] n. 种族主义者(one that believes one race is better than another)

(记)来自 race(种族)+ ist(者)→种族主义者

(例)The racist throws stones at the immigrants in their neighborhood.

radial [ˈreidjəl] a. 放射状的,射线的(arranged or having parts arranged like rays);半径的,沿半径转动的

(relating to or moving along a radius)
(记)radi(光线,射线)+al→放射状的,射线的

radiant [ˊreidjənt] a. 光芒四射的(sending out rays or reflecting beams of light);绚丽的(vividly bright and shining);喜悦的(marked by or expressive of love, confidence or happiness)
(记)radi(光线,射线)+ant→喜悦的
同根词:radiation(发光,传播),radiator(散热器)
(例)The earth is illuminated by the radiant sun. / Her radiant smile showed how happy she was.

radical [ˊrædikəl] a. 根本的,彻底的(of changes, thorough, complete);激进的(extreme; drastic; favoring extreme change)
(记)radic(根)+al→根本的
(例)The radical activist protested in front of city hall.

radius [ˊreidjəs] n. (复数为 radii)半径(the distance from the center of a circle to any point on the circle)
(记)来自 ray(射线),半径可以看作从圆心到圆周的一条线
(例)A circle's diameter is twice the length of its radius.

rage [reidʒ] vi. 大怒(to show extreme, violent anger toward sth. or someone);风(狂吹);盛行,(流行病)猖獗(to prevail uncontrollably; to be in tumult)
(例)The angry citizen raged against the new tax increase. / The disease raged through the city for months.

ragtime [ˊrægtaim] n. 拉格泰姆音乐(或舞蹈)(一种源于美国黑人乐队的早期爵士乐)
(记)分割记忆:rag(破衣服)-time(时候)→穿破

衣服的时候→黑人跳爵士舞，ragtime 还有滑稽、逗人发笑的意思（穿破衣服会逗人发笑）

raid [reid] v. / n. 突然袭击(a surprise attack, esp. by police or soldiers)

(记)不要和 rail(猛烈指责)相混

(例)The police raid resulted in the arrests of five people.

rampage [ˈræmpeidʒ] v. 狂暴地乱冲，暴怒(a course of violent, riotous, reckless action or behavior)

(记)分割记忆：ramp (发怒) - age →暴怒

(例)The boss's rampage frightened all the staff.

rancher [ˈræntʃə] n. 农场主(one who owns a very large farm where cattle or other animals are raised)

(记)来自 ranch(大农场) + er→农场主

(例)The rancher's cattle grazed on government land.

ransom [ˈrænsəm] n. 赎金(money demanded by kidnappers in exchange for releasing a hostage or someone who has been kidnapped); v. 赎回，解救(to free from captivity or punishment by paying a price)

(记)来自拉丁文 redemptio (redemption)

(例)The kidnappers demanded a $100,000 ransom for the child's return. / The firm ransomed the executive for a million dollars.

rapid(s) [ˈræpid] n. (常用复数)急流；湍滩(a part of a river where the current is very fast and active)

(记)来自 rapid(快速)，一般要加上 s

(例)Our rowboat was caught in the rapids, heading toward a waterfall.

rare [rεə] a. (肉类)半熟的，煮得嫩的(boiled lightly; cooked only a little)

(记)rare 的常用意义为"稀有"，中国人吃肉一般都煮得比较老，半熟的在国内属“稀有”
(例)The inside of the rare hamburger was pink.

rate [reit] n.费率(a charge, payment, price fixed according to a ratio, scale or standard)
(例)My health club's rates are cheaper than the rates at the one John goes to.

rating [ˊreitiŋ] n.级别，等级 (a classification according to grade)；(商人，商店等)信用程度(an estimate of an individual's or business's credit and responsibility)
(记)给国外商学院评级时就是用 rating 这个词
(例)Advertising costs are determined by a television show's ratings.

ratio [ˊreiʃiəu] n. 比例(the relationship between one amount as compared to another amount; a proportion)
(记)来自 rate(比率)
(例)The ratio of land to water on the earth is roughly 1 to 3.

ration [ˊræʃən] n.定量配给(an amount of sth., as prescribed by policy, rule or law)
(记)从 ratio (比例)一词转化而来
(例)The citizens received food rations one week at a time.

rationale [ræʃəˊnæl] n.基本原理，根本性的依据(an underlying reason; basis)；原理的阐述(an explanation of controlling principles of opinion, belief, practice, or phenomena)
(记)rational(理性的，合理的)+e→合理的东西→原理，根据
(例)My professor disagreed with the rationale of my argument.

rationality [ræʃən'æliti] n. 理性，理智(the quality or state of being rational or agreeable to reason)
(记)来自 ration(理性的) + ality(性质)→理智

ravenous ['rævinəs] a. 贪婪的(rapacious)；狼吞虎咽的，饿极的(very eager or greedy for food; very hungry)
(记)来自 raven(乌鸦，掠夺) + ous→贪婪的
(例)The ravenous student ate a whole pizza.

reactionist [ri'ækʃənist] n. 反动分子(one who advocates or practices a movement back to a former or less advanced condition, esp. in economics or politics)；a. 反动的
(记)re(反) + action(动) + ist→反运动的人→反动分子

reactor [ri(:)'æktə] n.【原】反应堆
(记)react(反应) + or→发生反应的东西→原子反应堆

real estate ['riləsteit] n. 不动产，房地产(land with all the buildings on it and all the minerals under it, which is bought and sold as a commodity)
(记)real(真正的) + estate(财产)→只有房子才是真正的财产→房地产
(例)I bought a piece of real estate in the suburbs.

realtor ['riəltə] n. 房地产经纪人(a real estate agent, esp. a member of the National Association of Realtors)
(记)Realtor 是美国房地产经纪人协会的一种资格；real(真正的) + tor→经营真正产业的人→经营房地产的人→房地产经纪人

rear [riə] v. 抚养，培养(to raise offspring)；饲养(to breed and raise 〔an animal〕 for use or market)；栽种(to cause 〔as plants〕 to grow)
(记)来自 raise(养孩子)
(例)My parents reared four children.

rebut [riˈbʌt] vt.【律】辩驳(to contradict or oppose by formal legal argument, plea or countervailing proof);揭露,戳穿(to expose the falsity of)

(记)re(反)+but(=butt 顶撞)→反顶撞→反驳,戳穿

(例)The scientist rebutted the cigarette company's claims.

recall [riˈkɔːl] n.公开回收(to request that a product be returned);撤销(cancel, revoke)

(记)re(重新)+call(叫,召集)→重新叫一遍,收集一遍→回收,撤回

(例)The company recalled the defective product.

recapture [riːˈkæptʃə] vt.重获,收复(to capture someone or sth. again)

(记)re(重新)+capture(夺取)→再次获得→收复,恢复

(例)The prisoner was recaptured the day after he escaped.

recast [riːˈkɑːst] vt.重新铸造(to cast again);彻底改造(remodel, refashion)

(记)re(从新)+cast(铸造)→彻底改变

receipt [riˈsiːt] n.收到(a state of having been received);收据(a statement that proves that sth. has been received or paid for);收入(money that is collected by a business or at a performance)

(记)来自 receive(收到)

(例)I expect receipt of the letter tomorrow. / I showed the guard my receipt for my purchases. / The accountant examined the records of the store's receipts.

receptor [riˈseptə] n.感受器;受体(a cell or group of cells that receives stimuli; sense organ); 接受器

(记)recept(接受)+or→受体,主要用于生物学领域

recession [riˈseʃən] n. 衰退时期,萧条时期(a period of reduced economic activity)

(记)re(反)+cess(走)+ion→反着走的时候→萧条期

(例)Many auto workers were laid off during the last recession.

reciprocal [riˈsiprəkəl] a. 相互的,交互的(shared, felt or shown by both sides);互惠的(giving and receiving at the same time);相应的(mutually corresponding)

(记)re(重新)+ciproc(=cip+pro 向前放下)+al→重新向前放下→互相给予→互惠

(例) John believed that all deeds were reciprocal, so if he did something nice for someone, someone would do something nice for him.

reciprocal [riˈsiprəkəl] n. 倒数(either of a pair of numbers [as 1/2 and 2 or 3/4 and 4/3] whose product is 1)

(记)相互(reciprocal)乘积为 1 的一对数

reclamation [rekləˈmeiʃən] n. 开垦;改造,感化;废料回收(restoration to use; recovery; reformation, rehabilitation)

(记)re(重新)+claim(拥有)+ation→重新拥有→回收,开垦

(例)The reclamation of the old mansion cost many thousands of dollars. / The reclamation of my possessions from the ashes was futile.

recoup [riˈku:p] vt. 赔偿,补偿,偿还(reimburse, compensate)

(记)re(反)+coup(意外的行动)→意外的反向行

动→赔偿

(例)The investor could not recoup the money she has spent on the stock.

recruit [riˈkruːt] n. 新兵,新成员(a newcomer to a field or activity; a newly enlisted or drafted member of the armed forces);v. 征募(to fill up the number of [as an army] with new members)

(记)re(重新)+cruit(=cres 成长)→重新成长→新兵

(例)The new recruits' heads were shaved. / The sergeant recruited college graduates to join the army.

recruiter [riˈkruːtə] n. 征兵人员;为学校招生的人

(记)recruit(新兵)+er→招新兵的人

rectangle [ˈrektæŋgl] n. 长方形

(记)rect(直)+angle(角)→每个角均为直角的多边形→长方形

(例)A square is a rectangle whose four sides are all equal.

recur [riˈkəː] vi. 再发生(to repeat; to happen again);重新提起(to bring up again for consideration)

(记)re(重新)+cur(=curr 跑)→跑回来→重现

(例)The same dream recurred night after night.

redress [riˈdres] v./n. 改正,修正(compensation for a wrong that has been done; correction)

(记)re(重新)+dress(穿衣,整理)→重新整理→改正

(例)The newspaper was fined to redress the injustice it had done with its libellous article.

reduce [riˈdjuːs] v. 降低(to diminish in size, amount, extent or number)

(记)与 deduct(扣除;演绎)一起记

(例)The politician promised to reduce taxes.

referendum [refəˈrendəm] n.(关于政治措施,法律等)公民投票(a direct vote by the voters of an area about a specific issue);复决权

(例)The voters' referendum was voided by the Supreme Court.

reflex [ˈriːfleks] n.(对刺激的)本能反应(movements of the body in response to an external stimulation);[~es]反应能力

(记)re(反)+flex(弯曲)→反过来弯曲→反应

(例)The doctor tested my reflexes by tapping my knee with a mallet.

refund [riːˈfʌnd] v.退款(to give back the money paid for a product or service);n.偿还额(money that is given back when someone returns a product to a store)

(记)re(重新)+fund(付钱)→再次付钱→偿还

(例)The store refunded $10 to Jane for the belt./John got a five-cent refund for returning his empty bottle.

regime [reiˈʒiːm] n.政权,政治制度(government; rule)

(记)reg(统治)+ime→统治机构→政权,政治制度

(例)the parliamentary regime(议会制度)/a capitalist regime(资本主义政体)

regiment [ˈredʒimənt] n.【军】团;v.严格控制(to treat someone strictly; to control someone)

(记)regi(=rigid 严格)+ment→严格控制;军队里的团

(例)The nutritionist regimented my diet.

regressive [riˈgresiv] a.(税率)递减的(decreasing in rate as the base increases);退化的(going back to an earlier condition or stage of development)

(记)re(后)+gress(走)+ive→向后走→退步的

(例)After a few regressive periods of severe pain, John began to recover from his surgery quickly.

rehabilitate [riːhəˊbiliteit] v. 修复(to restore or bring to a condition of health);恢复(职位等)(to restore to a former state [as of efficiency, good management, or solvency])

(记)reh(重新)+abilit(能力)+ate→重新获得能力→修复,恢复

参考:debilitate(使衰弱)

(例)David rehabilitated his car, and then he sold it. / The physical therapist rehabilitated Anne after her accident.

rehash [ˌriːˊhæʃ] vt. 以新形式处理旧内容,重复(to present or use again in another form without substantial change or improvement)

(记)re(重新)+hash(处理)→重复

(例)While debating, Anne rehashed the same arguments over and over.

reign [rein] n. 统治时期,王朝(the period of the rule of a king, queen, emperor, etc.);领域

(记)来自 reg(统治)的变体;注意与 regime(政权)的区别

(例)During the reign of King George III, the American colonies declared independence.

reimburse [ˌriːimˊbəːs] v. 偿还,给报销(to pay back to someone)

(记)re(重新)+im(进入)+burse(钱包)→重新进入钱包→偿还

(例)I reimbursed John for the $25 I had borrowed. / My company will reimburse my hotel bills.

reiterate [riːˈitəreit] vt. 重申，反复地说(to state repeatedly; to repeat an assertion)
(记)re(反复)+iterate(重申)→反复重申
(例)The teacher reiterated the most important points of the lecture.

rekindle [ˌriːˈkindl] v. 重新点燃(to start 〔a fire〕 burning again; to light again)
(记)re(重新)+kindle(点燃)→重燃

relay [ˈriːlei] n. 驿马；补充物资(a supply arranged beforehand for successive relief)；接替人员(a number of persons who relieve others in some work)；work in relays 轮班工作，接力赛跑
(记)re(重新)+lay(布置)→补充，接替
(例)New relays of men were sent to fight the flood.

relentless [riˈlentlis] a. 无情的，残酷的(without pity; severe, harsh, cruel)
(记)relent(动怜悯心，减弱)+less→不能变温和→残酷的
(例)The relentless landlord evicted the unemployed tenant.

relinquish [riˈliŋkwiʃ] v. 放弃；废除(to give sth. up; to let sth. go)
(记)re(再次)+linqu(=leave 离开)+ish→再次离开→放弃
(例)The king relinquished the throne because of the scandal.

remainder [riˈmeində] n. 余数(the number left after a subtraction; the final undivided part after division)
(记)来自 remain(剩余)，指减法之后的余数或除法中的商
(例)14 divides into 3 four times, leaving a remain-

der of 2.

remedy [ˊremidi] n. 治疗法，药物(a medicine, application, or treatment that relieves or cures a disease); 补救；纠正(an improvement of bad conditions or the correction of a problem)

(例)The doctor's remedy was to rest and drink lots of water. / The manager's remedy of the difficult situation was brilliant.

reminiscence [ˌremiˊnisns] n. 回忆，缅怀往事(the process of thinking or telling about past experiences); a. 回忆的；往事的(a remembered experience)

(记)re(重新) + mini(小的) + scence(= scene 情景)→重放小场景→缅怀往事

(例)The old friends shared happy reminiscences about their past.

renaissance [ˊrenəˊsɑːns] n. 新生；复活(rebirth, revival); 文艺复兴

(记)re(重新) + naiss(= nas 出生) + ance→新生；复兴

参考：reconnaissance(侦察)

(例)The old neighborhood enjoyed a renaissance as people began to repair their houses. / William Shakespeare was a famous playwright of the Renaissance.

rendition [renˊdiʃən] n. 表演(a performance of a piece of music, a drama or the reading of poetry); 翻译(translation)

(记)分割记忆：rend(撕碎) - ition→撕碎东西给人看→表演

(例)Bill's rendition of the sonata was flawless.

repeal [riˊpiːl] v.【律】废除，废止(to void a law; to cause a law to no longer be valid)

(记)re(反)+peal(=call 叫)→反过来叫→废除
同根词:appeal(呼吁)
(例)The 18th Amendment was repealed in 1933.

repertoire [ˈrepətwɑː] n.(剧团等)常备剧目(a list or supply of dramas, operas, pieces, parts that a company or person is prepared to perform)
(记)来自法语,re(反复)+pert(带)+oire→反复带着的剧目→常备剧目
参考:repertory(仓库)
(例)The dance company's repertoire was limited to ballet.

replete [riˈpliːt] a.饱满的,塞满的(fully or abundantly provided or filled)
(记)re(重新)+plete(满)→塞满
(例)He is a mind replete with learning.(他是位饱学之士。)/Their home is replete with every modern convenience.

replicate [ˈreplikeit] v.复制,重复(to make a copy of sth., duplicate; repeat)
(记)re(重新)+plic(重叠)+ate→折叠→复制
(例)The counterfeiter could not replicate the currency accurately.

repository [riˈpɔzitəri] n.贮藏室,仓库(a place, room, container where sth. is deposited or stored)
(记)re(反复)+pos(放)+itory→放东西的地方→仓库
(例)At city hall, there's a repository of birth records.

reproach [riˈprəutʃ] vt.斥责,非难(to express disappointment in or displeasure with [a person]);使丢脸,有辱…的名誉(to bring into discredit)
(记)re(反)+proach(靠近)→以反对的方式

靠近 → 谴责

(例)The teacher reproached the students for cheating.

reptile [ˈreptail] n. 爬行动物

(记)rept(爬) + ile→爬的东西→爬行动物

reptilian [repˊtiliən] a. 爬虫类的;卑下的(cold-bloodedly treacherous)

(记)来自 reptile(爬行动物),爬虫是卑下的

repudiate [riˊpjudieit] v. 拒付(to refuse to pay);拒绝,抛弃(to refuse to accept; to reject as untrue or unjust)

(记)re(反) + pudi(= put 放) + ate→放掉→抛弃

(例)The court repudiated John's claim to the disputed property.

repudiation [ripjuːdiˊeiʃən] n. 拒付

(记)参考上面的 repudiate

(例)waver between straight repudiation and moratorium(在断然拒付债款和延期清偿之间摇摆不定)

rescind [riˊsind] v. 废除(法律等)(to make void by action of the enacting authority or a superior authority; repeal)

(记)re(反) + scind(= cut 砍)→砍掉→废除

(例)The city council rescinded the tax increase.

resent [riˊzent] v. 憎恶,愤恨(to feel or express annoyance or ill will at)

(记)re(反) + sent(感情)→反感,憎恶

(例)Employees resent long hours without compensation.

reservation [rezəˊveiʃən] n. 保留(意见)(an act of reserving sth.; a limiting condition; a doubt about sth.)

(记)re(反复) + serv(= serve 保存) + ation→保留观点→谨慎

(例)I have reservations about going to unsafe neighborhoods at night.

resign [ri'zain] v. 辞职(to quit a job officially);顺从,听天由命(to give 〔oneself〕 over without resistance; to accept sth. as inevitable)
(记)re(再次)+sign(签字)→再次签字→辞职
(例)Richard Nixon resigned the office of President in 1974. / Anne resigned herself to her fate.

respire [ris'paiə] v. 呼吸(to breathe, to inhale and exhale air successively)

responsive [ris'pɔnsiv] a. 应答的(answering);易起反应的,敏感的(quick to respond or react appropriately; sensitive)
(记)respons(反应)+ive→有反应的→敏感的
(例)The patient was not responsive to the sound of my voice. / The teacher enjoyed the responsive students.

restitution [ˌresti'tjuːʃən] n. 归还(a restoration of sth. to its rightful owner);赔偿(the payment made to replace sth. that was lost, taken or stolen)
(记) re (重新) + stitut (站立) + ion → 重新站过去 → 归还
同根词:institution(创立,建立)
(例)Restitution of the stolen painting pleased the museum director. / John sought restitution when David damaged his car.

resurgence [ri'səːdʒəns] n. 复兴,复活(revival after defeat, destruction or disapperance)
(记)re(重新)+surg(=surge 浪潮)+ence→重起浪潮→复兴的
(例)After years of decline, downtown businesses experienced a resurgence.

resuscitation [riˌsʌsiˈteiʃən] n. 复活，苏醒(restoration of life or consciousness)

(记)re(重新) + sus(下) + cit(引起) + ation→重新引起生命→复活

(例)Doctors at the Emergency Care attempted resuscitation when the drowned man was brought in.

retail [ˈriːteil] v. / n. 零售(to sell commodities or goods in small quantities directly to the ultimate consumers); retailer 零售商

(记)re(再次) + tail(剪，玩)→剪下来卖→零售

同根词：tailor(裁缝)

(例)My new sofa retailed for $500.

retaliation [riˌtæliˈeiʃən] n. 报复，反击(the act of returning a bad deed to someone who has done a bad deed to oneself; revenge)

(记) re (反) + tail (邪恶) + ation → 把邪恶还回去→报复

参考：talisman(避邪物)；retaliatory(报复性的)

(例)He punched me, and I kicked him in retaliation.

retard [riˈtɑːd] v. 妨碍，推迟(to slow up, esp. by preventing or hindering advance or accomplishment; impede)

(记)re(使) + tard(迟缓)→使…迟缓→妨碍

同根词：tardy(行动慢的，迟到的)

(例)The inflation rate was retarded by the government policies.

retention [riˈtenʃən] n. 保留，保持(retaining, holding or keeping sth.)

(记)re(重新) + tent(拿住) + ion→重新拿住→保留

(例)As an aid to memory retention, I copied my

notes again after class.

retentive [ri'tentiv] a. 有记忆力的(able to remember, esp. by retaining knowledge easily)
(记)与 retention(保留,保持)一起记
(例)The retentive student did very well on the exam.

revenue ['revənjuː] n. 收入(the total income produced by a given source)
(记)re(回)+ven(来)+ue→回来的东西→收入
同根词:revenant(归来之人)
(例)The company's owner reinvested the company's revenue in real estate.

revere [ri'viə] v. 尊崇,尊敬(to have a deep respect for someone or sth.; to admire someone very much)
(记)re(一再)+vere(害怕,敬畏)→不断敬畏→崇敬
(例)The honest politician was revered by his constituents.

revise [ri'vaiz] vt. 修订,校订(to look over again in order to correct, improve or include new information)
(记)re(重新)+vise(签证)→校订
(例)The author revised her book for the second edition.

revisionist [ri'viʒənist] n. 修正主义者(one that advocated or participated in the movement of Marxian socialism favoring an evolutionary rather than a revolutionary spirit); a. 修正主义的
(记)来自 revise(修订)

revitalize [riː'vaitəlaiz] v. 使复活,使重新充满活力(to cause someone or sth. to have energy or power again; to give new life or vigor to)
(记)re(重新)+vital(有活力的)+ize→使…重新

有活力
同根词:vitality(生命力,活力)
(例)The new business revitalized the downtown area.

revival [ri'vaivəl] n.复活,复兴(the process of returning life or energy to someone or sth.)
(记)来自 revive(使复活),re(重新)+vive(有生气的)→复活
(例)The new factory was responsible for the industrial town's revival.

revokable [ri'vəukəbl] a.可撤销的(capable of being canceled or repealed)
(记)来自 revoke(废除),re(反)+voke(喊)→反过来喊→取消,revok(=revoke)+able→可废除的,可撤销的

rhetoric ['retərik] n.修辞学,辩术(the art of speaking or writing in a way that persuades or influences other people effectively);花言巧语(the words that are used when trying to persuade or influence other people)
(记)来自 Rhetor(古希腊的修辞学教师,演说家)
(例)The debater was highly skilled in the art of rhetoric. / The politician's rhetoric didn't persuade me to vote for him.

rhinoceros [rai'nɔsərəs] n.犀牛;犀属

rhombus ['rɔmbəs] n.菱形(a parallelogram with four equal sides and unequal angles)
(记)来自 rhomb(菱形)

rhythmical ['riðmikl] a.有韵律的,有节奏的(marked by or moving in pronounced rhythm)
(记)rhythm(节奏)+ical,也可以写作 rhythmic
参考:arrhythmic(无节奏的)

(例)We danced to the rhythmic drum.

rib [rib] n.【解】肋骨;(叶)脉,主脉;【动】翅脉,伞骨
(记)肋骨、脉和伞骨形状比较类似,可以类推

rigorous [ˊrigərəs] a. 严厉的,严格的(very strict, harsh or severe)
(记)rig(=rigid 严厉的)+orous→严厉的
(例)The soldiers' training was very rigorous.

rinse [rins] v. 冲洗,冲刷(to cleanse by flushing with liquid〔as water〕)
(记)rin(=rain 下雨)+se→冲洗
(例)Mary rinsed her dirty shoes with the garden hose.

rival [ˊraivəl] n. 竞争者,对手(someone against whom one competes or plays);匹敌者(one that equals another in desired qualities)
(例)The tennis player shook hands with her rival after the game.

rivalry [ˊraivəlri] n. 竞争,敌对(the act or state of rivaling; competition)
(记)来自 rival(对手)
(例)Bob and Anne encouraged sibling rivalry among their children.

robin [ˊrɔbin] n. 知更鸟

robust [rəuˊbʌst] a. 健壮的(having or exhibiting strength or vigorous health)
(记)分割记忆:ro(可看作 round)+bust(半身像)→圆圆的半身像→健壮的
(例)Robust children drink a lot of milk.

rodent [ˊrəudənt] n. 啮齿类动物
(记)rod(咬)+ent→咬的动物
同根词:erode(侵蚀);corrode(腐蚀)

rubble [ˊrʌbl] n.(一堆)碎石,瓦砾(broken stones, bricks

or other material)

(记)rub(摩擦)+ble→一堆碎石在一起会摩擦

(例)After the explosion, the building was reduced to rubble.

rudimentary [ˌruːdiˈmentəri] a. 基本的,基础的(consisting in first principles; fundamental)

(记)rudi(无知的,粗鲁的)+ment+ary→无知状态→初步的

同根词:erudite(深奥的)

(例)This manual provides a few rudimentary facts about computers. / This program is only rudimentary and is being developed for release next year.

runner [ˈrʌnə] n. 蔓藤植物,长匐茎

(记)run(跑)+ner→会在墙上跑的植物→蔓藤,该词另一常用意为"参加长跑者"

rupture [ˈrʌptʃə] v. / n. 破裂,断裂(to break or burst suddenly)

(记)rupt(断)+ure→断裂

(例)The cold weather ruptured the water pipes.

S

sabotage [ˈsæbətɑːʒ] n. 阴谋破坏,颠覆活动(secret, intentional damage done to property or a project)

(记)sabot(木鞋)+age,原指将木鞋扔进机器进行破坏

(例)The disgruntled employee committed sabotage against the firm.

sacralization [ˌseikrəlaiˈzeiʃən] n. 神化(the act or state of making someone or sth. holy or sacred)

(记)来自 sacred(神圣的)

salable [ˈseiləbl] a. 可出售的,卖得出的,有销路的(capa-

ble of being or fit to be sold; marketable)
(记)sal(=sale 卖)+able→可以卖的→有销路的

salience [ˊseiliəns] n.显著,突出(the quality or state of being standing out conspicuously; notably significant; prominent)
(记)sal(跳)+ience→跳起来→突出; a. salient (显著的,突出的)

saliva [səˊlaivə] n.唾液,口水
(记)sal(=salt 盐)+iva→盐吃多了会口渴→口水
(例)John spit some saliva onto the ground.

samurai [ˊsæmurai] n.(日本)武士阶层(the warrior aristocracy of Japan);陆军将校
(记)来自日语,指推崇武士道的人

sanction [ˊsæŋkʃən] n.认可,批准(approval by an authority to do sth.; permission);制裁(a restriction placed against a country that has done sth. wrong)
(记)sanct(神圣)+ion→神圣之物,原指教会的法令,引申为"批准";"赞许"
(例)The reporter had an official sanction to meet with the mayor. / Many years after the war, the United States finally lifted the sanctions against Vietnam.

sanctuary [ˊsæŋktjuəri] n.圣堂(a sacred or holy building; a holy place of worship);避难所(a state of safety or refuge traditionally provided by a house of worship)
(记)sanct(神圣)+uary(地方)→圣堂,圣堂经常会成为避难所
(例)The developer was not allowed to build on the ruins of the sanctuary. / The exiled king sought sanctuary in the church.

sandwich [ˊsænwidʒ] vt.把…做成三明治(to make into or

as if into a sandwich);夹入,挤进(to put someone or sth. tightly between or among other persons or objects)
(记)挤入的意思系由三明治的原意引申而来
(例)The librarian sandwiched the book into a tight space on the shelf.

sanitarium [ˌsæniˈteəriəm] n. 疗养院,休养地(a hospital where people who have a particular sickness, esp. tuberculosis or mental diseases, stay while they are getting better)
(记)sanit(卫生)+arium(场地)→卫生之地→疗养院
(例)The mental patient was placed in the county sanitarium.

sanitary [ˈsænitəri] a. 卫生的,清洁的(very clean; not dangerous to one's health)
(记)可与 sanitarium 一起记
(例)The doctor's office was extremely sanitary.

sap [sæp] n. 树液(a fluid in a tree that carries important nutrients to all of its parts); 活力(bodily health and vigor); v. 削弱,耗尽(to weaken or destroy)
(记)在古代,树液被认为是树的活力所在;另外,SAP 还是一家著名软件公司的名字
(例)The sap from the tree make my hands sticky when I touched it. / The continuing war sapped the nation's economy.

saturate [ˈsætʃəreit] v. 使饱和(to satisfy fully; to treat, furnish, or charge with sth. to the point where no more can be absorbed, dissolved, or retained); 浸透,湿透(to cause someone or sth. to become completely wet; soak)

(记)satur(饱,满)+ate

(例)The politician saturated her speech with promises. / The heavy rains saturated the farmland.

scale [skeil] n. 鱼鳞;(音乐)音阶(a graduated series of musical tones);v. 攀登(to climb up)

(记)这三个意思可以一起记,鱼鳞一层一层叠在一起,可以看作在逐渐升高

(例)John scraped the fish's scales off with a knife. / The opera singer warmed up her voice by practicing scales. / The climber scaled the mountain.

scan [skæn] vt. 粗略地看,浏览(to look through sth. quickly and carelessly);扫描(to put a picture or a text into a computer file by placing the picture or book on a scanner)

(记)扫描这个意思是新出现的,扫描仪是 scanner

(例)John scanned the reading assignment briefly before class. / Bill scanned a photo of himself and saved it in a file called "Me".

scapegoat [ˈskeipgəut] n. 替罪羊(someone who is blamed for the mistakes of others)

(记)来自圣经故事

(例)The inept worker was a scapegoat for all of the company's problems.

scarcity [ˈskɛəsiti] n. 缺乏,稀少(the quality or state of being scarce, esp. want of provisions for the support of life)

(记)来自 scarce(稀少的)

(例)There was a scarcity of fresh fruit during the war.

scatter [ˈskætə] v. 分散,扩散(to cause to separate widely; to distribute irregularly)

(记)注意与 scat(快走,乱叫)的区别
(例) Dozens of books were scattered across my desk.

scenario [si'nɑ:riəu] n. 剧情说明书,剧本(a summary of the plot of a story, movie or play)
(记)scen(=scene 场景)+ario→剧情梗概
(例)The teacher outlined the scenario of the play in class.

scintillate ['sintileit] v. 闪烁(to emit sparks);(谈吐)流露机智(to speak wittily, lively or stimulatingly)
(记)scintill(火花)+ate→闪火花,闪烁
(例)The stars scintillated in the winter sky.

scorch [skɔ:tʃ] v. 烤焦,烧焦(to dry or shrivel with intense heat; parch)
(记)可以与 torch(火炬)一起记
(例)The papers near the fire scorched but did not burn.

scour ['skauə] v. 四处搜索(to search a place thoroughly while looking for someone or sth.);擦洗,擦亮(to clean sth. by rubbing with a lot of force)
(例) The police scoured the area for the missing child. / Dave scoured the carpet with rug cleaner.

scramble ['skræmbl] v. 爬行,攀登(to move or climb hastily on all fours);争夺(to struggle eagerly or unceremoniously for possession of sth.);仓促地行动(to move with urgency or panic)
(记)分割记忆:scr 看作 scale(攀登) - amble(快走)
(例)The mountain goat scrambled up the hillside. / The six candidates all scrambled for the party's nomination.

scrap [skræp] n. 小片,碎屑(a small piece of sth., esp.

one that is left over from a larger piece); v. 废弃 (to throw sth. away)

(记)和 scrape(刮、擦)一起记

(例)Jane fed scraps of meat to her dog. / The manager scrapped the failed project.

screen [skri:n] v. 筛选,区分(to separate, conceal, shelter or protect with a screen);审查(to interview or test so as to separate according to skills, personality, aptitudes, etc.)

(记)screen 的动词意义都是由名词意思(屏幕,筛子)引申而来的,可以联系记忆

(例)A partition screened the contestants from the audience. / A butler screened the diplomat's visitors.

scrupulous [ˈskru:pjuləs] a. 多顾虑的,谨慎的(尤指道德方面)(full of scruples; hesitant, doubtful or uneasy, esp. constantly and obsessively, in deciding what is morally right or wrong);严格认真的,拘泥的(extremely careful to do the precisely right, proper or correct thing in every detail; most punctilious)

(记)来自 scruple(审慎,犹豫)

(例)A scrupulous man, he gave the money back to the owner. / This job needs scrupulous care.

scrutinize [ˈskru:tinaiz] vt. / vi. 细看,细阅,仔细检查(to look at very carefully; examine closely; inspect minutely)

(记)scrutin(检查)+ize→详细检查

(例)My lawyer scrutinized my contract carefully.

scurrilous [ˈskʌriləs] a. 下流的,恶言的(using indecent or abusive language; vulgar; foulmouthed)

(记)scurril(下流)+ous→下流的;可以和 scurry(急奔)一起记

scurvy [ˊskəːvi] a. 卑鄙的，可鄙的(disgustingly mean or contemptible; despicable)

(例)a scurvy trick / a scurvy fellow(卑鄙的家伙)

seance [ˊseiɑːns] n. [法]集会，会议，降神会(a meeting at which a medium seeks or professes to communicate with the spirits of the dead)

(记)来自法语，sea(海)+nce→人山人海→集会

(例)At seance, the medium(巫师)tried to contact the souls of the dead.

secretion [siˊkriʃən] n. 分泌(the production and release of fluid from living things)

(记)secret(秘密的)+ion→秘密的溢出→分泌

(例)The liver produces a secretion of bile.

secular [ˊsekjulə] a. 世俗的，尘世的(worldly; not sacred)

(例)Advancement of a religion is not permitted in secular schools.

secure [siˊkjuə] v. 获得(to get hold or possession of; obtain; acquire)

(记)与 secure 的通常意义"安全"联系起来记忆，获得安全

(例)Do you know where I can secure a good hotel room for the night?

sedan [siˊdæn] n. 轿子(亦作 sedan chair)；轿车(an enclosed automobile with four doors, a front seat and a back seat, a fixed roof and room for at least four people)

(记)sed(坐)+an→坐的东西→轿车；轿子、轿车的共同特征是四周封闭，并且开有窗户

(例)My friends and I rented a sedan when we drove to Texas.

sedentary [ˊsedntəri] a. 久坐的(marked by much sitting about and little travel; keeping one seated much of the time);固定不动的(remaining in one locality; fixed to one spot)

(记)sed(坐)+entary→久坐的

(例)Driving a car is a sedentary activity. / Our old dog has become very sedentary.

sediment [ˈsedimənt] n. 沉淀物,渣(pieces of solid matter that settle at the bottom of a liquid)

(记)sedi(坐)+ment→坐下去的东西→沉淀物

(例)The sediment in your orange juice is orange pulp.

seductive [siˈdʌktiv] a. 诱人的,有魅力的(tempting, alluring or enticing)

(记)se(分开)+duc(引导)+tive→引开→勾引

(例)Beware of the seductive power of greed.

segment [ˈsegmənt] n. 线段(any of the finite sections of a line)

(记)seg(=sect 部分)+ment→线的一部分→线段

参考:segmentable(可分割的),segmental(部分的、片断的)

segregation [segriˈgeiʃən] n. 隔离(the separation of someone or sth. from other things or people)

(记)se(分开)+greg(团体)+ation→和团体分开→隔离

参考:aggregate(集合)

(例)The jail enforced the segregation of dangerous criminals.

seismic [ˈsaizmik] a. 地震的,有关地震的(of or relating to earthquake)

(记)seism(地震)+ic→地震的

(例)The Japanese are used to small seismic tremors.

seismologist [saiz′ mɔlədʒist] n. 地震学者(someone who is trained in the study of earthquakes)
(例)After the quake, the seismologists said to expect additional jolts.

semiarid [ˌsemi′ærid] a. 半干旱的(characterized by little yearly rainfall and by the growth of short grasses and shrubs)
(记)semi(半)+arid(干旱的)→半干旱的

semiconductor [semikən′dʌktə] n. 半导体(a substance that allows electricity to pass through it, but not as well as some metals do)
(记)semi(半)+conductor(导体)→部分导电的物体→半导体
(例)Silicon is a common semiconductor.

seminal [′seminl] a. 有创意的(creative; original)
(记)semin(种)+al→种子的→有创见的
同根词:disseminate(播种)
(例)one of the most seminal of the great poets

seminar [′seminɑː] n. (大学的)研究班(a group of advanced students studying under a professor with each doing original research and all exchanging results through reports and discussions);专家讨论会(a meeting for giving and discussing information)
(记)semin(种子)+ar→培养种子的地方,产生创意的地方→研究班,讨论会;注意:seminary(神学院)
(例)The sales manager attended a motivational seminar.

semiotics [ˌsemi′ɔtiks] n.【哲】符号学(a general philosophical theory of sighs and symbols)
(记)来自希腊语 semeion(即 sign,符号)

seniority [ˌsiːni′ɔriti] n. 年长(the quality of being older than someone else)；资历深(the quality of having been employed at one's place of work for a relatively longer period of time than someone else)

(记)senior(年长的，老资格的)+ity→年长，资历深

(例)I respect my professors because of their seniority.

sensational [sen'seiʃənl] a. 耸人听闻的(flamboyant or exaggerated; designed to excite and appeal to a mass audience)；轰动的(very exciting or interesting; fantastic)

(记) sens (感觉) + ation (动) + al → 能感觉到动的 → 轰动的

同根词：sensible(明智的)，sensitive(敏感的)

(例)The singer gave a sensational performance yesterday.

sensible ['sensəbl] a. 明智的(having, containing, indicative of good sense or reason; wise)

(记)sens(=sense 感觉)+ible→有感觉的，明智的

(例)The sensible action would be to save as much money as possible.

sensuality ['sensju'æləti] n. 耽于声色(persistent or excessive pursuit of the pleasures and interests of eating, drinking, sex, etc.)

(记)sense(感觉)+ual+ity→沉迷于感官享受

(例)Sensuality occupies much of Bob's time.

sentient ['senʃənt] a. 有感觉能力的，有感觉的(responsive to or conscious of sense impressions; aware)

(记)sent(感觉)+ient→有感觉的

(例)be sentient of a tense atmosphere(意识到一种紧张气氛)

sentiment [ˈsentimənt] n. 思想感情,情操(a tender feeling or emotion);情绪(an attitude, thought or judgment prompted by feeling)
(记)senti(感觉)+ment→感情;观点
(例)Bill's sentiment was expressed in a poem. / We share the same sentiment about the death of our leader Deng Xiaoping.

sentinel [ˈsentinl] n. 哨兵(a soldier standing guard at a point of passage〔as a gate〕)
(记)senti(感觉)+nel→感觉者→哨兵,可与 sentry(哨兵)一起记
(例)The sentinel allowed me to pass when I said the password.

Seoul [səul] n. 汉城(韩国首都)

sequel [ˈsiːkwəl] n. 继续(subsequent development);继之而来的事(sth. that happens after sth. else, usually as a result);后果(consequence, result)
(记)sequ(跟随)+el→跟随,随之而来
(例)As a sequel to his traffic accident, Bill lost his job for being late.

sequential [siˈkwenʃəl] a. 连续的(following in sequence);一连串的(serial)
(记)sequ(跟随)+ent+ial→一连串的
参考:sequence(连续)
(例)sequential file system 系列文件系统

sequester [siˈkwestə] v.(使)隐退,隐居(seclude)
(记)注意不要和 sequestrate(扣押)相混,二个单词均来自 sequ(跟随)

sermonize [ˈsəːmənaiz] v. 说教(to speak didactically or dogmatically);讲道(to compose or deliver a sermon)
(记)sermon(布道)+ize
参考:homiletics(布道学)

session [ˊseʃən] n. 会议(a meeting or series of meetings);会期(a period of time during which a meeting is held); 一段时间(a period devoted to a particular activity)
(例)We chose to attend the morning session of the seminar and skip the afternoon session.

shatter [ˊʃætə] v. 粉碎(to break at once into pieces);使散开(to cause to drop or be dispersed);吹散;破坏(to damage badly; destroy; demolish)
(记)可以与 scatter(分散)联系记忆
(例)The vase shattered when it fell off the table. / The explosion shattered the peace of the rural farming village.

shield [ʃi:ld] n. 盾,庇护物(a device that serves as a protective cover or barrier; a protective structure);v. 保卫,庇护(to protect with or as if with a shield; provide with a protective cover or shelter);挡开(off)
(记)要牢记 shield 的原始意义"盾",其他意义均可引申而来
(例)This shield protects your eyes from damage. / The heavy coat shielded me from the cold.

shift [ʃift] v. 替换(to exchange for or replace by another);转移(to change the place, position or direction of; move)
(记)shiftless 是偷懒,没有决断力的意思
(例)The driver shifted gears as the car went up the hill.

shelter [ˊʃeltə] n. 隐蔽处,躲避处(常用来指住处)(sth. that covers or affords protection);v. 庇护(to constitute or provide a shelter for)
(记)注意不要与 shelve(搁置)相混淆

(例)The picnickers sought shelter from the rainstorm. / The tent sheltered the campers from the rain.

shoplifting [ˈʃɔpliftiŋ] n. 在商店行窃(the stealing of displayed goods from a store)

(记) shop (商店) + lifting (举起) → 进商店举东西→行窃

(例)A young thief was arrested for shoplifting.

shortfall [ˈʃɔːtfɔːl] n. 亏空,不足(a failure to come up to expectation or need; the amount of such failure)

(记) short (短) + fall (下落) → 因收入下降而短少→亏空

(例)The company treasurer hadn't anticipated a shortfall.

shrewd [ʃruːd] a. 判断敏捷的,精明的(marked by clever discerning awareness and hardheaded acumen)

(记)可以与 shrew(泼妇)一起记忆

(例)The shrewd business owner made large profits.

shrill [ʃril] a. 尖锐的,刺耳的(having or emitting a sharp high-pitched tone or sound; piercing)

(记)可与 thrill(发抖)一起记

(例)The referee's shrill whistle hurt my ears.

shuttle [ˈʃʌtl] n. (织机的)梭;穿梭运输工具(a bus or an airplane making regular trips back and forth between two places)

(记)航天飞机被称为 space shuttle

(例)I took a shuttle from school to the train station.

sickle [ˈsikl] n. 镰刀

(记)sick(病) + le→因病而弯曲→镰刀是弯的→镰刀

sidestep [ˈsaidstep] n.(侧面)台阶;拳击等横跨一步躲避打击(a step aside〔as in boxing to avoid a blow〕);v.[喻]回避(困难)(to avoid〔usu. sth. difficult or unpleasant〕)

(记)side(边)+step(步)→向边上跨出一步→回避

(例)The celebrity sidestepped the reporter's personal questions.

siege [siːdʒ] n.包围,围攻(a military blockade of a city or fortified place to compel it to surrender; a persistent or serious attack)

(例)During the enemy's siege, no one could leave or enter the city.

skepticism [ˈskeptisizəm] n.怀疑主义(an attitude of doubt or a disposition to incredulity)

(记)来自 skeptical(怀疑的)

(例)John's skepticism of evolution is based on his religious beliefs.

skeptic [ˈskeptik] n.怀疑者(sb. who doubts or suspects sth.)

sketch [sketʃ] n.素描(a rough drawing representing the main features of an object or scene)

sketchy [ˈsketʃi] a.概略的,粗略的(roughly outlined; without details)

(记)来自 sketch(素描)+y

(例)The reporter only had sketchy information about the bomb blast.

skull [skʌl] n.头骨

slander [ˈslændə] v.诽谤,中伤(to utter false charges or misrepresentations which defame and damage another's reputation)

(例)The newscaster slandered the politician by reporting gossip.

slice [slais] n. 薄片，切片(a thin flat piece cut from sth.)；部分(portion, share)
(记)可与 sly(狡猾的)一起记
(例)Mary put a slice of ham on her sandwich. / Taxes take a large slice of my income.

slip [slip] n. 疏忽(an unintentional and trivial mistake or fault)；v. 溜走(to move or happen quietly, quickly, smoothly, easily, secretly)
(记)拖鞋是 slipper
(例)Anne's slip at work caused her to be demoted. / The thief slipped out of the police station. / a slip of the pen (tongue) 笔(口)误

slowdown [ˊsləudaun] n. 减速；减退；怠工
(记)slow(慢)+down(下)→慢下来→减速

smallpox [ˊsmɔːlpɔks] n. 天花
(记)small(小)+pox(痘)→小痘痘→天花

smear [smiə] vt. 涂抹，弄脏(to spread sth. on a surface, especially in a careless or messy fashion)；诽谤，玷污(to ruin someone's reputation)
(例)The child smeared paint everywhere. / The gossip columnist smeared the celebrity's reputation.

smite [smait] vt. (smote, smitten)重击，打(to strike sharply or heavily, esp. with the hand or an implement held in the hand)；击败；侵袭(to attack or afflict suddenly and injuriously)
(例)smite the enemy with sword

smog [smɔg] n. 烟雾(a fog made heavier and darker by smoke and chemical fumes)
(记)这个词是由 smoke(烟)和 fog(雾)两个词组合而成

(例)Smog is more common in industrial areas than in rural areas.

sniper [ˊsnaipə] n. 狙击手(a person with a gun who shoots at people from a hidden position)
(记)snip(剪)+er→像剪刀一样快的人→狙击手
(例)The enemy sniper shot at the townsfolk from the mountainside.

soar [sɔː] v. 高飞(to sail or hover in the air, often at a great height);向上;高耸;猛增(to rise or increase dramatically[as in position, value or price])
(记)可按其发音记忆,"嗖"的一声猛冲上去
(例)The plane soared high in the sky. / The cost of gasoline soared during the oil crisis.

sodium [ˊsəudjəm] n.【化】钠

sojourn [səuˊdʒəː] v. / n. 逗留,寄居(to stay as a temporary resident)
(例)After a short sojourn in Dallas, I went back home.

solicit [səˊlisit] v. 恳求(to approach with a request or plea);教唆(to entice or lure esp. into evil)
(记)soli(=sole 惟一,全部)+cit(引出)→引出某人做事→教唆;恳求
(例)Anne solicited help from her doctor.

soloist [ˊsəuləuist] n. 独奏者,独唱者(a singer or musician who performs a solo);单飞者
(记)solo(单独)+ist→独唱者
(例)The soloist sang a beautiful ballad.

solvency [ˊsɔlvənsi] n. 溶解力(the ability to dissolve another substance);还债能力(the ability to pay all legal debts)
(记)solv(溶化,解决)+ency→溶解力
(例)A good borrower is a person with both finan-

cial needs and solvency.

somatic [səuˈmætik] a. 肉体的(of the body)
(记)somat(躯体)+ic→躯体的
同根词:somatology(人类躯体学)

sophisticated [səˈfistikeitid] a. 老于世故的(having a refined knowledge of the ways of the world, cultivated through wide experience);(仪器)精密的(highly complicated or developed)
(记)sophist(诡辩者)+icated→老于世故的
(例)The diplomat spoke in a sophisticated manner. / The sophisticated machinery is difficult to operate properly.

sophomore [ˈsɔfəmɔː] n. 大学二年级学生(a student in the second year at college);自以为样样都懂而实际上幼稚的人(one that is conceited and over confident of knowledge but poorly informed and immature)
(记)sopho(智慧)+more(多)→需要更多智慧→不成熟
(例)The sophomore showed the freshman around the campus.

soprano [səˈprænəu] n. 女高音(the highest singing voice of women); a. 女高音的
(记)sopor(=super 超过)+ano→声音超过别人→女高音
(例)The sopranos sang the melody, and the altos(女低音) sang only in the chorus.

span [spæn] n. 全长;一段时间(a period of time)
(记)桥的跨度也称为 span
(例)Bill was sick for a two-month span last year.

Spaniard [ˈspænjəd] n. 西班牙人

spark [spɑːk] vt. 发动(to set off in a burst of activity; activate, incite);激发感情,鼓舞

(记)激起火花→激发,鼓舞
(例)The professor sparked the students' interest in reading.

spate [speit] n.大批,大量(a large number or amount);(水)泛滥(flood)
(记)大量的水→泛滥
(例)They had a spate of bad luck.

spatial [ˈspeiʃəl] a.空间的(relating to, occupying or having the character of space)
(记)来自 space,注意 spatial 与 spate 无关
(例)The spatial arrangement of the furniture was pleasing to the eye.

speak out 大胆地说(to speak boldly; express an opinion frankly);清楚和响亮地说(to speak loud enough to be heard)
(例)The protesters spoke out against the mayor's policies.

specific [spiˈsifik] a.具体的(restricted to a particular individual, situation, relation, or effect);明确的(free from ambiguity; accurate)
(记)speci(=species 种类)+fic→具体的,明确的
(例)The witness gave specific facts and figures.

specimen [ˈspesimin] n.范例,样品(an individual, item, part considered typical of a group, class or whole);标本
(记)spec(看)+imen→看的东西→样品
(例)This tree is a good specimen of an oak tree. / The lab technician examines hundreds of blood specimens each day.

specter [ˈspektə] n.鬼魂,幽灵(a visible disembodied spirit; ghost);恐惧(sth. that causes fear or dread)
(记)spect(看)+er→引人注目的东西→鬼怪

(例)The psychic claimed to see the specter of my dead parents. / John was haunted by the specter of his past sins.

spectrum [ˊspektrəm] n. 范围(a continuous sequence or range; scope);光谱(the range of visible light)
(记)spectr(看)+um→看到颜色→光谱
(例)Raindrops or mist act as a prism through which the spectrum is seen as a rainbow. / Mary's spectrum of scientific knowledge ranged from anatomy to zoology.

speculate [ˊspekjuleit] v. 深思,思索(to think about sth., esp. without knowing all the facts; consider);投机(to assume a business risk in hope of gain, esp. to buy or sell in expectation of profiting from market fluctuations)
(记)spec(看)+ulate(做得多)→看得多→引起沉思
(例)The scientist speculated on the applications of the new medicine. / The investor speculated in companies formed by young geniuses.

spew [spjuː] vt. 呕出(to vomit),喷(to ooze out as if under pressure);n. 呕出物(matter that is vomited)
(例)Water spewed from the leaky pipe.

sphere [sfiə] n. 球,球面(a perfectly round object; a ball);天体(a planet or star)
(例)The sphere rolled across the floor.

spherule [ˊsferuːl] n. 小球(体)
(记)来自 sphere(球体)

spillover [ˊspiləuvə] n. 溢出(量)(an extension of sth., esp. due to an excess; the quantity that spills over);外流人口(大城市容纳不下的)
(记)spill(溢)+over(越过)→溢出量

spine [spain] n. 脊骨,脊柱;书脊;[喻]中心;支持因素(sth. resembling a spinal column or constituting a central axis or chief support)

(记)记住核心意义"脊柱",其他意思可以引申

(例)Mary's legs were paralyzed when her spine was injured. / Angrily, Bill pulled the pages of the book from its spine.

spiteful ['spaitful] a. 怀恨的,恶意的(full of spite; wanting to annoy someone else or get revenge)

(记)spite(怨恨)+ful→怀恨的

(例)The spiteful girl told lies about her teachers.

spleen [spliːn] n. 脾;脾气,怒气(feeling of anger or ill will often suppressed)

(记)据说脾与怒气有关

(例)Bon vented his spleen on his wife by shouting at her.

splinter ['splintə] n. 尖片,碎片(a thin, sharp broken-off piece of wood, glass, or some other material)

(记)splint(薄木条)和 split(分裂)有关,splinter 指裂开的碎片

(例)Be careful! There are splinters of glass all over the floor.

sponsor ['spɔnsə] v. 赞助;惠顾(to support someone or an organization, esp. financially); n. 赞助人;主顾(someone or an organization that supports and guides another person or organization)

(记)spons(支持)+or→支持者→赞助;赞助人

(例)The radio program was sponsored by local businesses. / Our program will continue after a message from our sponsors.

spray [sprei] n. 浪花(water flying in small drops or particles blown from waves or thrown up by a waterfall);小树枝(a usu. flowering branch or shoot);v. 喷(to direct a stream of small drops of liquid onto a surface)

(记)分割记忆:sp - ray(光线)→喷射出

(例)The spray from the vaporizer added moisture to the dry room. / David put a few sprays of flowers in the vase on the table. / John sprayed insecticide on the plants.

spruce [spruːs] n. 云杉; a. 整洁的;潇洒的(neat or smart in appearance)

(记)云杉是一种挺拔修长的树木

(例)Many raccoons lived in the forest of spruce. / The bathroom is spruce.

spur [spəː] v. 激励,鞭策(to persuade, urge, or encourage someone)

(记)spur 的原意是马刺,用于刺激马匹快走

(例)My parents spurred me on to study harder.

squash [skwɔʃ] n. 南瓜,西葫芦

stage [steidʒ] vt. 把…搬上舞台(to produce 〔as a play〕 in a stage)

(记)这是 stage(舞台)的动词形式

(例)Our theater company staged a new version of that play.

staggering [ˈstægəriŋ] a. 令人吃惊的(unbelievable, shocking)

(记)stagger(摇晃) + ing→令人摇晃的→令人震惊的

(例)Mary faced a staggering amount of work when she returned from vacation.

stagnant [ˈstægnənt] a. 停滞的,不流动的(not flowing in a current or stream);呆滞的(never changing; not developing; stale)

(记)stagn(= stand 站住) + ant→不动的

(例)Do not drink water from a stagnant pond. / No one laughed at the comedian's stagnant routine.

stale [steil] a. 不新鲜的,陈腐的(no longer fresh or new; not exciting or interesting)
(记)分割记忆:s + tale(故事)→陈旧的故事
(例)The stale bread was dry and hard. / The editor criticized the journalist's stale style.

stance [stæns] n. 站姿(a way of standing);立场(intellectual or emotional attitude)
(记)stan(站) + ce→站姿
(例)Peter took an antiwar stance.

standpoint [ˈstændpɔint] n. 立场,观点(a position from which objects or principles are viewed and according to which they are compared and judged)
(记)stand(站) + point(点)→站的地方→立场
(例)From the taxpayer's standpoint, taxes must be reduced.

staple [ˈsteipl] n. 钉书钉;主要产品(a chief commodity or production of a place)
(记)和 stable(稳定的)一起记,稳定的东西→主要产品
(例)Rice is a staple for many eastern Asians.

starch [stɑːtʃ] n. 淀粉;(复数)淀粉类食物(food that contains starch)
(例)Bill eats mostly starch on his diet.

stark [stɑːk] a. (外表)僵硬的(rigid in or as if in death);刻板的(rigidly conforming [as to a pattern or doctrine]);完全的(complete, absolute)
(例)The mail carrier fled from the angry dog in stark terror.

startling [ˈstɑːtliŋ] a. 令人吃惊的,惊人的(causing momen-

tary fright, surprise or astonishment)
(记)来自 startle(震惊)
(例)The startling explosion scared everyone in town.

stationary [ˈsteiʃənəri] a. 静止的(fixed in a station, course or mode; unchanging in condition)
(记)station(位置)+ary→固定在一个位置的→静止的;注意与 stationery(文具)的区别
(例)Because of an accident, traffic was stationary for an hour.

statute [ˈstætjuːt] n.【律】法令,成文律(a law enacted by the legislative branch of a government);章程,条例(an act of a corporation or of its founder intended as a permanent rule)
(记)stat(站)+ute→牢固竖立的→法令
(例)The city council passed a statute prohibiting smoking in restaurants.

statutory [ˈstætjutəri] a. 法定的;受法令所约束的(enacted, created or regulated by statute)
(记)来自 statute(法令)
(例)statutory control of wages(工资的法定控制)

stave [steiv] n. 桶板(any of the narrow strips of wood or narrow iron plates placed edge to edge to form the sides, covering, or lining of vessel [as a barrel] or structure)
(记)可与 starve(饿死)一起记

steep [stiːp] a. 极高的(extremely or excessively high);陡峭的(making a large angle with the plane of the horizon; mounting or falling precipitously)
(记)steep 还有一个意思是"浸泡,浸透"
(例)The children raced their sleds down the steep, snowy hill. / The new year began with a steep rise

in inflation)

steerage [ˊstiəridʒ] n. 驾驶,操纵(the act or practice of steering);下等客舱(a section of inferior accommodations in a passenger ship for passengers paying the lowest fares)

(记)来自 steer(舵)+age→驾驶

stellar [ˊstelə] a. 星的,星球的(of or relating to the stars);主要的(principal, leading, outstanding)

(记)来自拉丁文,stella(星)+r→星的

(例)The very bright star is actually a stellar explosion. / The author won an award for her stellar novel.

stench [stentʃ] n. 臭气,恶臭(a strong, unpleasant smell; a horrible odor)

(记)分割记忆:sten(=stern 严厉的)-ch→严厉的气→臭气;注意不要和 stanch(止住)相混

(例)The dead dog gave off a horrible stench.

steppe [step] n.(尤指东南欧或西伯利亚地区)无树林的大平原(one of the vast usu. level and treeless tracts in southeastern Europe or Asia)

(记)step(步)+pe→要走很多步→大平原

stereotype [ˊstiəriətaip] n. 铅版(a plate cast from a printing surface);陈规,旧框框(sth. conforming to a fixed or general pattern);v. 成固定形象

(记)stereo(立体)+type(形状)

(例)The teenager was angered by the stereotype of all young people as impolite. / The blonde actress feared being stereotyped as a silly woman.

stimulus [ˊstimjuləs] n. 刺激,刺激物(sth. that arouses or incites to activity)

(记)stimul(刺激)+us→刺激物

参考:stimulate(刺激,激励),stimulating(使人兴

奋的)

(例)Lisa's well-written book was a stimulus for Mary to write her own.

stinkwood [ˊstinkwud] n. 臭木(any of several trees with an unpleasant odor)

(记)stink(发出臭味的)+wood(木头)→臭木

stipend [ˊstaipend] n. 薪水,定期津贴(如奖学金等)(a fixed sum of money paid periodically for services or to defray expenses)

(记) stip (点) + end (结束) → 结束那一点上得到的→工资,薪水

(例) The university offered the best students a monthly stipend.

stipulate [ˊstipjuleit] v. 要求以…为条件(to specify as a condition or requirement of an agreement or offer); 约定(to make an agreement or covenant to do or forbear sth.; contract)

(记)stip(点)+ulate→点明,约定

(例) The workers' contract stipulated that they couldn't smoke on the job. / The rental agreement stipulated that I was to return the car with a full tank of gas.

stitch [stitʃ] n. 缝线,针脚(the thread that is seen after one movement of a threaded needle through an object while sewing)

(记)可与 stick(粘住)一起记,粘住→缝

(例)The stitches in the dress's hem match the color of the dress.

stock [stɔk] n. 股票(shares of a specific company); a. 普通的,惯用的(commonly used or brought forward)

(记)stock 可与 store 联系起来记,stock 就是 store 里的货物

(例)Lisa bought two stocks in the steel industry.

stockpile [ˈstɔkpail] n.(堆在路边为修路用的)料堆;贮存(a large amount of sth. that is stored for future use or in case of an emergency); vt.积聚(to accumulate a stockpile of)

(记)stock(储备)+pile(堆)→一堆储备→积聚

(例)During the winter, we keep a stockpile of canned goods in the pantry.

storefront [ˈstɔːfrʌnt] n.有铺面的大楼、房间或套间(a building, room or suite of rooms that face a street)

(记)store(商店)+front(前面)→沿街店面

(例)The small storefront clinic was open two days a week.

strain [ˈstrein] n.(人的)血缘,世系,种族(lineage; ancestry); 品质(inherited or inherent character, quality or disposition)

(记)strain 较常用的意思是"拉紧,压力",financial strain

(例)a strain of fanaticism; / This strain of wheat is only grown in Kansas.

strata [ˈstreitə] n.(stratum 的复数)地层(a sheetlike mass of sedimentary rock or earth of one kind lying between beds of other kinds);社会阶层(a socio-economic level of society comprising persons of the same or similar status)

(记)strat(=straight 直的,整齐的)+a→整齐的层次→地层,阶层

strategic [strəˈtiːdʒik] a.战略的(of, relating to marked by strategy);对全局有重要意义的(of great importance within an integrated whole or to a planned effect)

(记)strat(=strata 层次)+egic→有层次的→战略

的

(例)The general devised a strategic plan to win the war. / The soldiers gained control of the strategic port city.

strategy [ˈstrætidʒi] n. 谋略,策略(the skill or science of planning sth., esp. planning military movements)

(例)Because of our general's brilliant strategy, we won the war.

stratigraphical [ˌstrætiˈgræfikəl] a. 地层学的(of, relating to, or determined by the geology that deals with the origin, composition, distribution and succession of strata);n. stratigraphy 地层学

(记) strati (层) + graphical (绘画的) →一层层地画 → 地层学

strenuous [ˈstrenjuəs] a. 费力的(requiring hard work, a lot of energy, effort, etc.);精力充沛的(vigorously active; energetic)

(记)stren(=strength 力量)+uous→用力量的

(例)After a strenuous day at work, Bill slept for 12 hours.

stride [straid] v. 大步行走(to move with long steps);阔步(to take a very long step)

(记)与 strike(打击)一起记,大步走过去打,也可以将 ride 理解为 pride(骄傲)→骄傲地阔步走

(例)Mary quickly strode toward her house because it was raining.

strife [straif] n. 纷争,倾轧(bitter sometimes violent conflict or dissension)

(记)可以将 ife 理解作 knife(刀)→在纷争中可能会用刀

(例)The strife in her homeland caused the immigrant to flee.

stringent [ˊstrindʒənt] a.(规定)严苛的(marked by rigor, strictness, or severity);缺钱的(marked by money scarcity and credit strictness)
(记) 来自 string (线、绳) + ent → 像用绳限制住的 →严厉的
参考:astringent(收缩的)
(例) Our company has a stringent policy against smoking.

strive [straiv] vi.努力,奋斗(to devote serious effort or energy; endeavor);反抗(to struggle in opposition)
(记)可以将 ive 记作 live(生存)→为生存而奋斗
(例)The business owner strove for success.

stroke [strəuk] n.(病)突然发作(a sudden action or process producing an impact);中风(sudden diminution or loss of consciousness, sensation, and voluntary motion)
(记)stroke 的基本意思是一击,打击→发作;中风
(例) Bill's stroke paralyzed the left side of his body.

strut [strʌt] n.支柱,撑杆(a structural piece designed to resist pressure);vt.支撑(to provide, stiffen, support with a strut);炫耀(to walk somewhere arrogantly, as though one were more important than one is)
(记)可与 structure(结构)一起记,结构需要支撑
(例)The arrogant student strutted around campus. / The roof collapsed when termites destroyed the struts in the attic.

stultify [ˊstʌltifai] vt.使显得愚蠢(to cause to appear or be stupid, foolish or absurdly illogical);使无效,使无价值(to impair, invalidate or make ineffective)
(记)stu(=stupid 愚蠢) + ltify→使显得愚蠢

(例)The stultifying effect of uninteresting work.

stunt [stʌnt] vt.阻止…发育(或成长)(to prevent someone or sth. from reaching full growth);n.发育迟缓,矮小的人(或东西)(one that is stunted)

(记)分割记忆:stun(使震惊)-t→矮得惊人→矮人

(例)Malnutrition stunts the growth of children around the world.

sturdy [ˈstəːdi] a.(身体)强健的(marked by or reflecting physical strength or vigor);结实的(firmly built or constituted)

(记)可与study(学习)一起记,身体强健才能学习

(例)Anne piled heavy weights on top of the sturdy table.

subconscious [sʌbˈkɔnʃəs] a.下意识的,潜意识的(existing in the mind but not immediately available to consciousness)

(记)sub(下)+conscious(有意识的)→下意识的

(例)Something subconscious kept him from expressing his feelings.

subcontract [sʌbˈkɔntrækt] n.转包合同,分包合同(a contract between a party to an original contract and a third party);v.承做,转包(to engage a third party to perform under a subcontract)

(记)sub(下)+contract(合同)→向下分包合同

(例)The contractor kept track of each subcontract for the project. / The contractor subcontracted the electrical work to an electrician.

subdue [sʌbˈdjuː] v.征服(to conquer and bring into subjection);压制(to bring under control, esp. by an exertion of the will);减轻(to reduce the intensity or degree of)

(记)sub(在下面)+due(=duce)引导→引到下面→征服

(例)The army subdued the neighboring tribes. / The police subdued the excited suspect. / Because the lighting was subdued, I couldn't see across the room.

subject [ˊsʌbdʒikt] n. 臣民(someone who is ruled by a government or a ruler)

(例)The queen is supported by her subjects' tax money.

subordinate [səˊbɔːdənit] vt. 把…列在下级;使服从(to make subject or subservient)

(记)sub(下面)+ordin(顺序)+ate→顺序在下面→使附属,使服从

(例)Emperors of the Song Dynasty sometimes had to subordinate themselves to the Tartars.

subscriber [sʌbˊskraibə] n. 订购者(a customer who receives a newspaper, magazine, or newsletter on a regular basis);捐献者(a person who pledge [a gift or contribution] by writing one's name with the amount)

(记)来自 subscribe,sub(下面)+scribe(写)→签署,写下订单→订购

(例)Advertising rates are based on the number of subscribers a publication has.

subscription [səbˊskripʃən] n. 捐助(the act of subscribing);订购(a purchase by prepayment for a certain number of issues [as of a periodical])

(记)同样来自 subscribe

(例)Mary has a yearly subscription to the local newspaper.

subsequent [ˊsʌbsikwənt] a. 继…之后的,后来的(following in

time, order or place)
(记)sub(向下的)+sequ(跟随)+ent→下面跟着的→后来的
(例)The magazine informed its readers that subsequent issues would cost one dollar more.

subsidiary [səb'sidjəri] a. 辅助的;次要的(of secondary importance)
(记)sub(下面)+sid(坐)+iary→坐在下面的→辅助的

subsidize ['sʌbsidaiz] v. 补助,资助(to help a company or a person by paying part of its cost)
(记)来自 subsidy(补助金)
(例)The federal government subsidized my college education because I couldn't afford to pay for it myself.

substantial [səb'stænʃəl] a. 物质的(consisting of or relating to substance);实际的(not imaginary or illusory);坚固的(firmly constructed; sturdy);大量的(ample; rather large)
(记)substant(事实,物质)+ial→物质的,实际的
参考:substance(物质)
(例)The substantial tree withstood the violent winds. / The TV news program received a substantial number of complaints about poor reporting.

substantiate [səb'stænʃieit] v. 证实,确证(to establish by proof or competent evidence; verify)
(记)substant(事实,物质)+iate→用事实来证明→证实
(例)His experiment substantiated his claims.

substantive ['sʌbstəntiv] a. 独立存在的(being a totally independent entity);实质性的
(记)sub(下)+stant(=stand 站立)+ive→站在下

面的→独立存在的
(例)a substantive nation(独立国家)

substrate [ˈsʌbstreit] n.底层(the base on which an organism lives);地层
(记)sub(下面)+strate(层次)→下面一层→底层,地层

subterfuge [ˈsʌbtəfjuːdʒ] n.诡计;托辞(lies or dishonesty used to hide sth. or evade sth.)
(记)subter(私下)+fuge(逃跑)→诡计;借口
(例)The boss remained unaware of the problem because of the employee's subterfuge.

subtract [səbˈtrækt] v.减(to take away by deducting)
(记)sub(下面的)+tract(拉)→拉到下面→减去
(例)Tom subtracted the smaller number from the larger number.

succumb [səˈkʌm] v.屈从(to yield to superior strength or force);因…而死亡(to be brought to an end [as death] by the effect of destructive or disruptive forces)
(记)suc(下面)+cumb(躺)→躺下去→死亡
(例)The politician succumbed to pressure and resigned. / Hundreds of soldiers succumbed on the battlefield.

sue [sjuː] v.控告,控诉(to start a lawsuit; to file a claim against someone or sth. in court)
(记)可以用其发音来记忆,sue 近似"诉"→控诉,控告
(例)The worker who had been fired sued for compensation.

suffice [səˈfais] vt.使满足,使满意(to meet or satisfy a need)
(记)与 sufficient 一起记

(例)You don't need a coat outside. A sweater will suffice.

sugarcane [ˈʃugəkein] n. 甘蔗

(记)来自 sugar(糖) + cane(棍杖)→含糖的茎→甘蔗

sulfur [ˈsʌlfə] n.【化】硫磺; vt. 用硫处理

(记)硫的化学符号为 S

sultan [ˈsʌltən] n. 苏丹(某些伊斯兰国家最高统治者称号)

superb [sjuːˈpəːb] a. 上乘的,出色的(marked to the highest degree by grandeur, excellence, brilliance or competence)

(记)super(上等,超越) + b→上乘的

(例)This excellent restaurant serves superb steaks.

superficial [ˌsjuːpəˈfiʃəl] a. 肤浅的,表面上的(concerned only with the obvious or apparent; shallow)

(记)super(上面) + fic(做) + ial→在上面做→表面的

(例)The engineer has only superficial knowledge of ancient philosophy.

supernova [ˌsjuːpəˈnəuvə] n.【天】超新星

(记)super(超) + nova(新星)→超新星

supersede [ˌsjuːpəˈsiːd] v. 替代,取代(to take the place, room, or position of);淘汰(to displace in favor of another)

(记) super (在…上面) + sede (坐)→坐在别人上面→取代

(例)The new law superseded several old ones.

superstition [ˌsjuːpəˈstiʃən] n. 迷信(an irrational fear of what is unknown or mysterious)

(记)super(超过) + stit(站) + ion→超越人理智的东西→迷信

(例)Fear of the number 13 is an old superstition.

supplement [ˈsʌplimənt] v./n. 增补,补充(sth. that completes or makes an addition)

(记)supple(=supply 提供)+ment→提供补充

(例)As a supplement to my regular exercise program, I joined a softball team.

supplicant [ˈsʌplikənt] n. 乞求者,恳求者(one who asks humbly and earnestly of)

(记)sup(下面)+plic(重叠)+ant→双膝重叠下跪→恳求

suppressant [səˈpresnt] n. 抑制物(an agent 〔as a drug〕 that tends to suppress or reduce in intensity rather than eliminate sth.)

(记)sup(在上面)+press(压)+ant→在上面压→抑制物

surface [ˈsəːfis] v. 浮上水面(to go up to or above the surface of the water)

(记)由 surface 的原意"表面"引申而来

(例)The submarine surfaced when it entered the port.

surpass [səˈpɑːs] vt. 超越(to go beyond);胜过(to become better, greater or stronger than; exceed)

(记)sur(上面)+pass(经过)→从上面经过→超越

(例)Mary surpassed all of her siblings in school.

surplus [ˈsəːpləs] n. 过剩,剩余,盈余(the amount that remains when use or need is satisfied)

(记)sur(下面)+plus(加,多余的)→剩余的

参考:nonplus(难堪)

(例)The clothing factory donated its surplus to charity.

susceptible [səˈseptəbl] a. 易受影响的(easily influenced or harmed by sth.)

(记)sus(在…下面)+cept(接受)+ible→在下面接受→容易接受→易受影响的

(例)Infants and the elderly are more susceptible to illness than other people. / The young revolutionaries were susceptible to propaganda.

sustain [səˊstein] v. 支撑;维持(to give support or relief to);供养(to nourish and care for living plants and creatures)

(记)sus(下面)+tain→在下面支撑住

(例)The arts agency was sustained by government funds. / Mary sustained her plants with plenty of water and sunshine.

swell [swel] v. 膨胀;增长壮大(to expand [as in size, volume or numbers] gradually beyond a normal or original limit);隆起(to form a bulge or rounded elevation);骄傲(to become filled with pride and arrogance)

(例)My ankle began to swell when I injured it. / The crime rate swelled during the economic recession.

switch [switʃ] v. 转换,转变(to change sth. or change to sth.; to move from one to another)

(记)switch 的原意为开关→转换

(例)I switched pens when the one I was using ran out of ink. / The coffee drinker switched to a new brand of coffee.

syllable [ˊsiləbl] n. 音节(a unit of spoken language)

(例)The word "watermelon" has four syllables.

symmetrical [siˊmetrikəl] a. 对称的(having the opposite sides of sth. being or looking exactly alike.)

(记)sym(共同)+metr(测量)+ical→两边测量相同的→对称的

(例)The painting of a vase of flowers and its mirror image was symmetrical.

symptom [ˈsimptəm] n. 征兆(sth. that indicates the existence of sth. else);(病)症状(subjective evidence of disease or physical disturbance)

(记)sym(共同)+ptom(现象)→症状

(例)High unemployment is a symptom of a troubled economy. / A running nose and coughing are symptoms of the common cold.

syndicate [ˈsindikit] n.【经】辛迪加,企业联合组织(people or businesses that are joined together for specific business reasons)

(记)syn(共同)+dicate(=dictate 命令)→共同发命令→联合组织,也可通过发音来记住"辛迪加"一义

(例)The office building was owned by a multinational syndicate.

syndrome [ˈsindrəum] n.【医】综合病症(a group of signs and symptoms that occur together and characterize a particular abnormality);同时存在的事物(a set of concurrent things [as emotions or actions])

(记)syn(共同)+drome (跑)→症状一起跑来→综合病症

(例)The doctor noticed the symptoms of a serious mental syndrome in the patient.

synonymous [siˈnɔniməs] a. 同义的(having the same meaning as sth. else)

(记)来自 synonym(同义词),syn 共同+onym(名字)→同义词

(例)Very few words are exactly synonymous.

synthesize [ˈsinθəsaiz] v. 合成(to make sth. by combining and organizing many parts)

(记) syn (共同) + thesize (=thesis 放) → 放在一起→合成
同根词:antithetic(对应的)
(例)Mary synthesized her report from interviews with dozens of people. /The substance was rare in nature so it will have to be synthesized in the laboratory.

T

tablet [ˈtæblit] n. 药片(a pill);便笺簿(a thin slab or one of a set of portable sheets used for writing);碑,匾(a flat slab or plaque suited for or bearing an inscription)
(记)table(桌子)+t→放在桌上的→便笺簿
(例)Aspirin comes in the form of a tablet or a capsule. /The teacher instructed the students to take notes in their tablets.

taboo [təˈbuː] a. 讳忌的(forbidden to profane use or contact banned on grounds of morality or taste);n. 禁忌(a prohibition imposed by social custom or as a protective measure)
(例)Many cultures have taboos concerning sex.

tack [tæk] n. 平头钉(a small short sharp-point nail); v. 钉住(to fasten or affix with tacks);添加(to add as a supplement)
(记)注意不要和 tact(机智)相混
(例)David repaired the door frame with a few tacks. /Mary tacked her child's drawing to the wall. /Bill tacked an extra clause on to his will.

tactic [ˈtæktik] n.(达到目的)手段(a skillful way of doing sth. in order to reach a goal);战术(a method

of employing forces in combat)
(记)tact(机智)+ic→机智的技巧→手段
(例)Anne's tactic of confronting her boss directly was successful.

tactical [ˈtæktikl] a. 手段的,战术的(of or about tactics)
(记)来自 tactic(战术,手段)
(例)The army's tactical maneuvers helped it win the war.

tactile [ˈtæktail] n. 触觉的(of or relating to the sense of touch);tactile hair【动】【植】触毛
(记)tact(接触)+ile→触觉的
同根词:contact(联系),tactometer(触觉测量器)
(例)The paralyzed man had lost the tactile senses in his hands.

tag [tæg] vt. 装包头于(鞋带等);加标签于(to provide or mark with or as if with a label);连接,合并(to attach as an addition)
(例)The scientist tagged the deer with a metal clip so the animal could be identified.

takeover [ˈteikəuvə] n. 接管,接任(the assumption of control or possession)
(记)take(取得)+over(过来)→取过来→接管
(例)The board of directors executed a takeover of a weaker company.

tally [ˈtæli] n. 账,记录(a recorded reckoning or account);v. 计算(to make a count of; reckon);记录(to record on a tally)
(例)The final tally of the votes indicated that the incumbent had won. / The computer tallied the votes automatically. / The witness's testimony tallied with (与…一致) the defendant's.

tamper [ˈtæmpə] v. 窜改(to alter sth. secretly, especially

without permission)；玩弄(to fiddle around with sth.)
(例)The terrorist tampered with the president's food.

tangent [ˈtændʒənt] a.相切(meeting a curve or surface in a single point if a sufficiently small interval is considered)
(记)tang(接触)+ent→和圆接触的线→切线,相切的
(例)straight line tangent to a curve

tangible [ˈtændʒəbl] a.可触摸的(capable of being perceived or felt, esp. by the sense of touch)
(记)tang(接触)+ible→可接触的,可触摸的
(例)One tangible benefit of my new job is a company car.

tardive [ˈtɑːdiv] a.(疾病)延迟发作的
(记)tard(迟缓)+ive→延迟的
同根词:retard(阻碍);tardigrade(缓步的)

tariff [ˈtærif] n.关税(a schedule of duties imposed by a government on imported or in some countries exported goods)
(例)The government imposed a higher tariff to discourage imports.

tartan [ˈtɑːtn] n.格子花(a plaid textile design of Scottish origin consisting of stripes of varying width and color)；格子织物(a twilled woolen fabric with tartan design)
(记)tartan 是一种原产于苏格兰的格子呢,常用于制作围裙
(例)The dress was made of a beautiful tartan.

tease [tiːz] vt.取笑,戏弄(to taunt someone; to make fun of someone)

(例) Jane is always teasing Bill about his poor grades. / Mary .teased Bill for weeks and then started dating Tom.

technocrat [ˈteknəkræt] n. 技术专家型官员(a techical expert who has become a politician)
(记)techno(技术) + crat(统治)

tedious [ˈtiːdiəs] a. 沉闷的,冗长的(tiresome because of length or dullness)
(记)来自 tedium(单调乏味)
(例)The tedious lecture went on endlessly.

temblor [temˈblɔː] n. [美]地震(earthquake)

temperance [ˈtempərəns] n. 自制,节制(moderation in action, thought, or feeling; restraint);禁酒(abstinence from the use of intoxicating drink)
(记)temper(掺合, 使平衡) + ance→控制脾气→节制
(例)The nondrinkers urged temperance among the population.

tempo [ˈtempəu] n. (生活的)步调,速度(rate of motion or activity; pace of living or working)
(记)来自 tempor(时间)
(例)The tempo of life at our house seems to decrease as we grow older.

tenet [ˈtenit] n. 信念,信条(a principle, belief or doctrine generally held to be true)
(记)ten(握住) + et→(握住的)信念
(例)Honesty is a tenet of good business.

tenor [ˈtenə] n. 男高音(the highest natural adult male singing voice; a person having such voice);要点,要旨(the drift of sth. spoken or written)
(记)ten(握住) + or→握住的东西→要点
(例)The director cast a tenor as the lead in the mu-

sical.

tentative [′tentətiv] a. 试探性的(not fully worked out or developed; uncertain)
(记)tent(测试)+ative→测试性的
(例)Sue and Bill made a tentative date for Saturday night.

terminate [′tə:mineit] vt.(时间上)使停止,使终止(to bring to an end; close)
(记)termin(结束)+ate→结束,停止
(例)The author terminated his contract with the publisher.

terminology [tə:mi′nɔlədʒi] n. 术语(the technical or special terms used in a business, art, science or special subject);术语学(nomenclature as a field of study)
(记)term+(术语)+inology→术语(学)
(例)I did not understand the terminology of the computer manual.

terrestrial [tə′restriəl] a. 地球的,地球上的(of or relating to the earth or its inhabitants);陆地的(of or relating to land)
(记)terr(地)+estrial→地球的
(例)The astronauts returned to their terrestrial home. / The eagle preys on small terrestrial creatures.

territory [′teritəri] n. 地区(an area of land)
(记)terr(地)+itory→地区,区域
(例)All the territory north of the river belongs to the Indians.

terrorism [′terərizəm] n. 恐怖主义(the use of violence and te-rror to achieve political goals)
(记)terror(恐怖)+ism→恐怖主义
(例)The country suffered many attacks of terror-

ism.

terse [tə:s] a. 简洁的(concise; succinct; using few words)

(记)可按发音记为"特少"→简洁的

(例)The professor wrote a few terse comments on my research paper.

testimony [ˊtestiməni] n. 证据(firsthand authentication of a fact; evidence);【律】证言(the statements of a witness, especially in a court of law)

(记)testi(见证)+mony→证言

(例)John's testimony contradicted the defendant's testimony.

thereafter [ðεərˊɑ:ftə] ad. 此后(after that);据此(according to that)

(记)there(那)+after(后来)→那之后→此后

(例)It rained until 8:30, and it snowed thereafter.

threshold [ˊθreʃhəuld] n. 门槛;入门,开始(the place or point of entering or beginning);界限,临界点(a level, point, value above which sth. is true or will take place and below which it is not or will not)

(记)thresh(反复击打)+old(老)→反复击打变旧了→门槛→入门

(例)China is now on the threshold of an economic rennaisance.

thrive [θraiv] v. 兴旺,繁荣(to gain in wealth or possessions; prosper);茁壮成长(to grow vigorously; flourish)

(例)The banker thrived in New York. / Most plants thrive in sunlight.

throttle [ˊθrɔtl] v. 掐脖子,扼杀(to compress the throat of; to kill by such action);节流阀(a valve for regulat-

ing the supply of a fluid〔as steam〕to an engine)
(记)throt(=throat 喉)+tle→掐脖子
(例)The mugger throttled his victim and then stole his wallet. / Turn off the throttle to stop the engine.

thwart [θwɔːt] v. 阻挠(to effectively oppose or baffle);使…受挫(to defeat the hopes or aspirations of)
(记)可与 dwarf (侏儒)一起记,矮人 → 成长受挫→阻挠
(例)The young hero thwarted the tyrant's evil plans. / The police thwarted the criminal's escape.

tickle [ˈtikl] v. 呵痒(to touch〔as a body part〕lightly so as to cause laughter)
(记)tickler 是难题的意思
(例)Mary tickled me until I was laughing hysterically.

tilt [tilt] v. 倾斜(to move or shift so as to lean or incline; slant)
(记)参考:stilt(高跷)
(例)If you tilt your glass any more, it will fall over!

tinge [tindʒ] n.(较淡的)色调,色彩(a slight staining or suffusing shade or color),气息(a very small amount of sth., such as odor or an emotion);vt. 着色于,染(to color with a slight shade or stain)
(例)I felt a tinge of guilt for eating Mary's cookie. / The sun tinged the afternoon clouds with red.

tinker [ˈtiŋkə] n.(流动的)补锅工人(a usu. itinerant mender of household utensils);v. 做拙劣修补(to repair, adjust or work with sth. in an unskilled or experimental manner)

(记)tink(=tinkle 叮当作响)+er→发出叮当响的人→补锅匠

(例)Bob damaged the broken toaster even more when he tinkered with it.

tissue [ˈtisjuː] n.【生】组织(a part of a plant or an animal that is made of many cells having the same function);薄纱,织物(a fine lightweight, often sheer fabric);连篇谎言(a tissue of lies)

(记)卫生纸也叫 tissue

(例)Layers of fatty tissue keep animals warm in the winter.

titanic [taiˈtænik] a.巨人的,力大无比的(having great magnitude, force, or power; colossal)

(记)来自希腊神话中的巨神 Titan,联想 Titanic "泰坦尼克"号沉船

(例)Residents evacuated as the titanic storm approached.

toddler [ˈtɔdlə] n.蹒跚而行的人,学步小孩(one that walks with short tottering steps, esp. a young child who is just learning to walk)

(记)toddle(东倒西歪地走)+r→蹒跚学步的小孩

(例)Mary stopped her toddler from walking up the staircase.

tonality [təuˈnæliti] n.音质,音调(tonal quality)

(记)ton(声音)+ality(=quality 品质)→音质

topographical [ˌtɔpəˈgræfikl] a.地形的,地形学的;地形测量的

(记)topo(地方)+graph(写)+ical→地形学的

同根词:toponym(地名)

topple [ˈtɔpl] v.倾覆(to fall from);推倒(to cause to topple; overthrow; defeat)

(记)分割记忆:top(顶)-ple→顶向下→推翻

(例)The ladder toppled when I walked into it. /

Jimmy toppled a glass of milk at the dinner table.

topsoil [ˈtɔpsɔil] n. 表层土(the top layer of soil; the highest layer of soil)
(记)top(顶)+soil(土)→表层土
(例)The farmer plowed the rich topsoil.

torture [ˈtɔːtʃə] n. 酷刑,折磨(the act or method of inflicting pain in a cruel way);v. 对…施以酷刑(to cause someone to suffer pain in a cruel way)
(记)tort(扭)+ure→扭打,折磨
(例)The hostages underwent torture while they were held captive. / The cruel king tortured his political enemies.

totalitarian [təuˌtæliˈtɛəriən] n. 极权主义者(an advocate or practitioner of the centralized control by an autocratic leader or hierarchy);a. 极权主义的
(记)total(全部)+itarian→控制全部权力的→极权主义的
(例)The citizens of the totalitarian society had very little freedom.

tout [taut] v. 招徕(to publicize or advertise sth. in an insistent or demanding way);极力赞扬(to praise someone or sth. very much, esp. in an extravagant way)
(例)The computer company touted its new product with heavy advertising. / The political party touted its presidential candidate endlessly.

toxic [ˈtɔksik] a. 有毒的(of, relating to caused by a poison or toxin; poisonous);中毒的(affected by a poison or toxin)
(记)tox(毒)+ic→有毒的
同根词:detoxify(解毒);toxication(中毒)
(例)Some toxic waste was illegally buried in the

landfill.

toxin [ˈtɔksin] n. 毒素,毒质(a poisonous chemical produced by a bacterium, plant or animal)
(例)The toxin in the snake's venom killed the rat.

trait [treit] n. 品质;物性;性格(a distinguishing quality [as of personal character])
(例)The color of one's eyes is a genetic trait.

traitorous [ˈtreitərəs] a. 叛徒的,卖国贼的(guilty or capable of treason)
(记)来自 traitor(叛徒)

trajectory [trəˈdʒektri] n. (抛射物)弹道轨道(the path through space or through the air that sth. travels)
(记)tra(横向)+ject(扔)+ory
(例)The ballistics expert determined the trajectory of the bullet.

transcribe [trænˈskraib] v. 抄写(write down; record);转录(to make a copy of)
(记)trans(互相)+scribe(写)→照着写下→抄写
(例)The reporter transcribed the tape she made during the interview. / The sociologist transcribed the story told by the old man.

transform [trænsˈfɔːm] v. 将…变形,变化(into)(to change in composition or structure; to change the outward form or appearance of)
(记)tran(改变)+form(形状)→变形
(例)The sculptor transformed the clay into the form of a bird. / John's personality transformed when he started meditating.

transistor [trænˈsistə] n.【无】晶体管;晶体管收音机
(记)晶体管的名称由来是因为它用一个 resistor(电阻器)来 transfer(传递)电子信号,所以叫 transfer+resistor→transistor

transmit [trænz'mit] v. 传送,传播(to send or convey from one person or place to another; to send information by way of electricity or radio waves)
(记)trans(横过)+mit(送)→送过去→传送
(例)The radio station plans to transmit its broadcasts from a satellite.

transmitter [trænz'mitə] n. 传送者(one that transmits);发射机(an apparatus for transmitting radio or television signals)
(例)The TV station went off the air when its transmitter was damaged.

trapezium [trə'piːziəm] n. 梯形
(记)来自希腊语,tra(四)+pezium(peza"脚"的复数形式)→有四个脚→梯形

trauma ['trauːmə] n. 创伤,精神创伤(a disordered psychic or behavioral state resulting from mental or emotional stress or physical injury)
(记)来自希腊语"受伤",原来指肉体的,现在也包括精神上的
(例)The victims of the crash underwent serious trauma.

traverse [træ'vəːs] v. 横过;扫过(to go or travel across or over; to move or pass along or through)
(记)tra(横)+verse(转)→横过
(例)The soldiers traversed the battlefield on foot.

treasury ['treʒəri] n. 宝库,宝藏(a place in which stores of wealth are kept);国库(one where public revenues are deposited, kept and disbursed);国库券(a government security〔as a note or bill〕issued by the Treasury)
(记)来自treasure(财宝)
(例)treasury department(财政部)

trench [trentʃ] n. 沟,壕沟(a long cut in the ground, esp. one used for military defense)
(记)注意构词:entrenched(牢固的,确立的)
(例)The soldiers slept in the wet, dark trench.

trenchant [ˈtrentʃənt] a. 一针见血的,精辟的(vigorously effective and articulate; sharply perceptive)
(记)trench(沟)+ant→说话像挖沟,入木三分
(例)a trenchant critic(一针见血的批评家)

tribal [traibl] a. 部落的,宗族的(of, relating to, or characteristic of a tribe)
(记)来自 tribe(部落)
(例)tribal customs(宗族习惯)

trim [trim] v. 修剪(to make sth. neat esp. by cutting or clipping); a. 井井有条的(exhibiting neatness, good order or compactness of line or structure)
(记)可以与 slim(苗条)一起记
(例)The gardener trimmed the hedges. / trim houses(整洁的房间)

triple [ˈtripl] v. 三倍于(to become three times as great or as many)
(记)tri(三)+ple→三倍于
(例)The inflation rate tripled last month from 0.1% to 0.3%.

trite [trait] a. 陈腐的,陈词滥调的(hackneyed or boring from much use; not fresh or original)
(记)tri(三)+te→用了多次("三"在中文里也有"多"的意思)→陈腐的
(例)The movie was filled with trite generalizations about teenagers.

trivial [ˈtriviəl] a. 琐屑的(of little worth or importance); 平庸的(commonplace, ordinary)
(记)来自 trivia(琐事)+l→琐屑的

(例)I didn't bother Bob with my trivial concerns because he was busy.

tuberculosis [ˌtjuːbəːkjuˈləusis] n. 结核病,肺结核(略作 TB)
(记)tuber(结块)+culo+sis→结块的→肺结核

tubular [ˈtjuːbjulə] a. 管的(having the form of a tube);由管构成的(made or provided with tubes)
(记)tubu(=tube 管子)+lar→管子的

tumble [ˈtʌmbl] v. 跌倒(to fall suddenly and helplessly);翻腾(to roll over and over, toss)
(记)tum(肿)+ble→摔肿了→跌倒
(例)I tripped on my shoelace and tumbled into a bush.

turbine [ˈtəːbain] n. 汽轮机,涡轮(机)(a large engine or motor that is powered by pressure from wind, water, or some other liquid or gas)
(记)turb(搅动)+ine→搅动的→涡轮机
(例)Dozens of turbines at the dam produced electricity.

turbulent [ˈtəːbjulənt] a. 骚动的,骚乱的(causing unrest, violence or disturbance);汹涌的,湍流的(violent, unruly or wild, as with water, air, the stock market or emotions)
(记)turb(搅动)+ulent→搅得厉害→骚乱的
(例)The turbulent protest resulted in 50 arrests. / Turbulent winds buffeted the airplane.

turmoil [ˈtəːmɔil] n. 混乱,骚乱(a condition of extreme confusion or trouble; agitation)
(记)tur(=turbulent)+moil(喧闹)→吵作一团→骚乱
(例)The refugees had suffered from the turmoil of war.

turn [təːn] n. 倾向,才能(distinctive quality or charac-

ter)
(例)an optimistic turn of mind 乐观的性格

turnover [ˊtəːnəuvə] n.(人员)流动,变更(movement〔as of goods or people〕into, through, and out of a place);流通(a cycle of purchase, sale, and replacement of a stock of goods);营业额,成交量,证券交易额(the amount of business done, esp. the volume of shares traded on a stock exchange)
(记)turn(转动)+over(过来)→转过来→流通,交易额
(例)The manager was pleased with the turnover this month.

tyrannical [taiˊrænikl] a.暴君的,专制的(of or like an absolute ruler unrestrained by law; oppressive);残酷的(cruel)
(记)来自 tyrant(暴君)
(例)The tyrannical ruler killed all of his opponents.

U

ulcer [ˊʌlsə] n.溃疡;[喻]腐烂的事物,腐败的根源(sth. that festers and corrupts like an open sore)
(例)The doctor noticed ulcers on the bedridden woman's skin.

ultimate [ˊʌltimit] a.最终的,结果的(final and conclusive; eventual)
(记)ultim(最远,落后)+ate
参考:ultimatum(最后通牒)
(例)The ultimate decision in hiring is made by the company president.

unbridled [ʌnˊbraidld] a.(马等)脱缰的(not confined by a

bridle);放纵的,无约束的(unrestrained)
(记)un(放开)+bridle(缰绳)+d→松开缰绳的→放纵的

undercut [ˌʌndəˈkʌt] v.从下部切开(to cut away the underpart of);与…抢生意(to beat a competitor by selling the same goods at a lower price)
(记)under(底,下)+cut(切)→从下面切
(例)When one airline undercut its major competitor, the others followed suit.

undergo [ˌʌndəˈgəu] vt.经历,经受(to go through; experience);忍受(to submit to; endure)
(记)under(底下)+go(走)→从底下走→忍受
(例)Bob must undergo surgery to remove a tumor.

underlying [ˌʌndəˈlaiiŋ] a.在下面的(lying beneath or below);基础的(basic; fundamental)
(记)under(下)+lying(躺着的)→在下面的,基础的;注意与underling(下属,手下)的区别
(例)Lack of money was the underlying reason that I didn't go on vacation.

undermine [ˌʌndəˈmain] vt.削弱(to weaken sth. gradually by wearing away support)
(记)under(在下面)+mine(挖)→在下面挖→破坏
(例)The project was undermined by lazy workers.

underpin [ˌʌndəˈpin] vt.在…下面加基础(to form part of, strengthen, replace the foundation of);巩固(support, substantiate)
(记) under (下) + pin (别针,扣牢)→从下面扣牢→巩固
(例)The new legislation needs enforcement mechanism to underpin it.

unicameral [ˌjuːniˈkæmərəl] a.(议会)一院制的,单院的(having or consisting of a single legislative chamber)

(记)uni(一个)+cameral(立法机构的)→单一立法机构的→一院制的

unification [ˌjuːnifiˈkeiʃən] n. 统一,联合,一致(the act, process or result of making sth. into a unit or a coherent whole)

(记)来自 unify(统一,使成一体)

(例)political unification

unison [ˈjuːnizn] n. 一致,调合(a harmonious agreement or union);【音】同度,齐唱,齐奏(identity in musical pitch)

(记)uni(一个的,统一的)+son(=sing 唱)→齐唱

(例)In unison, all of the workers voted "yes" for the new contract. / This part of the piece is performed in unison.

universality [ˌjuːnivəˈsæliti] n. 普遍性,一般性(the quality or state of being existent or operative everywhere or under all conditions);(知识,才能,兴趣等)多方面性(comprehensiveness in range)

(记)uni(全的)+vers(转)+ality→可以到处转动的→普遍

unparalleled [ʌnˈpærəleld] a. 无比的,无双的,空前未有的(without equal or match; unique in kind or quality; superior)

(记)来自 parallel(相同的,类似的),没有类似的→无比的

(例)Such a daring feat is unparalleled in history!

unprecedented [ʌnˈpresidentid] a. 前所未有的(not having happened before)

(记)来自 precedent(先例),pre(前)+ced(走)+ent→在前面走的→先例

(例)Such extremely cold weather is unprecedented

in this century.

untenable [ʌn'tenəbl] a.难以防守的(not able to be defended);站不住脚的(not able to be occupied)
(记)un(不能)+ten(拿住)+able→拿不住的→难以防守的
(例)His argument is untenable.

unviable [ʌn'vaiəbl] a.不能单独生存的(incapable of existence or development as an independent unit);行不通的(unable to work, function or develop adequately)
(记)un(不能)+via(道路)+able→无路可走的→无法生存的

unwarranted [un'wɔrəntid] a.未经保证的(not guaranteed);无根据的(not justified)
(记)un(不能)+warrant(保证)+ed→未经保证的
(例)The patron's unwarranted complaints offended the waitress.

unwieldy [ʌn'wiːldi] a.笨重的,笨拙的(not easily managed, handled, moved or used [as because of bulk, weight, complexity or awkwardness]; cumbersome)
(记)un(不)+wieldy(支配的,控制的)→不可控制的→笨重的
(例)Moving the unwieldy piano up the stairs was difficult.

unwitting [ʌn'witiŋ] a.不知不觉的(not knowing; unaware)
(记)un(不)+witting(知道的,有意的)→不知不觉的
(例)Bill kept the truth from their unwitting friends.

updraft ['ʌpdrɑːft] n.向上排气,通风(an upward move-

ment of gas [as air])
(记)up(向上) + draft(排水,排气)→向上排气→通风

upgrade [ʌp'greid] n. 升级(to raise or improve the grade of),增加,上坡;vt. 使升级,改良(to raise the quality of)
(记)up(向上)grade(等级)→向上提高等级→升级
(例)The quality of the company's products is on the upgrade. / The office manager upgraded the software on my computer.

upheaval [ʌp'hiːvəl] n. 动乱(extreme agitation or disorder);大变动(radical change; a violent social or political movement)
(记)来自 upheave(举起,鼓起),up(向上) + heave(举起,胀起)→大变动
(例)The prime minister called on the army to end the upheaval. / The historian studied the upheaval caused by the war.

upstate ['ʌp'steit] ad.(指美国的一州内)远离大城市;a. 在州北部的(away to the north from an important city or in the northern part of a state)
(记)up(上) + state(州)→地图上位于州上方的→州北部的
(例)We traveled upstate in the fall to see the leaves' changing colors. / The new student is from one of the upstate counties.

upsurge [ʌp'səːdʒ] n. 高潮(a rapid or sudden rise)
(记)up + surge(浪潮)→浪潮向上→高涨

upturn [ʌp'təːn] n.(情况)好转;(价格)提高;向上的趋势(an upward turn, esp. toward better conditions or higher prices)

(记)up(向上)+turn(转动)→向上转动→提高，好转

(例)The economist predicted an upturn in the economy.

urchin [ˈəːtʃin] n. 海胆；刺猬；小淘气，顽童(a mischievous youngster)

(记)可以将两个意思联系起来记忆，刺猬是淘气的→顽童

usurp [juːˈzəːp] v. 篡夺，霸占(to seize and hold in possession by force or without right)

(记)分割记忆：use(用)－urp，看作 up 用(阴谋)上台→篡夺

参考：usury(高利贷)

(例)The army usurped the prime minister's power.

utilize [ˈjuːtilaiz] v. 利用，使用(to make use of; turn practical use)

(记)ut(用)+ilize→利用

(例)Efficient workers utilize time wisely.

V

vacancy [ˈveikənsi] n. 空闲(an interval of leisure)；空缺(a job or position that is not filled)

(记)vac(空)+ancy→闲置，空缺

(例)Bill's retirement left a vacancy in the production division.

vaccine [ˈvæksiːn] n. 牛痘苗，疫苗(a substance that is given to people in order to protect them from a certain disease)

(记)vacc(牛)+ine→牛痘苗

(例)The scientist was awarded a prize for developing a life-saving vaccine.

vacuum [ˊvækjuəm] n. 真空(emptiness of space; a space that is completely empty and does not have any air in it)
(记)vac(空的)+uum→真空
(例)The vegetables were packed in a vacuum to ensure freshness.

vague [veig] a. 模糊的(not having a precise meaning; not clearly felt, sensed or understood)
(记)vag(游移)+ue→游移不定的→模糊的
(例)Tom evaded Jane's question by giving her a vague answer.

valance [ˊvæləns] n. 窗帷(a short, gathered curtain hung at the top of a window)
(例)Dave hung the valance above the kitchen window.

validity [vəˊliditi] n. 有效,合法性(a state of having legal efficacy or force);正当,正确(a state of being logically correct)
(记)来自 valid(有效的,合法的)
(例)The doorman at the bar questioned the validity of my identification card.

vanity [ˊvæniti] n. 虚荣,自负(inflated pride in oneself or one's appearance; conceit)
(记)van(空)+ity→空虚→虚荣
同根词:vanish(消失)
(例)Anne's vanity would not allow her to cut off her long hair.

variable [ˊvɛəriəbl] n. 可变物(sth. that is able or apt to vary);变量(a quantity that may assume any one of a set of values);变项(a symbol representing a variable)

(记)vari(变化)+able→可变的东西→变量
同根词:variation(变动),varied(各式各样的)
(例)Anne plotted the graph of an equation with two variables.

vascular [ˊvæskjulə] a. 血管的,脉管的
(记)vascul(血管)+ar→血管的

vegetarian [vedʒəˊtɛəriən] a. 吃素的人(one who lives on a diet made up of vegetables, fruits, grains and nuts);食草动物
(记)veget(植物)+arian→吃植物的人→素食主义者
参考:vegetable(蔬菜)
(例)These vegetarians get their protein from rice and beans.

vegetation [vedʒiˊteiʃən] n. 植被(plant life or total plant cover [as of an area])
(记)veget(植物)+ation→植物的集合→植被
(例)Thick vegetation grows in tropical jungles.

vehement [ˊviːimənt] a. 猛烈的,强烈的([of expression] passionate, strong or fierce)
(记)vehe(带来)+ment→带来情绪的→猛烈的
参考:vehicle(交通工具)
(例)The vehement politician gestured wildly as he spoke.

velocity [viˊlɔsiti] n. 速度(quickness of motion; speed);速率(speed at one particular moment);迅速(rapidity of movement)
(记)veloc(速度)+ity
(例)At the current velocity, this plane will land in London in one hour.

velvet [ˊvelvit] n. 天鹅绒;鹿茸的嫩皮
(例)The smooth velvet felt nice against my skin.

vendor [ˊvendə] n. 小贩(one that sells, esp. a peddler or hawker);【律】卖主
(记)来自 vend(出售)+or
(例)That vendor sells cheap jewelry on the street corner.

veneer [viˊniə] n. 镶面板(a thin layer of wood or other decorative material that is glued on top of a surface);劣质物品上的装饰(a pleasant appearance that covers up an unpleasant feeling)
(例)The countertop's veneer was beginning to peel away. / John hid his anger behind a veneer of politeness.

venerable [ˊvenərəbl] a. 可尊敬的,年高德劭的(worthy of honor, esteem or respect, especially because of age, experience, position or importance)
(记)vener(尊敬)+able→值得尊敬的
同根词:venerate(崇敬,尊敬)
参考:reverence(尊敬,崇敬)
(例)It is my honor to introduce the venerable mayor of this fine city.

vengeance [ˊvendʒəns] n. 报仇,报复(punishment inflicted in retaliation for an injury or offense)
(记)venge(报复)+ance→报复
同根词:vengeful(报仇心切的),revenge(报复)
(例)Bob's urge to achieve vengeance after the fight was very strong.

venom [ˊvenəm] n. 毒液(the poisonous liquid in the bite or sting of a snake, scorpion, and other similar creatures);恶毒,痛恨(ill will, malevolence; extreme hatred)
(例)The snake's deadly venom killed the careless hiker. / John's criticism of Jane was laced with

venom.

vent [vent] n. 孔,口(an opening for the escape of gas or liquid or for the relief of pressure)

(例)Jane vented her frustration by kicking the tires on her car. / Cool air came through the ceiling vent in the office.

venture [ˊventʃə] n. 冒险行事,冒险事业(a risky undertaking)

(记)vent(发泄)+ure→发泄精力的事→冒险事业

(例)John's venture into business wasn't very succ-essful.

verdict [ˊvəːdikt] n. 判决(the decision of a judge or a jury at the end of a trial);结论(a conclusion, judgment or opinion)

(记)ver(真实)+dict(说)→认真地说→判决

(例)The jury could not reach a verdict. / The critic's verdict was that the movie was worth seeing.

verge [vəːdʒ] n. 边缘(sth. that borders, limits, or bounds; the very beginning of doing sth.)

(记)来自古法语 verge,"杆、棍"

(例)Susan was on the verge of laughter, so she left the lecture hall.

verifiability [ˊveriˊfaiəˊbiliti] n. 可证实性 (the possibility of being verified)

(记)来自 verify(证实),ver(真实)+ify→证明真实,可证明为真→可证实性

verisimilitude [verisiˊmilitjuːd] n. 逼真(the appearance of being true to reality)

(记)veri(真实)+simil(相像)+itude→与真实情况相像→逼真

(例)The jury was not sure of the witness's testimony in spite of its ostensible verisimilitude.

vernacular [və'nækjulə] n. 本国语,地方语(the common spoken language of the people of a country or area)
(记)来自拉丁语 vernaculus,意为"家奴的,土生土长的"
(例)Formal writing should be done in the standard, not the vernacular.

versatility [vəːsə'tiliti] n.(才能,用途等)多面性(the quality or state of being embracing a variety of subjects, fields, or skills);多才多艺
(记)versa(转)+tility→可以转动→多面性
同根词:verse(诗歌);versant(精通的)
(例)Leonardo da Vinci is an artist of great versatility.

version ['vəːʃən] n. 译本(a translation from another language);改写本(an adaptation of a literary work);版本(a form of sth. that is different from another form of it)
(记)vers(转)+ion→转动之后产生的→改写本,版本
(例)The class read the English versions of famous Russian poems. / I saw the movie version of that story before I read the book.

vessel ['vesl] n. 血管;船只(a watercraft bigger than a rowboat; ship)
(记)注意不要和 vassal(陪臣,诸侯)相混
(例)The clot blocked an important blood vessel. / The vessel contained exotic cargo from a distant port.

vestige ['vestidʒ] n. 痕迹,残余(a trace, mark or visible sign left by sth);【生】退化器官(a bodily part or organ that is small and degenerate or imperfectly developed)

(记)vestige 可作词根,如:investigation(调查)
(例)A few artifacts were the only vestige of the once powerful city.

viable [ˊvaiəbl] a. 可行的(capable of working, functioning, or developing adequately);能活下去的(capable of living)
(记)via(道路)+able+有路可走→可行的
(例)The bank offered loans to viable businesses. / Only two of the six plans were determined to be viable.

vicinity [viˊsiniti] n. 附近,接近(a surrounding area or district)
(记)vicin(邻近)+ity→邻近(地区)
同根词:vicinage(周围地区)
(例)What stores are in the vicinity of 23rd Street and 7th Avenue? / The storm hit the downtown area but passed over the outlying vicinities.

victim [ˊviktim] n. 牺牲品,受害者(someone or an animal that dies, suffers or loses sth. because of someone else's actions, a sickness, an accident or a natural disaster)
(例) The flood victims were given emergency funds.

victor [ˊviktə] n. 胜利者,得胜者(one that wins a fight, game, contest, race, etc.; winner)
(例) Susan was declared the victor of the chess tournament.

villainy [ˊviləni] n. 邪恶,腐化堕落,道德败坏(the quality or state of being villainous);(复)犯罪行为(villainous conduct)
(记)来自 villain(恶棍)+y

vintner [ˊvintnə] n. 酒商(a wine merchant; a person who

makes wine)
(记)vint(酒)+ner→酒商
同根词:vintage(酒的,最佳酿造期的)

visionary [ˈviʒənəri] a.梦幻的,想象的(existing only in imagination; unreal);不实际的(incapable of being realized or achieved)
(记)vision(幻影,景象)+ary→只能出现在幻影中的→想象的,不切实际的
(例)John ridiculed Bill's visionary ideas as unrealistic.

visual [ˈvizjuəl] a.看的,视力的(of, relating to, or used in vision)
(记)vis(看)+ual→看的,形象的
(例)Special glasses corrected David's visual disorder.

vitriolic [vitriˈɔlik] a.刻薄的,恶毒的(caustic; virulent)
(记)vitri(玻璃,引申为硫酸盐,因为硫酸盐具有玻璃光泽,再引申为刻毒)+olic
(例)The man divorced his wife because he could no longer stand her vitriolic nagging.

vividness [ˈvividnis] n.鲜艳([of a color] very strong or bright);活泼,生动(the quality or state of being vigorous or fresh)
(记)来自 vivid(生动的,鲜明的),viv(活)+id
(例)The speaker told the story with such vividness that it captivated the whole audience.

vocal [ˈvəukəl] a.有声的(of, relating to or resembling the voice);口述的(uttered by the voice; oral);畅言无忌的(expressing oneself freely or vociferously; outspoken)
(记)voc(声音)+al→有声的
(例)The singer did some vocal exercises before

performing. / The more vocal citizens did not hesitate to complain about waste in government.

volatile [ˊvɔlətail] a. 反复无常的(characterized by or subject to rapid or unexpected change);挥发性的(readily vaporizable at a relatively low temperature)

(记)volat(飞) + ile→飞走的;挥发性的

同根词:volant(飞行的;敏捷的);volary(大型鸟舍)

(例)I avoid Bill because his temper is so volatile. / The volatile substance changed directly from solid to gas.

voluminous [vəˊljuːminəs] a. 长篇的(filling or capable of filling a large volume or several volumes);庞大的(having or marked by great volume or bulk; large)

(记)volum(= volume 容量) + inous→容量大的→庞大的

(例)The mayor faced the voluminous task of improving the schools.

W

wage [weidʒ] v. 开展运动,进行斗争,作战(to engage in or carry on)

(记)wage 作为"工资"这一意思大家比较熟悉,可以理解为"为了工资而斗争"

(例)The United States waged many wars against other nations. / The residents waged a battle against the proposed landfill.

warrior [ˊwɔriə] n. 战士,斗士(a man engaged or experienced in warfare)

(记)war(战争) + rior →战斗的人→战士

(例)The warriors fought on the battleground.

wayside [ˈweisaid] n. 路边(the side of or land adjacent to a road or path)
(记)way(路) + side(边)→路边
(例)We finally found a wayside inn that has a vacancy.

wedge-shaped [ˈwedʒʃeipt] a. 楔形的
(记)来自 wedge(楔子,楔入)

weld [weld] v. 焊接,熔接,结合(to join two pieces of metal together with high heat, sometimes using additional metal)
参考:solder(焊接)
(例)The metal worker welded the metal frame together.

well-being [ˌwelˈbiːiŋ] n. 健康,幸福,福利(good health and prosperity; a state of having a comfortable life and good health)
(记)可以理解为 be well 的名词形式→幸福
(例)Parents are concerned for their children's well-being.

whim [wim] n. 多变,怪念头(a sudden wish to do sth., esp. an unreasonable wish);at whim 随意
(记)是 whim-wham 的简写,表示多变(从 whim 跳到 wham)
(例)On a whim, Mary decided to buy a new car.

whirligig [ˈwəːligig] n. 旋转木马;循环变迁(a whirling or circling course [as of events])
(记)whirli(= whirl 旋转) + gig(旋转物,马车)→旋转木马,再引申为循环变迁

wholesale [ˈhəulseil] n. 批发(the sale of commodities in a large quantity, usu. for resale)
(记)whole(全部) + sale(卖)→整个地卖→批发
(例)Wholesale prices are much cheaper than retail

prices. / The war criminal was accused of wholesale slaughter.

wig [wig] n. 假发(a head covering simulating one's own hair)

(记)是 periwig 的简写,注意不要和 wag(幽默的人)相混

(例)The cancer patient wore a wig after his hair fell out.

willy-nilly [ˈwilinili] a. / ad. 不管愿不愿意,强迫地(by compulsion; without choice)

(记)是由 will I nill(不想,不愿)变形而来

(例)The city council introduced the new ordnance willy-nilly.

windshield [ˈwindʃiːld] n. 挡风玻璃(the large, curved piece of glass in the front of a car above the dashboard)

(记)wind(风) + shield(挡)→挡风的→挡风玻璃

(例)I cleared the snow and ice from my windshield.

wingspan [ˈwiŋspæn] n. 翼展(the distance between the tip of one wing to the tip of the other when both wings are opened as wide as possible) = wingspread

(记)wing(翅膀) + span(跨度)→翅膀的跨度→翼展

(例)An eagle's wingspan is much larger than a robin's wingspan.

wither [ˈwiðə] v. 枯萎,凋零(to become dry and sapless; to lose vitality, force, or freshness)

(记)联想记忆:with(和…一起) + er(可以记为饿)→和饿在一起久了就会枯萎

(例)I forgot to water my plant and it withered.

without [wiðˈaut] n. 外面,外部(an outer place or area)

(记)without 的常用意义为"没有",可以理解为没有遮挡→在外面

(例)come from without

withstand [wið'stænd] v. 承受(to resist successfully);抵制(to stand up against; to oppose with firm determination)

(记)with(相反)+stand(站)→反着站→承受,抵制

(例)The protected town withstood the onslaught of the enemy's army. / The coastal town withstood the hurricane's force.

witty ['witi] a. 机智的(having good intellectual capacity; intelligent);措辞巧妙的,诙谐的(amusingly or ingeniously clever in conception or execution)

(记)来自 wit(智力,才智)

(例)The friends' witty conversation was entertaining.

womb [wu:m] n.【解】子宫;发源地,孕育处(a place where sth. is generated)

(记)可与 tomb(坟墓)一起记

(例)Jane's baby shifted in her womb. / from the womb to the tomb(一生)

wreak [ri:k] vt. 泄(怒)(to cause the infliction of [vengeance or punishment]);露出(恶意)发脾气(to give free play to [malevolent feeling])

(记)可与 leak(泄漏)一起记,注意不要与 wreck(失事,残骸)相混淆

(例)The gangster wreaked revenge on his brother's murderer.

wreath [ri:θ] n. 花圈,花冠,花环(an ornament of flowers and leaves arranged in a certain shape, esp. a circle); 圈状物(sth. intertwined into a circular shape)

(记)注意不要与 wreak(泄怒)相混淆

(例)A mourner put a wreath of pine boughs (树枝) on the casket (棺材).

wristband [ˈristbænd] n.(衬衫等的)袖口(the part of a sleeve covering the wrist)
(记)wrist(手腕)+band(镶边)→手腕处的镶边→袖口

write-off [ˈraitɔf] v.注销,勾销(债款等)(to remove from the books of account an asset that has become worthless)
(例)The company has to write-off the huge bad debt.

X

xenophobia [ˈzenəˈfəubiə] n.仇外,排外(fear and hatred of strangers or foreigners)
(记)xeno(外国人)+phob(恨)+ia→恨外国人→排外
同根词:xenomania(媚外)

Y

yeast [jiːst] n.酵母;兴奋(something that causes ferment or activity)
(记)分割记忆:y+east(东方)→东方有令人兴奋的事物→兴奋

yellow fever n.【医】黄热病

yield [jiːld] n.产量(the amount or quantity produced or returned)
(记)yield 还有服从、顺从的意思
(例)The field's high yield made the farmer rich.

Z

zing [ziŋ] n.(子弹等的)尖啸声(a shrill humming noise);活力(an enjoyably exciting or stimulating quality; zest)

(例)the zing of machine-gun bullets(机枪子弹的尖啸声) / put some zing into business(给商业注入活力)

zoning [ˈzəuniŋ] n.分区制

(记)来自 zone(区域,时区)

(例)zoning ordinances(分区法规)

zoom [zuːm] v.急速上升,(价格)猛增(to go speedily; to increase sharply)

(记)zoom 还有变焦和图像缩放的意思

(例)The rocket zoomed up into the clouds. / Sugar is zooming upwards.(食糖的价格在飞涨。) / The president's popularity zoomed.(总统的声望大增。)

GMAT 常考科技词汇

以下是 GMAT 中已经考过的科技词汇。这些词汇经常出现在阅读理解的文章之中,表明了阅读考试的一些倾向;比如:医学、生物、化学、地理、地质的词汇较多,表示这些领域的内容出现的频率较高。当然经济学的内容更是 GMAT 的常考内容;经济学的词汇更多地收录在前面的单词列表中。以下这些科技词汇并不一定要背出来,只要看二三遍就行了,这样在以后考试中碰到时不会显得太陌生。

abscisic acid	*n*.【生化】脱落酸
abscissa	[æb'sisə] *n*.横坐标
acridine	['ækridi:n] *n*.【化】氮蒽
acrylic	[ə'krilik] *a*.【化】丙烯酸;丙烯酸衍生物的
adrenal	[ə'dri:nl] *a*.肾上腺的,肾上附近的
aerobe	['ɛərəub] *n*.需氧生物
aerobic	[ə'rəubik] *a*.有氧代谢的
aerosol	['ɛərəsɔl] *n*.烟雾;【化】气溶,烟雾剂
algebra	['ældʒibrə] *n*.代数
amino acid	['æmi:nəu'æsid] *n*.【生】氨基酸
amphetamine	[æm'fetəmi:n] *n*.【药】氨基丙苯,苯基丙,安非他明
anaerobe	[ə'neiərəub] *n*.厌氧微生物
anaerobic	[æneiə'rɔbik] *a*.厌氧的
anopheles	[ə'nɔfili:z] *n*.【动】疟蚊属
antipsychotic	[ˌæntisai'kɔtik] *a*.抑制精神的;*n*.安定药
binary	['bainəri] *a*.二,双,复;【化】二元的;【数】二

进制的

biota [baiˊəutə] n. 生物区系
bipedalism [ˊbaipedəlizəm] n.二足类
brandling [ˊbrændliŋ] n.(作钓饵用的)一种红纹小蚯蚓
broccoli [ˊbrɔkəli] n.硬花球花椰菜,花茎甘蓝
bubonic [bju:ˊbɔnik] a.腹股沟腺炎的
budworm [ˊbʌdwə:m] n.芽虫
carcinogen [kɑ:ˊsinədʒən] n.【医】致癌物,诱癌物
cardiopulmonary [kɑ:diəuˊpʌlmənəri] a.心肺的
cardiovascular [kɑ:diəuˊvæskjulə] a.【医】心血管的
caries [ˊkerii:z] n.[拉]【医】龋;骨疡
carpal [ˊkɑ:pl] n.【解】腕骨;腕的
charge [tʃɑ:dʒ] n.【物】电荷
chiaroscuro [kiˌɑ:rəsˊkuərəu] n.(绘画中的)明暗对照法;用明暗对照法绘的图画
chlorofluorocarbon [ˊklɔ:rəuˌfluərəuˊkɑ:bən] n.含氯氟烃
cholesterol [kəˊlestərəul] n.【生化】胆固醇
chordate [ˊkɔ:deit] n.脊索动物
circadian [sə:ˊkeidjən] a.【生】生理节奏的
coleslaw [ˊkəulslɔ:] n.酸卷心菜丝
coriander [ˌkɔriˊændə] n.【植】芫荽,香菜
coronary angiography n.【医】冠状血管照相术
cytokinin [ˌsaitəuˊkainin] n.【生】细胞分裂素
cytology [saiˊtɔlədʒi] n.细胞学
cytoplasm [ˊsaitəplæzəm] n.【生】细胞质
diapir [ˊdaiəpiə] n.【地】挤入构造
dopamine [dəupəˊmi:n] n.【生化】多巴胺
electromagnetic [iˌlektrəumægˊnetik] a.电磁的
encephalitis [ensefəˊlaitis] n.脑炎
endorphin [enˊdɔ:fin] n.【生化】内腓肽
ethylene [ˊeθili:n] n.【化】乙烯,次乙基
eukaryotic [ju:ˌkæriˊɔtik] a.【生】真核细胞的;真核生物

的

fallout	[ˈfɔːlaut]	*n*.【原】微粒回降;放射性尘埃
follicle	[ˈfɔlikl]	*n*.【解】小囊,滤泡 ,卵泡
formaldehyde	[fɔːˈmældihaid]	*n*.【化】甲醛
gel	[dʒel]	*n*.【物】【化】凝胶(体),冻胶; *v*.胶化
gibberellin	[ˈdʒibəˈrelin]	*n*.【生化】赤霉素
gingivitis	[ˌdʒindʒiˈvaitis]	*n*.【医】(齿)龈炎
glycerol	[ˈglisərɔl]	*n*.【化】甘油
haberdashery	[ˈhæbədæʃəri]	*n*.(总称)男子服饰用品;缝纫用品
hadron	[ˈhædrən]	*n*.【物】强子(一种基本粒子)
helium	[ˈhiːljəm]	*n*.【化】氦
hemoglobin	[ˌhiːməuˈgləubin]	*n*.【生化】血红蛋白
hydrocarbon	[ˈhaidrəuˈkɑːbən]	*n*.【化】烃, 碳氢化合物
hypertherm	[ˈhaipəθəːm]	*n*.【医】人工发热器
hypothalamus	[haipəˈθæləməs]	*n*.【生】视下丘
hysterectomy	[histəˈrektəmi]	*n*.【医】子宫切除术
ibuprofen	[ˌaibjuˈprəufin]	*n*.布洛芬(镇痛药)
improper fraction		假分数
indomethacin	[ˌindəuˈmeθəsin]	*n*.消炎痛
intracellular	[ˌintrəˈseljulə]	*a*.细胞内部的
ion	[ˈaiən, aiɔn]	*n*.【物】离子
iridium	[aiˈridiəm]	*n*.【化】铱
isotope	[ˈaisəutəup]	*n*.【化】同位素
jasper	[ˈdʒæspə]	*n*.【矿】碧玉;墨绿色
kelp	[kelp]	*n*.海草,巨藻;海草灰(从中可提取碘)
lepidopter	[ˈlepiˈdɔptə]	*n*.(昆虫)鳞翅目
leprosy	[ˈleprəsi]	*n*.【医】麻风病
leucine	[ˈljuːsiːn]	*n*.【生化】白氨酸
leukemia	[ljuːˈkiːmiə]	*n*.【医】白血病
lipid	[ˈlipid]	*n*.【化】类脂化合物
lipoprotein	[lipəˈprəutin]	*n*.脂蛋白, lipo \ 脂肪的

logotype	[ˊlɔgətaip]	*n*.【印】连合活字;广告等用的标识
lymph	[limf]	*n*.【医】淋巴,淋巴液;(淋巴液似的)浆,苗
lymphatic	[limˊfætik]	*a*.【医】(含)淋巴的;淋巴腺的;(思想行动)迟缓的
lymphocyte	[ˊlimfəsait]	*n*.【解】淋巴细胞
lysis	[ˊlaisis]	*n*.【医】(病的)渐退;消散;【生化】细胞溶解
macaque	[məˊkɑːk]	*n*.猕猴,恒河猴;短尾猴
macrophage	[ˊmækrəfeidʒ]	*n*.【生】巨噬细胞
matrix	[ˊmeitriks]	*n*.【数】矩阵;模子
methane	[ˊmiːθein]	*n*.甲烷,沼气
migraine	[ˊmigrein, ˊmai-]	*n*.[法]【医】周期性偏头痛
mitochondria	[ˌmaitəˊkɔndriə]	*n*.(mitochondrion 的复数)【生】线粒体
morphogenetic	[ˌmɔːfəudʒiˊnetik]	*a*.形态基因的
morphological	[ˌmɔːfəˊlɔdʒikəl]	*a*.形态(学)的;【语】词法的,形态的
mouflon	[ˊməuflɔn]	*n*.摩弗伦羊(南欧产的一种野生羊)
neurogenesis	[ˌnjuərəuˊdʒenisis]	*n*.神经发生(形式)
neuroleptic	[ˌnjuərəuˊleptik]	*a*.抑制精神的,安定的
neuron	[ˊnjuərɔn]	*n*.【物】中子
neuron	[ˊnjuərɔn]	*n*.神经元,神经细胞
nightshade	[ˊnaitʃeid]	*n*.茄属植物(有毒)
nitric	[ˊnaitrik]	*a*.(含)氮的 nitric acid 硝酸
novocaine	[ˊnɔvəkein]	*n*.奴佛卜因(一种麻醉药)
nucleotide	[ˊnjuːkliətaid]	*n*.【生化】核苷酸
number lines		数轴
obstetrical	[ɔbˊstetrikəl]	*a*.产科(学)的,助产的
ocher	[ˊəukə]	*n*.【矿】赭石;(黄)褐色

ohydrate metabolism 糖类代谢作用
oligosaccharide [ˌɔligəˈsækəraid] *n*. 寡糖素
organelle [ɔːgəˈnel] *n*.【生】细胞器
orthogenetic [ˌɔθədʒiˈnetik] *a*.【生】直向演化的;直生现象的
osprey [ˈɔspri] *n*.【动】鹗,鱼鹰;白色装饰羽毛
paleoclimatologist [ˈpæliəuˌklaiməˈtɔlədʒist] *n*. 古生物气象学家
paleontologist [pæliˌɔnˈtɔlədʒist] *n*. 古生物学家
parallax [ˈpærəlæks] *n*.【物】【天】视差;【天】周年(日)视差
parameter [pəˈræmitə] *n*.【数】参;【物】参量
pelvic [ˈpelvik] *a*.【解】骨盆的
peptide [ˈpeptaid] *n*.【生化】肽,缩氨酸
periwinkle [ˈperiˌwiŋkl] *n*.【植】常春花
phagocytosis [fægəsaiˈtəusis] *n*.【医】吞噬(细胞),噬菌作用
phosphate [ˈfɔsfeit] *n*. 磷酸盐,磷酸酯; phosphate fertilizer 磷肥
photon [ˈfəutɔn] *n*.【物】光子;【医】见光度
pituitary [piˈtjuːitəri] *a*.【解】脑垂体的;粘液的
plasma [ˈplæzmə] *n*.【解】血浆,淋巴液;【生】原生质;【物】等离子区
Pleistocene [ˈplaistəusiːn] *n*. / *a*.【地】更新世(的)
plutonium [pluːˈtəunjəm] *n*.【化】钚
polymorph [ˈpɔlimɔːf] *n*. 多形体;【化】多晶形物
potassium [pəˈtæsjəm] *n*.【化】钾
prokaryotic [prəuˌkæriˈɔtik] *a*.【生】原核生物的
prostaglandin [ˌprɔstəˈglændin] *n*.【生化】前列腺素
prostatectomy [ˈprɔstəˈtektəmi] *n*.【医】前列腺切除术
prosthetic [prɔsˈθetik] *a*.【医】修复术的,弥补性的;prosthetic hand 假手
protoplasm [ˈprəutəplæzm] *n*. 原生质,原浆;细胞质

pseudomer	[ˌ(p)sjuːdəumə]	*n*.【化】假异构体
psychotherapy	[saikəuˈθerəpi]	*n*.【医】心理疗法,精神疗法
pterosaur	[ˈterəsɔː]	*n*.翼龙
pulsar	[ˈpʌlsɑː]	*n*.【天】脉冲星
radiometric	[ˌreidiəuˈmetrik]	*a*.公制辐射仪的
rem	[rem]	*n*.雷姆,人体伦琴当量
rheumatoid	[ruːˈmətɔid]	*a*.风湿病的,类风湿病的
rhinovirus	[ˈrainəuˈvaiərəs]	*n*.鼻病毒
ribosome	[ˈraibəsəum]	*n*.【生化】核糖体
schistosomiasis	[ˌʃistəsəuˈmaiəsis]	*n*.【医】血吸虫病,裂体吸虫病
schizophrenia	[skizəˈfriːniə]	*n*.【医】精神分裂症
seltzer	[ˈseltsə]	*n*.一种矿泉水;苏打水
serotonin	[sirəˈtəunin]	*n*.血清素
silicone	[ˈsilikən]	*n*.【化】硅酮,聚硅酮
sinusitis	[sainəˈsaitis]	*n*.【医】窦炎 (sinus 窦)
snapdragon	[ˈsnæpˌdrægən]	*n*.【植】金鱼草属植物;金鱼草
stratosphere	[ˈstrætəusfiə]	*n*.【天】平流层
strep throat		*n*.【医】脓毒性咽喉炎
streptomycin	[streptəuˈmaisin]	*n*.【药】链霉素
sulphate	[ˈsʌlfeit]	*n*.【化】硫酸盐;*vt*.用硫酸处理
synthetase	[ˈsinθiteis]	*n*.【生化】合成酶
tamarind	[ˈtæmərind]	*n*.【植】罗望子树;罗望子果(味酸,常做清凉轻泻剂用)
tektite	[ˈtektait]	*n*.【地】熔融石
terra-cotta	[ˈterəˈkɔtə]	*n*.赤土,赤陶;一种带褐色的柑子
thyroid	[ˈθairɔid]	*a*.【解】甲状腺的; *n*.甲状腺
tonsillectomy	[ˌtɔnsiˈlektəmi]	*n*.【医】扁桃体切除术
tortillas	[tɔːˈtiljəs]	*n*.(墨西哥人用以代替面包的)未经发酵的玉米饼
trichotomy	[traiˈkɔtəmi]	*n*.三分法(尤指神学中将人性分

为肉体，灵魂，精神三部分)

tryptophan	[ˊtriptəfæn]	*n*.【生化】色氨酸
typology	[taiˊpɔlədʒi]	*n*.【语】类型学；象征论
tyrosine	[ˊtaiərəsiːn]	*n*.【生化】酪氨酸
uranium	[juəˊreinjəm]	*n*.【化】铀
varicose	[ˊværikəus]	*a*.【医】静脉曲张的；治疗静脉曲张用的
vector	[ˊvektə]	*n*.【数】矢量，向量；飞机航线；动力；干劲
vinyl	[ˊvainil]	*n*.【化】乙烯基，塑料
white dwarf		*n*.【天】白矮星
woodchuck	[ˊwudtʃʌk]	*n*.【动】土拨鼠

GMAT 常考短语及词组

GMAT 中并不专门考词组，所以词组的变化并不多。GMAT 考的是一种整体上的理解和观察能力。以下这些词组是 GMAT 中常出现的一些实义词组，组合词组和介词词组。熟悉这些词组对大家迅速理解句子的上下文意义和结构有很大好处，列出如下词组供大家参考。

air envelope	大气层
an encounter action	遭遇战
antitrust law	反托拉斯法
assembly line	装配线
as-yet-unexploited	尚未开发利用的
at one stroke	一笔，一举
at stake	存亡攸关，危若累卵
average out	达到平均数，最终得到平衡
bargain on doing sth.	商定做某事
be at a disadvantage	处于不利地位
be at issue	在争论中，不和的；待裁决的
be priced out of	(价格太高而)被排挤出
black hole	【天】黑洞
blind spot	【物】盲点，【无】静区
bona fides	[拉] 诚意，善意
call for	要求
capitalize on the opponent's mistake	利用对手的错误
capitalize on	利用
cash in on	靠…赚钱，趁机利用
center on	集中于

clerical supplies	文具供应
cling to	坚持,墨守;依靠,依恋
closed-circuit television	闭路电视
compound interest	复利(即以本和利为基础的利率)
daylight saving time	夏时制
delve (into)	深入探究,钻研
digital audiotape	数字音带
dote on	溺爱,过分喜爱
draw in	收(网),引诱;天近黄昏;紧缩开支
draw on	戴上(手套);吸收,利用,凭靠;向…支取
ecological systems	生态系统
fall into a rut	陷入陈规,落入俗套
fly by	(一架或几架飞机)在低空飞过指定地点,飞越;宇宙飞船飞近天体
fool around	闲荡,干蠢事(或无用,琐碎的事)
free market	自由竞争的市场
get by	通过,走过;勉强混过
get through	到达;办完,花光;通过;打通(电话)
give rise to	引起,发生
give way to	让位于…
government intervention	政府干预
hit show	风行一时的演出
housing start	楼房破土动工
import relief	进口援助(设置壁垒以保护民族工业)
in full bloom	全盛时期
in kind	以货代款,以实物(援助等)
in sb's favor	对某人有利;得某人欢心
in so far as	在…的限度内,在…的范围内
laissez-faire caplitalism	自由资本主义
lay off	解雇;(临时)解雇期;关闭;停止活动
list price	标价

live show	现场表演
look to	指望
make allowances	留出余地,体谅
make(both)ends meet	使收支相抵,量入为出;靠微薄收入为生
mark up	涨价
mark down	降价
more often than not	经常,时常(=often)
more than ever	尤其
on pain of death	(违者)以死论处
other than	除了
pass up	[俚]放弃,拒绝机会
play off	使暴露弱点,使出丑;把…假装
prime-time ratings	黄金时间收视率
prior to	在…之前
processed food	腌制食品
pull away	脱身,离开;脱出
purchasing price	买价
put away	把…收起来,放好;储存
recruiting agent	征兵员
resort to	求助,凭借;诉诸
roller coaster	娱乐场的环形滑车道
rule of thumb	单凭经验来做的方法,比较简单但有效的方法
shut off	关掉(煤气等);切断,使隔绝,脱离
side effect	副作用
simple interest	单利
sluggish economy	萧条的经济
speculative fever	投机热
speed velocity	速度
status quo ante	[拉] 原状,以前的状态
status quo	[拉] 现状

stumbling block	障碍物,绊脚石
take issue with	与…争论
take over	接收,接管,接任
take precedence over	优先于…; 地位在…之上
trade off	交替换位;通过交换抛掉;弊病,某事的不利之处
trade in. . . for	以…对换;购买
transatlantic migrate	横越大西洋的移民
transnational cooperation	跨国公司
turn down	拒绝,摒斥;把(音量)调低
upscale clientele	高层次的顾客
vichy government	二战时期法国维希政权
virgin soil	未开垦的土地
wall street	华尔街(美金融业集中之地)

GMAT 数学常用符号及术语

数学术语是 GMAT 的重要词汇，因为对数学术语的理解错误会导致做题的错误。因此，所有的考生在开始做数学题以前，都应该首先熟悉数学术语。

一、数学中常用符号

−：subtract	÷：divide
+：plus	×：multiply
=：is equal to	≠：is not equal to
>：is greater than	<：is less than
√ ：square root	|…|：absolute value
//：is parallel to	⊥：is perpendicular to
⩾：is greater than or equal to	（或：no less than）
⩽：is less than or equal to	（或：no more than）

二、表达相应数目的前缀

1：uni-，mono-，	6：hex-，sex，
2：bi-，du-，di-，	7：sept-，hapta-，
3：tri-，ter-，	8：oct-，
4：tetra-，quad-，	9：enn-，
5：penta-，quint-，	10：dec-，deka-

三、数学中常用单词术语

abscissa	横坐标
absolute value	绝对值
acute angle	锐角
addition	加

adjacent angle	邻角
algebra	代数
altitude	高
angle bisector	角平分线
arc	弧
area	面积
arithmetic mean	算术平均值(总和除以总数)
arithmetic progression	等差数列(等差级数)
arm	直角三角形的股
at	总计(乘法)
average	平均值
base	底
be contained in	位于…上
bisect	平分
center	圆心
chord	弦
circle	圆形
circumference	圆周长
circumscribe	外切,外接
clockwise	顺时针方向
closest approximation	最相近似的
combination	组合
common divisor	公约数,公因子
common factor	公因子
complementary angles	余角(二角和为 90°)
composite number	合数(可被 1 及本身以外其他的数整除)
compound interest	复利
concentric circle	同心圆
cone	圆锥(体积 = $13\pi r^2h$)
congruent	全等的

consecutive integer	连续的整数
coordinate	坐标的
cost	成本
counterclockwise	逆时针方向
cube	①立方数 ②立方体(体积 = a^3 表面积 = $6a^2$)
cylinder	圆柱体
decagon	十边形
decimal	小数
decimal point	小数点
decrease by	减少了
decrease to	减少到
decreased	减少
define	①定义 ②化简
degree	角度
denominator	分母
denote	代表,表示
depreciation	折旧
diagonal	对角线
diameter	直径
difference	差
dimension	维数
discount	折扣
distance	距离
distinct	不同的
divided evenly	被整除
dividend	①被除数 ②红利
divisible	可整除的
division	①除

	②部分
divisor	除数
down payment	预付款,定金
equation	方程
equilateral triangle	等边三角形
even number	偶数
expression	表达
exterior angle	外角
face	(立体图形的)某一面
factor	因子
fraction	①分数 ②比例
geometric mean	几何平均值(n 个数的乘积再开 n 次方)
geometric progression	等比数列(等比级数)
have left	剩余
height	高
hexagon	六边形
hypotenuse	斜边
improper fraction	假分数
in terms of...	用…表达
increase	增加
increase by	增加了
increase to	增加到
inscribe	内切,内接
integer	整数
intercept	截距
interest rate	利率
interior angle	内角
intersect	相交(注:a if only b 表示 b⇨a)
irrational	无理数

isosceles triangle	等腰三角形
least common multiple	最小公倍数
least possible value	最小可能的值
leg	直角三角形的股
length	长
list price	标价
margin	利润
mark down	降价
mark up	涨价
maximum	最大值
median, medium	中数(把数字按大小排列,若为奇数项,则中间那项就为中数;若为偶数项,则中间两项的算术平均值为中数。例:1,3,8 其中数为 3;1,3,8,9 其中数为 $\frac{3+8}{2}=5.5$)
median of a triangle	三角形的中线
mid point	中点
minimum	最小值
minus	减
multiple	倍数
multiplication	乘法
multiplier	乘数
multiply	乘
natural number	自然数
negative number	负数
nonzero	非零
number lines	数线
numerator	分子
obtuse angle	钝角
octagon	八边形(注:a only if b

	是 a⇨b）
odd number	奇数
ordinate	纵坐标
overlap	重叠
parallel lines	平行线
parallelogram	平行四边形
pentagon	五边形
per capita	每头
perimeter	周长
permutation	排列
perpendicular lines	垂直线
phramid	角锥
plane	平面
plus	加
polygon	多边形
positive number	正数
power	次方（2^5 = the fifth power of 2）
prime factor	质因子
prime number	质数
product	乘积
profit	利润
proper fraction	真分数
proportion	比例
purchasing price	买价
quadrant	象限
quadrihedron	三角锥
quadrilateral	四边形
quotient	商
radian	弧度
radius	半径（复数为 radii）
ratio	比例

rational	有理数
real number	实数
reciprocal	倒数
rectangle	长方形
rectangular prism	长方体
reduced	减少的
regular polygon	正多边形
remainder	余数
retail value	零售价
rhombus	菱形
right angle	直角
right triangle	直角三角形
round	四舍五入
sale price	卖价
scalene triangle	不等边三角形
segment	线段
sequence	数列
set	集合
side	边长
simple interest	单利
slope	斜率
solution	(方程的)解
speed	速度
sphere	球体(表面积 $=4\pi r^2$ 体积 $=\frac{4}{3}\pi r^3$)
square	①平方数,平方 ②正方形
square root	平方根
straight angle	平角
subtract	减
subtraction	减法
sum	和

surface area	表面积
tangent	相切
tenth	十分位
tenths' digit	十分位
tie	并列,打平
times	倍
to the nearest	最接近的
total	①总数(用在加法中,相当于+) ②总计(用于减法中,相当于-)
trapezoid	梯形
triangle	三角形
two digits	2位
units' digit	个位
velocity	速度
vertex angle	顶角
vertical angle	对顶角
volume	体积
whole number	整数
width	宽
3-digit number	三位数

图书在版编目（CIP）数据

GMAT词汇精选／俞敏洪著．—北京：世界知识出版社，1999.6

ISBN 7-5012-1193-0

Ⅰ.G... Ⅱ.俞... Ⅲ.英语-词汇-研究生-入学考试-自学参考资料 Ⅳ.H313.1

中国版本图书馆CIP数据核字（1999）第27214号

责任编辑／吴新杰 孟淑贤

封面设计／文 敏

责任出版／车胜春

出版发行／世界知识出版社

地址电话／北京市东城区干面胡同51号 （010）65265933

E-mail:gcgjlz@public.bta.net.cn

邮政编码／100010

经 销／新华书店

排 版／东远先行彩色图文中心

印 刷／北京京科印刷有限公司

开本印张／850×1168 1/32 13印张

版 次／1999年5月第一版 2003年8月第八次印刷

印 数／77001—87000

书 号／ISBN 7-5012-1193-0/G·319

定 价／24.00元